The Bedside Guardian 2021

EDITED BY
CLARE MARGETSON

guardianbooks

Published by Guardian Books 2021

2 4 6 8 10 9 7 5 3 1

First published in Great Britain in 2021 by
Guardian Books
Kings Place, 90 York Way
London N1 9GU

www.guardianbooks.co.uk

A CIP catalogue record for this book is available from the British Library

ISBN 978-1-9162047-2-0

Cover design by Guardian News & Media Ltd
Typeset by seagulls.net

Printed and bound in Great Britain by
CPI Group (UK) Ltd, Croydon CR0 4YY

MIX
Paper from
responsible sources
FSC® C020471

Contents

Foreword

KATHARINE VINER

I remember the day, in late March 2020, when I first worried that we might not be able to publish a newspaper, for what would have been only the second time in the *Guardian*'s history. I had driven in to the office – no one was taking the train any more. Classed as an essential worker, I was permitted to travel, but the streets were utterly silent, with every school, cafe and shop closed.

I sat down with colleagues, spaced apart by yellow tape, to work out whether we could gather enough people to produce a print edition. We could publish the digital *Guardian* from anywhere, but, to publish the newspaper, we needed a small number of people in the office. A handful of colleagues volunteered, but I wondered how we would be able to keep everything going. People were anxious for their families and friends and themselves – and frightened, too, for what kind of world we were entering, and what we would be left with.

So, as the editor-in-chief, I did what I have often done in difficult times, and looked to the history of the *Guardian*. How did they get the paper out during the 1918 flu pandemic, which killed 228,000 people in Britain and more than 50 million worldwide? What was it like for journalists on the *Manchester Guardian*? Did many staff fall ill or even die from the virus that the paper itself warned was 'very fatal'?

The second wave of the flu pandemic, in autumn 1918, hit Manchester hard: all schools were closed, mortuaries were full and doctors announced they could not attend to everyone. The lives of our journalists were surely affected – unusually, the 1918 flu was more deadly for people between the ages of 20 and 40. And yet there is nothing in the history books about the pandemic's impact on the *Guardian* as an institution or the individuals who made it. Not a word.

This absence does not surprise Laura Spinney, whose brilliant 2017 book about the 1918 pandemic, *Pale Rider*, was an essential text in the early months of 2020 as we watched our world transformed by a new coronavirus. She recalls that when she started her research, there were more than 80,000 books about the first world war, but only around 400 about the 1918 flu, which took more lives than the war. 'People didn't know how to think about it,' Spinney writes. 'They still don't.'

The Covid-19 pandemic will certainly not be so invisible to future generations. Ours is 'the first worldwide digitally witnessed pandemic', writes Astrid Erll, an academic who studies historical memory, 'a test case for the making of global memory'. The question is what shape that memory will take. Already there is a sense of trauma slipping from our collective recollection. Many people died quickly and could not be buried properly. (Remember the images of Ismail Mohamed Abdulwahab, a 13-year-old from Brixton, buried without his family present?) There are one-year-olds who have hardly met anyone but their parents, and a generation of children trapped at home for a large proportion of their lives.

Covid's impact is likely to be vast and enduring. Spinney writes that the 1918 flu pandemic 'resculpted human populations more radically than anything since the Black Death'. But, as historians have observed, the aftereffect of a global shock depends on the prevailing mood of the times. Positive changes do not automatically emerge from periods of crisis; you have to fight for them. Thomas Piketty says that 'the nature of the impact depends on the theories people hold about history, society, the balance of power ... It always takes major social and political mobilisation to move societies in the direction of equality.'

The *Guardian* is not the only newspaper to declare that it has a higher purpose than transmitting the day's events in order to make a profit. But it might be unique in having held on to that sense of purpose for two centuries. 'A newspaper has two sides to it,' as former editor CP Scott wrote in his essay commemorating our first 100 years. 'It is a business, like any other ... But it is much more than a business; it is an institution; it reflects and it influences the life of a whole community ... It has, therefore, a moral as well as a material existence.' This conviction was present from the start: the prospectus that announced the *Guardian*'s founding in 1821, in response to the Peterloo massacre, asked how the 'great diffusion of Education' in the country, which had excited a 'greatly increased interest' in politics, could be 'turned to beneficial account'.

We are a long way from Peterloo and the 1918 flu. But, once again, events have sparked the intense interest of readers, who are asking how we can emerge from this crisis with something better. The first question for the *Guardian*'s third century is what role we can play in shaping the memory of this catastrophe. How our reporting – in words, pictures, video and audio – will have an impact on the struggle to make sense of the pandemic and the new world it shapes, how our commentary and analysis illuminates the decisions that led us here, and how the past has determined the possibilities for the present. In Arundhati Roy's electrifying long read about India's Covid nightmare (reproduced here on page 155), she shows how the meek acceptance of earlier travesties paved the way for this political catastrophe. 'Grenfell was a rehearsal for Covid,' says Naomi Klein, 'just as Covid is a rehearsal for climate breakdown, if we don't radically change course.' If the pandemic is 'an opening', in Rebecca Solnit's words, making 'room for change that wasn't there beforehand', how can the *Guardian* help create a better kind of world than the one we had before?

There cannot be a person alive who has not been touched by the events of the past year, but this pandemic is simultaneously universal and infinitely particular. There is no one common experience we have all shared, even as it is happening at the same time to all of us. How do we reckon with these abrupt and enormous shifts in our lives and routines? How do we process this trauma without any shared ritual? How do we relate to the deaths of people we do not know? How do we reckon with the fact that the pandemic is not simply a tragedy but also a scene of gross political negligence and outrageous profiteering? How do we understand what the pandemic is doing to society, the way it is accelerating inequality and hitting the most vulnerable hardest, at a time when our empathy has been dulled by lockdown and taxed by fear?

These are challenges for everyone. But they are particularly urgent for journalists, who must chronicle these events in all their shock and immediacy, while trying to connect our audiences to the events in a human way. Reporting on Covid has given us fresh ideas and new energy for covering some of the biggest stories of our time, such as the climate crisis, which shares some of these same qualities – universal, yet affecting different people in different ways; global, and yet not easily located in specific places and times. How do we report a disaster that is happening everywhere all at once, and inspire our audience to understand its gravity without thinking it's too big and too scary to comprehend?

Moments of crisis tend to raise the question of what the role of journalism should be. The need for reliable information is a reminder of why journalism is necessary – but also a reminder that simply recording what has happened is not enough. In fact, this is what has always distinguished the *Guardian* throughout its history: its purpose.

The *Manchester Guardian* (as the *Guardian* was called until 1959) was founded in 1821 in a mood of great hope – to capitalise on a demand for representation that followed the 'earthquake' of Peterloo. Right from the beginning, the *Guardian* was not just about the news of the day, but about how people can use information to make the world a better place – the facts, but not only the facts. This is what we mean when we say that our purpose is to provide hope through clarity and imagination.

CP Scott's essay on journalism was written in 1921, and it is striking just how enduring the mission that it laid out has proved to be. Scott was editor of the *Guardian* for 57 years, and he made it what it is today. Scott listed the values of the *Guardian* as 'honesty, cleanness [integrity], courage, fairness, a sense of duty to the reader and the community', and emphasised that the *Guardian* must be editorially led, and the journalists free from commercial or political interference. He set the terms for pluralism, so crucial to a news organisation without a proprietor: 'The voice of opponents no less than of friends has a right to be heard. It is well to be frank; it is even better to be fair.' He stressed the primacy of fact with the line 'comment is free, but facts are sacred'.

The Scott Trust – the ownership model put in place by CP's son John in 1936, a few years after Scott's death – codifies Scott's essay and underpins the *Guardian* today: the idea that it has a 'moral as well as a material existence', and all that entails, is guaranteed by the trust in perpetuity. It is no wonder that the Scott Trust ownership model has been adopted by other journalistic organisations working in the public interest around the world.

As the *Guardian* enters its third century, nothing must change our mission, but the digital revolution might change how we interpret that mission for the modern age. We are now in a more levelled world, where journalists are no longer so separate from their audience. Yes, we do the work and pound the streets and dig around for documents, but we no longer deliver our journalism from 'on high' to an uninitiated audience. To be successful today – to get the stories that really matter to readers, and to convey the information they need in ways they want – journalists must be part of the social fabric of the world they report on. The *Guardian* is a community of journalists and readers, all of us equal citizens of that community.

It is inevitable that the Gutenberg-era *Guardian* was a one-way street, an ivory tower, since a mutually engaged conversation with a reader in real time was beyond imagination. Scott might have been shocked by such a possibility – he might have been shocked that there was a woman sitting in his editor's chair, too – but ultimately I think he would have embraced both innovations. Privileged as he was, he was resolutely part of his community. He believed powerfully in a 'sense of duty to the reader and the community', and would surely have enjoyed the interaction and accessibility enabled by the web. (And his beard would surely have been a massive social-media hit.)

If the mission that defined the *Guardian*'s first century was the idea that everyone deserves knowledge and facts that they can use, then our second was defined by the vision of Scott's essay: of a newspaper built on facts and guided by its values, a newspaper with a moral as well as a material existence.

What is the mission for the *Guardian*'s next century? We are still guided by the principles that shaped our first 200 years, with two crucial additions: we must always be a part of the community we represent, and we must remember that that community is now a global one, confronting crises on a global scale.

The *Guardian*'s mission is one that allows – and even encourages – its editor to make decisions in the public interest; to challenge the powerful, whatever the consequences. There is no politically motivated proprietor to tell you otherwise, no shareholders demanding commercially minded coverage in order to get a dividend. The public interest is rarely popular with the powerful. The biggest *Guardian* stories of the past few decades – the Edward Snowden revelations, the phone-hacking scandal, the Panama and Paradise papers, the Windrush scandal – were fiercely disputed and fought by powerful interests, bringing unfriendly contacts from the police, government ministers and intelligence agencies. Even last year's scoop revealing Dominic Cummings had broken lockdown – which 'gripped the public in a way we've never seen before', as one pollster later wrote – was subject to vociferous pushback from minister after minister.

Our duty to serve the public interest has not changed, but our 'public' is no longer the liberals of Manchester, or even the people of the UK – it is now local and national and international, British and European, American and Australian, and everywhere else that our readers and supporters live. Since 2016, alongside our subscriptions, the *Guardian* has been generously supported by contributions from readers, who pay voluntarily so that our journalism can be a public good, free to all. (Our readers now contribute far more revenue than our advertisers.)

Making payment voluntary, in an era where many organisations were putting up expensive paywalls, was a controversial decision at the time, portrayed as desperate begging. The belief was that people would never pay for what they could get for free. But in a world filled with political demagogues and

algorithmically enhanced junk news, *Guardian* readers understood the value of keeping trusted, reliable information and
progressive perspectives freely available around the world. They
saw how this would matter in a democracy.

What defines this community is not geography, or even reading
or supporting the *Guardian*; it is a community of those who share
our hope for the future, who know that the way things are now is
not the way they have to be, and who want to see this pandemic
'turned to beneficial account', to make a different world from the
suffering and solidarity that we have all experienced in this difficult year.

This crisis has not changed the values that have guided the
Guardian for 200 years. What it has produced is a new conviction
that making connections really matters – not only with each
other, but ones that help us understand how the world works. The
pandemic showed everyone how interconnected we all are, and
yet how separate – atomised, and yet all fighting the same virus.

Our reporting is not about telling our readers what they
should think, or broadcasting 'the Truth' from Guardian Towers.
It is about connecting, empathising, listening. It's about hearing
what people are telling us, not what we expect them to say. The
disruption to every aspect of our lives has produced a new appreciation of human connection, of what we missed without touch,
without contact; a new softness, a new slowness, a chance for
creativity and community. As Naomi Klein says, 'when you slow
down, you can feel things. When you're in the constant rat race,
it doesn't leave much time for empathy.'

It's about making the connections between the dinner delivered to your door and where that food came from and the life of
the courier who brought it to you. It's about making the connections between the politicians who presided over pogroms then

and pandemics now, as Arundhati Roy has done. Getting close to our readers means building the kind of trust that whistleblowers and victims need. It means community-based journalism, making contact with readers everywhere, from Hong Kong protesters to NHS doctors. It means embedding ourselves in an area, as we have with our *Made in Britain* video series. It means a more diverse group of journalists, helping to redefine what constitutes 'news'. It means being open to different points of view, to accepting that we might not agree on everything. It means restoring a better balance – between humans and technology, between the super-rich and everyone else, between society and the environment.

We will find ways, as we are doing already, to get out and speak to people, to get away from our screens and understand what life is like for others. We will dig out the truth, as the powerful try to get away with things under cover of the pandemic. We will understand how we're all connected, and try to make a difference. The post-Covid journalism that I am seeking will be more urgent, more essential. It must be rooted in real conversations, fact-based reporting, information you can trust, and it must have the imagination to understand other people's lives and other people's points of view. It must also be aware of the pleasures, diversions and enjoyment of life. Wit is often just as important as gravity.

It may seem hard to imagine things changing for the better when so many people are desperate just to go back to normal. But the tranquillity of plane-free skies, the crescendo of bird-song, that sustenance so many of us have felt from nature, the solidarity we felt during collective clapping or singing – that was real, and that was special. Astrid Erll points out that there is much evidence that events from late adolescence are remembered best, and so that generation, just entering adulthood now, will remember these urgent times even more acutely. We have all learned that terrible things can happen on a truly global scale.

We've all seen what can be achieved if we work together, united in a collective effort. Can we now work together to vaccinate the world, then stop an environmental catastrophe?

The pandemic has also highlighted some of the obstacles that might hinder that collective spirit. When the pandemic struck England, you were far more likely to die if you came from a deprived area. As epidemiologist Michael Marmot wrote, 'enduring social and economic inequalities mean that the health of the public was threatened before the pandemic and during it, and will be after it'. Meanwhile, the 10 richest men on earth saw their wealth increase by £400 billion during the pandemic – enough to pay for vaccines for all, according to Oxfam – while ordinary employees' wages have stagnated for more than a decade. Will we stand for this? Or is it a chance to demand fair taxation, a new impetus for the social state, to build a fairer society?

The unequal impact of Covid along racial lines has spotlighted the extent to which 'the social determinants of health' are affected by structural racism. Covid has had a much greater impact on people of colour in Britain and the US. Meanwhile, domestic violence surged in lockdown as women were trapped at home with violent men. The killing of Sarah Everard, a young woman walking home along a busy road in London in the evening, was met with a torrent of protest – a feeling that enough was enough. The Black Lives Matter protests took place in this moment too, in cities, towns and villages around the world, because, in Klein's words, 'what was bad before the disaster has been downgraded to unbearable'.

All *Guardian* staff know that their work is not done to generate profits for others, or to buy influence. We are all here for a reason, and that is the biggest unifier. We all work for an organisation, as laid out by CP Scott, that 'is a public service, not an instrument of private profit or power'. Our mission is based on a moral conviction: that people long to understand the world they are in, and to create a better one. To use our clarity and imagination to build hope.

There are not many companies, in any business, that last for two centuries, and it says something about the role the *Guardian* plays in the world that it has got this far. I think it's because we know who we are: we have roots, we have principles, we have philosophy, we have values. When I was appointed editor-in-chief in 2015, I was given one instruction: to carry on the *Guardian* 'on the same lines and in the same spirit as heretofore', which is assumed to mean that 'fidelity to principle is to be put before profit'. There is so much power in that – something we must never forget. I am grateful to the 11 editors who served with such distinction in the decades before me; to 200 years' worth of *Guardian* staff, from star reporters to stable boys, ad execs to copytakers, columnists to cleaners; to my current colleagues, a brilliant, energetic, resilient team who have shown in the past year exactly what they're made of; and to our readers, who've stuck with us in good times and bad, in times when the *Guardian*'s politics were in the ascendancy and the times when they were needed more than ever, who know that there's nothing quite like the *Guardian*, anywhere in the world. Thank you. Times change. Technologies change. Principles don't. Two hundred years, and we've only just begun.

Introduction

CLARE MARGETSON

It wasn't meant to be like this. Last year we had hoped – even if we knew deep down it might not be the case – that the pandemic might be a thing of the past by now.

When the publisher first called me about doing this book, her one steer was: 'Well, it would be good not to make it too dominated by coronavirus. That was last year's edition.' Back in April, when we spoke, that seemed possible; optimistic, but not completely implausible. Vaccines had come to our rescue. Their development and rollout have been one of the truly great scientific and logistical successes of our era.

Yet even though they have made a massive difference, as I write this, 8,000 people are in hospital in the UK, children and young people are picking up the virus in ever greater numbers and the prime minister is preparing to set out his winter Covid plan. There is clearly some way to go.

The first step on the long path to something resembling pre-Covid normality, however, was taken when the first woman was vaccinated in the UK, as recorded by Aamna Mohdin last December. This was an incredible moment of joy and relief; it offered a glimpse of a better future. Scientists in different countries had worked at an extraordinary pace to produce a vaccine for Covid 19. And in an unprecedented period of time, a mass vaccination programme was put into place.

Here in the UK, we have been incredibly fortunate. Almost two thirds of the population have been fully vaccinated and we are now looking at potential booster jabs for some of the most vulnerable.

That isn't the case for billions of other people around the world. The crucial question of how we share vaccines with countries unable to develop and buy their own is still being debated – and, to date, the programme for western countries to donate supplies is floundering. This poses urgent ethical and moral questions.

As Katharine Viner asks in her foreword: 'How do we understand what the pandemic is doing to society? ... These are challenges for everyone. They are particularly urgent for journalists, who must chronicle these events in all their shock and immediacy, while trying to connect our audiences to the events in a human way.'

But 2021 need not only be defined as the second year of the pandemic. We saw some extraordinary events; some shocking, others awe-inspiring.

This was the year the US voted out President Donald Trump. The year he then refused to go. The year that Capitol Hill in Washington was stormed. The supposed seat of American democracy seemed to wobble, terrifying people not only in the US but around the world.

This was also the year that Trump's successor, Joe Biden, decided to pull out of Afghanistan, 20 years after 9/11. The so-called 'war on terror' ended as it began – with the Taliban back in government.

The sight of men, women and children running for flights out of Kabul airport, clambering onto the side of planes in their desperation to flee the grip of the Taliban, was horrifying and heartbreaking. President Biden said the withdrawal was no 'Saigon'. Yet that is exactly how it looked. Take Ramin Rahman, the 27-year-old Afghan journalist, who gave a first-hand account of the panic, crowds and shooting, having to decide whether to give up his space on the plane as others squashed in around him.

In such a tumultuous year, perhaps it is unsurprising that mental health problems have soared. Inequality is rising. The pandemic will have many stings in its tail.

The havoc being wrought by the climate crisis is ever more apparent, most noticeably with increasingly intense weather phenomena – flooding in Germany and China; wildfires in Greece and the US; unprecedented temperatures in Russia; storms in Indonesia; the list is long. As Damian Carrington, our environment editor, wrote in July: 'As a verdict on the climate crimes of humanity, the Intergovernmental Panel on Climate Change report could not be clearer: guilty as hell.'

And so our heads are now focused on the upcoming COP26 convention in Glasgow.

The repeatedly ignored warnings of scientists over decades have now become reality. Never has the world needed wisdom, compassion, courage and good leadership more.

This year has also of course been one of hope and happiness. Sport, as so often, provided us with many exhilarating moments that brought families and friends together. England reaching the finals of the delayed Euro 2020 tournament was enough to lift so many of our hearts. For a few weeks, millions of people were distracted and Gareth Southgate seemed a surprisingly inspiring and thoughtful leader.

Then came the Olympics in Tokyo, where our journalists had to quarantine and isolate themselves before making their way to echoey, empty stadia. Medallists from all corners of the UK – from Tom Daley to Duncan Scott, Hannah Mills to Kellie Harrington – certainly made a damp, rainy summer more bearable.

The American gymnast Simone Biles won as many hearts for what she didn't do. Suffering from mental health problems, she had to pull out of events she might have won. But when she came back to compete in the balance beam, she claimed bronze – and it felt like triple gold.

Another female athlete who stood out this year was Emma Raducanu. Before this summer no one had really heard of her and yet, by the second week of September, this incredibly talented, engaging teenager from Kent had become the first qualifier – male or female – to win a Grand Slam title when she became US Open champion. A measure of her success is that during Wimbledon she dropped out of the fourth round, overcome by the occasion, yet she had the resilience and strength of mind to bounce back two months later.

Our writers also did so much to reveal our interior lives, how they have changed over the last year, from Paula Cocozza's wonderful piece about how a lack of physical touch affected us in lockdown to Laura Barton's insights on friendship and Emma Beddington's relationship with her beloved dog.

It has been an immense privilege to sift through a year's worth of *Guardian* reporting and choose some stand-out pieces to include in this book. I wanted to thank those section editors who reminded me of their favourite articles. I enjoyed reading every single one of them. Given more time, I could have come up with many more volumes. Even then, I would have had to miss out so many deserving pieces. So I apologise now to all those brilliant journalists whose work I haven't been able to fit in.

I have laughed and laughed at pieces the *Guardian* has published. Marina Hyde, thank you. I have also sat rigid, numb, damp-eyed, reading some of the brave and deeply impressive work our reporters have produced to shine light on the more horrific events of this year.

Thank you to Katherine Butler, my predecessor as editor of *The Bedside Guardian*, who was kind enough to give me advice – and to warn me that my weekends might be rather busy come the summer. How right she was.

And lastly, a big thank you to the wonderful Lindsay Davies, whose judgment was spot-on all the way through and whose calm and upbeat tones made every call to discuss where we'd got to a delight.

I hope as we look over the brow of this hill into 2022 that my successor as editor of the next *Bedside Guardian* will truly be able to focus on stories and events beyond the pandemic that has so blighted our lives.

Autumn

At 31, I have just weeks to live. Here's what I want to pass on

ELLIOT DALLEN

The first three decades of my life were pretty standard. Well, actually they were awesome, and everything was going pretty perfectly with regard to work, health, relationships and friends. I had plans for the future, too: learn some Spanish, see more of Central America, and get a bit more out of it with some volunteering too.

I imagined settling down in my thirties or forties with kids, a mortgage and so on. Or maybe I wouldn't. Maybe my friends' children would call me Uncle Elliot as their parents gathered in the kitchen looking slightly concerned for their single 45-year-old friend about to set off travelling around Mongolia. Either way, growing older with my mates and living my life to the full was always my ambition.

Of course, the second part of this storyline won't be written now. It's a shame I don't get to see what happens. But everybody dies, and there will always be places and experiences missing from anyone's life – the world has too much beauty and adventure for one person to see. I will miss marriage or children, blossoming careers and lives moving on. But I'm not alone in my life being cut short, and I think my time has been pretty good. I haven't asked for a specific prognosis, as I don't believe there's much to gain from doing so, but I think it's a matter of weeks. Medicine has luckily turned this into quite a gentle process. That really does take a lot of the fear away. And I'm hoping impending death now grants me the licence to sound prematurely wise and overly grandiose. Because I've had time to think about the things that are really important to me, and I want to share what I've discovered.

First, *the importance of gratitude*. During my worst moments – the shock of cancer diagnosis, the mental lows and debilitating symptoms of chemotherapy – it was difficult to picture any future moments of joy, closeness or love. Even so, at those times I found comfort in remembering what I have: an amazing family, the friends I've made and times I've shared with them, the privilege of the life I've had.

Second, *a life, if lived well, is long enough*. This can mean different things to different people. It might mean travel. I've had the good fortune to be able to do this, and can confirm that the world is a wonderful place full of moments of awe and amazement. It may mean staying active, as much as possible – the human body is a wonderful thing. You only appreciate this when it starts to fail you. So, when you find yourself slipping into autopilot, catch yourself, and take simple pleasure in movement, if you can.

Look after your body because it's the only one you have, and it's bloody brilliant. Knowing that my life was going to be cut short has also changed my perspective on ageing. Most people assume they will live into old age. I have come to see growing old as a privilege. Nobody should lament getting one year older, another grey hair or a wrinkle. Instead, be pleased that you've made it. If you feel like you haven't made the most of your past year, try to use your next one better.

Third, it's important to let yourself *be vulnerable and connect to others*. We live in a society that prizes capability and independence, two things that cancer often slowly strips away from you. This was naturally a very difficult pill to swallow for a healthy, able late-twentysomething male, but having to allow myself to be vulnerable and accept help has given me the best two years of my life, which was pretty inconceivable at the time of diagnosis.

Fourth, *do something for others*. Against the backdrop of Covid-19, Black Lives Matter and the desperate attempts of migrants to cross the Channel, my thoughts really turned to those who have not had my privilege – whether that's by virtue of socio-economics, ethnicity or the country I was born in. I always try to remind myself of this.

Fifth, *protect the planet* – I can't leave this off because it's so important. I'll be gone soon, but humanity will still be faced with the huge challenge of reducing carbon emissions and saving habitats from destruction. In my time here, I've been lucky enough to see some natural wonders and understand how precious they are. Hopefully future generations will be able to say the same. But it will take a massive collective effort.

If you asked me what I'd want to leave behind, it would be a new awareness of these things among my friends – and anyone who'll listen, really. I now find myself in a position where people are asking me how they can help or what they can do that would make me happy. Apart from the obvious – looking after each other once I've gone – I'm going to push for people to give, be that money or time. I've already had so many people ask which causes I recommend, and there are loads, but I'd say any that align with the 'values' I've sketched out would have my blessing. Among friends and family there is talk of setting up a small charity in my memory.

Despite some very low times, it's worth repeating that the period since being diagnosed has been made not just bearable but actually fantastic. I've had new experiences that haven't seemed tainted by cancer – and those experiences were, as always, much better shared. In a situation that is pretty new for most of my loved ones and friends (I am yet to meet anyone I grew up with who has had to deal with cancer or a similar chronic illness at my age), it has been amazing watching them all rise to the challenge. I'm not sure if it's just that I know a high proportion of amazing people (possible) or if most human beings have this capacity for connecting and recognising what's truly important (very likely).

After the gut-punch of cancer diagnosis, I've really struggled to define a purpose for my own life. I found in time this came naturally. Life is for enjoyment. Make of it what you can.

Elliot Dallen was diagnosed with adrenocortical carcinoma in 2018, aged 29. He died the night after this piece was published.

2 OCTOBER

Hicks, hubris and not a lot of masks: the week Trump caught Covid

LUKE HARDING

Donald Trump's presidency has been full of plot surprises. But no single tweet has had the same meteor-like impact as the one sent by the president just before 1am yesterday. It felt like a season finale moment. 'Overnight, @Flotus and I tested positive for Covid-19,' Trump wrote. He added, in matter-of-fact style: 'We will begin our quarantine and recovery process immediately. We will get through this TOGETHER!'

The announcement was astonishing. And yet – seen through the timeline of Trump's recent activities – it appears wholly unremarkable and perhaps even inevitable. In recent days he has behaved with the same reckless disregard for public health rules that has characterised his response throughout the global pandemic.

Viewed with hindsight, his meetings during the last week look ill-judged, to say the least. On Saturday he appeared in the White House Rose Garden to announce his choice for the supreme court, Judge Amy Coney Barrett. Trump appeared on stage with Barrett and her family. About 200 people watched.

One person at the ceremony was Republican senator Mike Lee of Utah. Another was the president of Notre Dame University, John Jenkins. Rev Jenkins sat without a mask. Lee had a mask but held it loosely in his hand as he hugged friends. Both men subsequently tested positive for the virus, in what now looks to be a super-spreader episode.

On Monday, Trump returned to the Rose Garden to announce new measures to distribute Covid-19 test kits to US states – to defeat what he referred to as the 'China virus'. The president was upbeat. He confidently predicted the pandemic would soon be over. 'We're rounding the corner,' he declared.

His audience was made up of members of Congress and state officials. Few wore masks. Neither did Trump or the vice-president, Mike Pence. Also present were the health secretary, Alex Azar, and the education secretary, Betsy DeVos.

On Tuesday, Trump was preparing for his first televised debate with Joe Biden, his Democratic challenger. These practice sessions took place in the West Wing of the White House. As has been frequently noted, masks are rarely seen inside the White House building. It was almost as if this area of executive power had been deemed off limits to the virus – a fantasy that would soon prove to be spectacularly wrong.

Later on Tuesday, Trump boarded Air Force One en route to Ohio. With him was a large entourage including his wife, Melania, his adult children and senior staff. Also there was his trusted aide, Hope Hicks. Since joining his campaign in early 2015, Hicks was often at Trump's side. She returned to his administration in spring, following an earlier spell as press secretary. None were seen wearing masks while getting off the plane. Hicks was seen climbing into a staff van together with Bill Stepien, the president's campaign manager, the *New York Times* reported. Those onboard included: a strategist, Jason Miller, the White House chief of staff, Mark Meadows, and Stephen Miller, a policy adviser.

In the debate hall, the two rivals were placed some distance apart. It was a rancorous and unpleasant evening, memorable for Trump talking over his rival. One moment now stands out. On stage, Trump mocked Biden for wearing a mask in public so often. He said both of them had been tested for the virus, before the TV clash. 'I put a mask on when I think I need it,' he added.

And then Trump went on the attack. Speaking to Biden directly, Trump suggested his rival's precautions were over the top. And ridiculous: 'I don't wear a mask like him. Every time you see him, he's got a mask. He could be speaking 200ft away from them and he shows up with the biggest mask I've ever seen.' To emphasise his point, Trump spread his arms. Biden was in close proximity to Trump for 90 minutes.

Trump's family watched from the audience. None wore masks. This was in clear breach of host rules, which called for blue surgical masks to be worn. A doctor from Cleveland Clinic in a white lab coat had even approached the Trump family guests, offering a mask. She was unsuccessful. Someone shook their head at her as she came close, according to a press pool report.

But it was Wednesday that turned out to be the most consequential moment so far of the 2020 election. Trump carried on with his campaign activities – a fundraiser at the home of a private donor in Minneapolis and then a rally in Duluth. Everything was as normal: warm-up music for the tightly packed crowds waiting for Trump, followed by the theatrical arrival of Air Force One. Trump emerged, looking solemn. He waved at his supporters. Arriving on stage, he embarked on his usual stump speech: how he had 'won big' in his debate with 'Sleepy Joe', and how he would put the US first during his second term. Curious observers might have noticed that he wrapped up after just 45 minutes.

Behind the scenes, something was wrong. Hicks had accompanied Trump to Minneapolis. By this point she was feeling unwell. Her symptoms were ominous: probably a cough, a headache or both. On the trip home, she was isolated in a separate part of the cabin. Upon landing, she exited from the plane's rear.

Until Wednesday, Trump's behaviour might have been defended. After all, Hicks had cut herself off from other White House staff as soon as she fell sick. Over the next 24 hours, however, Trump continued as if nothing had happened. It was a remarkable act of hubris that may have caused the virus to spread. Key members of his administration also failed to isolate.

On Thursday, Hicks tested positive. The news shook the White House like a bomb blast, shattering the complacency that had prevailed. White House staff began wearing masks. News of Hicks's diagnosis was not made public. The hope among senior staff was this might be kept secret. The mood was one of growing panic, according to reports.

Meanwhile, some of Trump's aides said they had sensed on Wednesday that he was feeling unwell. They put this down to tiredness caused by an intense schedule. The president had seemed exhausted, one person familiar with the situation told Bloomberg. Apparently unconcerned, Trump flew to his Bedminster golf resort in New Jersey for a private fundraising event. Several aides who had been in close proximity to Hicks were due to go too. They cancelled. At the golf club, Trump made a speech and mingled with supporters. As usual, he was not wearing a mask. The White House press secretary, Kayleigh McEnany, who had been with Hicks on Wednesday, did not use a face covering when briefing reporters.

Trump was tested for Covid-19 later on Thursday, after returning to the White House. For a little while longer it was business as usual. The president gave a telephone interview to Sean Hannity on Fox News. He sounded a little raspy. Trump explained that he and the first lady were both being tested for the coronavirus. The result – delivered via Twitter – came when much of the US was asleep.

Over the past nine months, Trump has sought to diminish the significance of the virus which has killed more than 208,000 Americans, and more than 1 million people worldwide. He has mostly spurned social distancing.

For a long time he downplayed the importance of wearing masks. The president even blithely predicted the virus would disappear, as if by magic.

It didn't. And now Trump has become its most famous victim.

12 OCTOBER

Black people will not be respected until our history is respected

BENJAMIN ZEPHANIAH

I wish we didn't need a Black History Month. But we really do. We need it now more than ever. Once upon a time there was no such month here, but there was one in the United States. Talk about the need for a British version went round and round for years, until in 1987 the idea was put to the Labour politician

Linda Bellos. Bellos was someone I had met a couple of times, and we had stood together on many protests and demonstrations. She was able to stay revolutionary and lead Lambeth council at the same time.

It was Bellos who pioneered the first Black History Month across London schools, and by doing so *she* made history. We are of the same generation, so I can understand that when she used the term 'black', it was political, and not a reference to skin colour – something that many people find difficult to understand these days.

I wasn't interested in history at school, because I was being taught that black people had no history. We were usually being 'discovered' by great white explorers, civilised by the great white conquerors and missionaries, or freed by the great white abolitionists. It was only when I started to listen to reggae music that I began hearing about my own history. I am not going to mention Bob Marley, he did his bit, but there was Pablo Moses, Fabienne Miranda, Peter Tosh, Fred Locks, Burning Spear, I-Roy, Big Youth, Judy Mowatt and many more. These were my teachers.

Black people were being beaten down in school, and beaten up on the streets, so we started to set up Saturday (supplementary) schools in people's front rooms and in community centres. We were that hungry for knowledge. There were racist gangs and skinheads on the streets, and sometimes we were forced to defend ourselves.

And the police didn't help us. I did a count and the reality is that I got beaten more times by the police than I did by the National Front – and something I can say for sure about all the cops who beat me up is that they thought I had no history, no intelligence, no rights and no humanity. They weren't taught well at school.

The racists that I used to fight on the streets of east London have not disappeared: they now have respectable jobs, they wear suits, and are much better organised. They have organisations, so they can distribute brutality from their office desks. That's why people nowadays often talk about racism being 'systemic' and a 'system of power'.

Empowered bigots have learned how to sugar-coat their racism, and make it more 'acceptable', so they can blend into the mainstream and even debate with you on TV shows in the name of free speech and 'balance'. They will tell you they want to put up borders not because they hate immigrants, but because they love their country. You know them, they start sentences by saying, 'I'm not a racist, but ...'

The uprisings we see happening all over the world now are not happening in a vacuum. They are happening because history is being ignored – and, ultimately, it's all of our history. Many statues of white supremacists should be toppled, and those that remain, if they remain, need to do so with context, and with their history explained. But it's not just about tearing down statues, it's also about being honest. If we tear down everything to do with slavery, because of Britain's involvement and role in the slave trade, there might be nothing left.

When I saw George Floyd die, I saw my cousin Mikey Powell die. When I see the insults black women get when they dare to speak up for freedom and justice, I remember the way the media treated Angela Davis in the US, and Linda Bellos in England. How can those who write hate about us, those who unlawfully police us, and those who judge us unjustly, respect us if they don't respect our history?

Now I love history. It is fascinating, illuminating and stimulating, but I don't want to live there. Black history is not perfect. We have had our dictators, our massacres, our warmongers and our evil-doers, and we should not shy away from that. But we have also had our pioneers, our universities, our inventors, great writers, great poets, scientists, cartographers, teachers and philosophers. The police who beat me up didn't know that.

But there is hope. A few years ago, when the Black Lives Matter protests first started, it was a black thing but this year all that changed. Some of my white students were contacting me and demanding that I join them on demonstrations. I saw a Black Lives Matter protest in Lincolnshire, and it was a case of 'spot the black person'.

I smiled when I saw someone with a banner that read 'Black Lives Matter, don't you understand, dad?' So this was a young white girl telling her father to stop being racist. The younger generations are speaking up. They are rising up. Black and white together, and it feels good. But our history must rise up too.

I might be old. I might be history myself. But I am trying to play my part in the creation of the Black Writers' Guild, to make sure our history is told by us, and our future is visualised by us. I won't plug my book, *Windrush Child*. I'll just quote my friend and fellow poet Linton Kwesi Johnson, who said: 'It is noh mistri / Wi mekkin histri.' Now translate dat.

Mainstream party politics are far divorced from reality. Those players haven't got a clue. Anti-racists are being called racists, we who seek peace are called dreamers. They refuse to learn from our history, but they say things like 'Happy Black History Month' as if it's Christmas, or Easter, or some pray day imposed on us by the church.

We need Black History Month now more than ever before. If we really want to understand what's happening in the world and change it for the better, we must confront the past and learn from the past. Good or bad. We owe it to ourselves, and future genera-tions. Now, go and listen to some reggae. Go on. Turn up the bass.

26 OCTOBER

Statistical illiteracy isn't a niche problem. During a pandemic, it can be fatal

CARLO ROVELLI

A few years ago, a rare, non-infectious illness hit five colleagues in quick succession in the institute where I worked. There was a sense of alarm, and a hunt for the cause of the problem. In the past, the building had been used as a biology laboratory, so we thought there might be some sort of chemical contamination, but nothing was found. The level of apprehension grew. Some looked for work elsewhere.

One evening, at a dinner party, I mentioned these events to a friend who is a mathematician, and he burst out laughing. 'There are 400 tiles on the floor of this room; if I throw 100 grains of rice into the air, will I find five grains on any one tile?' We replied in the negative: there was only one grain for every four tiles: not enough to have five on a single tile.

We were wrong. We tried numerous times, actually throwing the rice, and there was always a tile with two, three, four, even five or more grains on it. Why? Why would grains 'flung randomly' not arrange themselves into good order, equidistant from each other?

Because they land, precisely, by chance, and there are always disorderly grains that fall on tiles where others have already gathered. Suddenly the strange case of the five ill colleagues seemed very different. Five grains of rice falling on the same tile does not mean that the tile possesses some kind of 'rice-attracting' force. Five people falling ill in a workplace did not mean that it must be contaminated.

The institute where I worked was part of a university. We, know-all professors, had fallen into a gross statistical error. We had become convinced that the 'above average' number of sick people required an explanation. Some had even changed jobs for no good reason.

Life is full of stories such as this. Insufficient understanding of statistics is widespread. The coronavirus pandemic has forced us all to engage in probabilistic reasoning – from governments having to recommend behaviour on the basis of statistical predictions, to people estimating the probability of catching the virus while taking part in common activities. Our extensive statistical illiteracy is today particularly dangerous.

We use probabilistic reasoning every day, and most of us have a vague understanding of averages, variability and correlations. But we use them in an approximate fashion, often making errors. Statistics sharpen and refine these notions, giving them a precise definition, allowing us to reliably evaluate, for instance, whether a medicine or a building is dangerous or not.

Society would gain significant advantages if children were taught the fundamental ideas of probability theory and statistics – in simple form in primary school, and in greater depth in secondary school. Reasoning of a probabilistic or statistical kind is a potent tool of evaluation and analysis. Not to have it at our disposal leaves us defenceless. To be unclear about notions such as mean, variance, fluctuations and correlations is like not knowing how to do multiplication or division.

This lack of familiarity with statistics leads many to confuse probability with imprecision. Early during the pandemic, scientists mapping and modelling the spread of the virus in the UK were criticised for estimating rather than accurately depicting how severe the virus might be. Criticisms of their 'dodgy predictions' proceeded from a misunderstanding: dealing in uncertainty is exactly why statistics is helpful.

Without probability and statistics, we would not have anything like the efficacy of modern medicine, quantum mechanics, weather forecasts or sociology. To take a couple of random but significant examples, it was thanks to statistics that we were able to understand that smoking cigarettes is bad for us, and that asbestos kills. In fact, without knowing how to deal with probability, we would be without experimental science in its entirety, from chemistry to astronomy. We would have very little idea about how atoms, societies and galaxies operate.

What is probability? A traditional definition is based on 'frequency': if I roll a dice many times, one-sixth of these times the number 1 will show, hence I say that the probability of rolling a 1 is one in six (1/6). An alternative understanding of probability is as a 'propensity'. A radioactive atom, physicists say, has a 'propensity' to decay during the next half an hour, which is evaluated by expressing the probability that this could happen.

In the 1930s, the philosopher and mathematician Bruno de Finetti introduced an idea that proved to be the key to understanding probability: probability does not refer to the system as such (the dice, the decaying atom, tomorrow's weather), but to the knowledge that I have about this system. If I claim that the probability of rain tomorrow is high, then I am characterising my own degree of ignorance of the state of the atmosphere.

We know many things, but there is a great deal more that we don't know. We don't know whom we will encounter tomorrow in the street; we don't know the causes of many illnesses; we don't know the ultimate physical laws that govern the universe; we don't know who will win the next election; we don't know if there will be an earthquake tomorrow. If I catch the virus, I do not know if I will survive.

But lack of complete knowledge does not mean that we know nothing, and statistics is the powerful tool that guides us when we do not have complete knowledge, which is to say: virtually always. Death rates, case rates and R numbers are now a feature of everyday news coverage. A better understanding of statistics and probability would help us all not only to better understand what we know of the pandemic, but also to take wiser decisions – for instance, in balancing risks and evaluating whether certain behaviours are safe. There is no certainly safe behaviour, nor a certain way to get ill.

In this uncertain world, it is foolish to ask for absolute certainty. Whoever boasts of being certain is usually the least reliable. But this doesn't mean that we are in the dark. Between certainty and complete uncertainty there is a precious intermediate space – and it is in this intermediate space that our lives and our decisions unfold.

3 NOVEMBER

The fall of Johnny Depp: how the world's most beautiful movie star turned very ugly

HADLEY FREEMAN

Johnny Depp is 'a wife-beater'. This is the verdict of the UK courts. Just writing that sentence feels genuinely shocking, and yet by now perhaps it should not. For a start, the allegation that he was physically abusive to his ex-wife Amber Heard emerged more than four years ago, after she applied for a temporary restraining order against him following their divorce, citing domestic abuse. It should also not be a shock, given how many other hugely famous men have been accused of abusing women. Sean Connery was alleged to have beaten his first wife and frequently defended hitting women. His death this weekend sparked online arguments about how much the coverage should focus on the professional achievements of a man who repeatedly insisted it was fine to hit women, 'if the woman is a bitch, or hysterical, or bloody-minded continually', as he said in 1965.

But Depp is a very different figure from Connery. The latter represented alpha masculinity and aggressive sexuality. No one ever said it explicitly, but Connery's defences of beating women fit in, on some level, with his image, and so that side of him was never going to be a problem with his audience. Depp, however, represented something else. He sued the *Sun* for defamation when it described him as 'a wife-beater', something Connery would never have done, and it is why, for a certain kind of fan (me), this feels like the death of yet another childhood hero.

And yet, unlike the ends of Kurt Cobain and River Phoenix, perhaps you couldn't describe this one as a shock. After the judge gave his verdict on Monday morning, Depp's notoriously virulent online followers (a different kind of fan) made sure they got the predictable hashtags trending, all proclaiming Depp's innocence. I often wonder about these online Depp fans, given that they are most likely in their thirties or forties. Such online stanning from the middle-aged is unusual, and yet that it is Depp who inspires it says a lot about him: both what he represented to my generation, and how far he has fallen.

Depp could still appeal. 'The judgment is so flawed that it would be ridiculous for Mr Depp not to appeal this decision,' said

Jenny Afia, a solicitor at the London law firm of Schillings, which represented Depp.

But, by now, most of the world has seen the photos of Heard's bruised face, and the court case presented a relationship that had become gruesomely toxic. The court heard recordings of Heard verbally abusing Depp and admitting to 'clocking' him and throwing pots and pans at him. But none of that could change the fact that the judge, Mr Justice Nicol, found the majority of Heard's allegations that Depp abused her proved to the civil standard, and that, therefore, the *Sun* was entitled to describe him as a 'wife-beater'.

It was always risky for Depp to pursue this case. Next year in the US he has a $50 million (£38 million) defamation case against Heard regarding an opinion piece she wrote about being the victim of domestic abuse; the verdict of this case will surely have some impact on the next one.

But it's not just the judge's verdict that has decimated Depp's reputation. For a while, his life has been absurdly over the top: when he was asked in 2018 if it was true, as his managers alleged, that he spent $30,000 a month on wine, he replied that this was 'insulting ... because it was far more'. So testimonies about private jets, cocaine for breakfast and arguments over – in perhaps the most memorable part of the trial – whether Heard or her yorkshire terrier had defecated in Depp's bed were titillating, but little more. More destructive to Depp's career, and to those who have followed him from the early days, was how low he had fallen: throwing phones at his wife's head; zonked out and covered in ice-cream; so riddled with jealousy of Heard's male co-stars he referred to Leonardo DiCaprio as 'pumpkin head' and Channing Tatum as 'potato head'; sending vicious emails and texts to friends about Heard in which he referred to her as a 'flappy fish market'. Aside from everything else, Depp had always been unusually eloquent for an A-lister, with a courtly, old-fashioned conversational style. That was part of his appeal; now he was lobbing insults like a six-year-old. Somewhere, amid all the drugs and the drink, Depp seemed to lose his mind. As I looked at the photos of him, turning up to court looking like a self-parody in his perma-present piratical scarf and blue-tinted sunglasses, to argue over whether it was human or terrier excrement in his bed, I felt horrified, of course, but I also felt sad. This was not how it was supposed to go. To those watching, the verdict felt inevitable, Depp's trajectory less so.

For those who came of age in the 90s, Depp represented a different way of being famous. He complicated the narrative. Along with Phoenix and Keanu Reeves, he was part of a holy trinity of grunge heart-throbs. They were the opposite of the *Beverly Hills, 90210* boys, or Brad Pitt and DiCaprio, because they seemed embarrassed by their looks, even resentful of them. (Depp reportedly turned down Pitt's cheesecake role in *Thelma & Louise*.) This uninterest in their own prettiness made them seem edgy, even while their prettiness softened that edge. They signified not just a different kind of celebrity, but a different kind of masculinity: desirable but gentle, manly but girlish. Depp in particular was the cool pin-up it was safe to like, and the safe pin-up it was cool to like. We fans understood that there was more to Depp, Phoenix and Reeves than handsomeness. They were artistic – they had bands! – and they thought really big thoughts, which they would ramble on about confusingly in interviews. If we dated them, we understood that our role would be to understand their souls.

He would never put it like this, but Depp cultivated this image. He decided almost from the start that he didn't want to be just a celebrity but a cultural figure. In 1987, he was cast in Fox's teen cops show *21 Jump Street*, and at first he gave enthusiastic interviews about how much he enjoyed his 'clean' and 'slick' character, Tom Hanson. But he soon appeared to realise he wanted more and regularly derided the show as 'borderline fascist', mentioning his own youthful drug experiences and how he lost his virginity at 13.

Nevertheless, *21 Jump Street* was a huge hit, largely thanks to Depp. Sunday evenings for me, growing up in the US, quickly became about watching Depp bust some drug-dealing adolescents. There were reports from the set that he would refuse to do scenes, leading to him getting a reputation as difficult, but to us fans this just proved that he had an artistic soul and was better than the TV show (although we also loved the TV show). They paid him $45,000 an episode to make him stay – a dream for a poor boy from Kentucky, the youngest child of a waitress, who had lived in more than 20 different places before he was seven and whose parents divorced when he was a teenager. But to Depp it was hell. 'Lost, shoved down the gullets of America as a young Republican TV boy, heart-throb, teen idol, teen hunk. Plastered, postered, postured, patented, painted, plastic!! Novelty boy, franchise boy. Fucked and plucked with no escape from this nightmare,' he wrote about the show.

Depp was supposed to be a teen idol, but he complicated the narrative by choosing John Waters' *Cry-Baby* for his big movie lead debut, kitschily satirising his image as a heart-throb, and spiking any producers' attempts to pigeonhole him as just another pin-up. In his next role, as Edward Scissorhands, he went further, entirely obscuring his good looks – not even James Dean did that – and relying instead on subtlety and acting skills, neither of which had been in much evidence on *21 Jump Street*. But he was good, or certainly good enough, and in the 90s Depp carved out one of the more interesting careers a teen pin-up has ever managed. He worked with Lasse Hallström in *What's Eating Gilbert Grape?*, Jim Jarmusch in *Dead Man*, Roman Polanski in *The Ninth Gate* and Mike

Newell on *Donnie Brasco* (in which he probably gave his best performance). And he took his audience with him; a whole generation discovered indie films and auteurs through Depp. He was that rarest of things: a celebrity who was, genuinely, cool.

He was also known as a romantic. He was married briefly at 20, then developed a proposal habit, getting engaged to Sherilyn Fenn, Jennifer Grey and Winona Ryder, whose name he had tattooed on his arm: 'Winona Forever' (changed to 'Wino Forever', when the booze lasted longer than the relationship. Similarly, he had 'Slim' tattooed on his hand for Heard; after their divorce, he changed it to 'scum', then to 'scam').

We Depp fans loved Ryder. They made sense as a couple and, with her delicate gothic looks, she confirmed our image of him as a friend of the outsider (as though a gorgeous Hollywood actress could ever really be considered an outsider). We were less pleased when he started dating a model, which felt a bit lame, but at least it was Kate Moss, and at least she seemed absolutely bananas about him, clutching his arm on the Cannes red carpet. During their relationship, he notoriously tore up a hotel room they were staying in together, causing $8,000 worth of damage. But again, we told ourselves, this was just his artistic nature. And it was the 90s – destroying hotel rooms was what male celebrities did, right?

While Phoenix tended to come across as quite surly in interviews, and Reeves was monosyllabic to the point of incomprehensibility, back in the 90s Depp seemed more fun. Onscreen, he had a tenderness the others didn't; off-screen, journalists loved him, and he would drive them around LA talking gnomically about his love life and showing them cool tricks he could do with a cigarette. In the 90s, loving Depp was as uncontroversial as liking chocolate, and yet, unusually, the universality of appeal only added to his credibility. He had Oscar nominations and was the highest-paid star in the world. And yet, unlike any other actor who has achieved that – Jimmy Stewart, Tom Hanks – he was still cool. Back then, everyone loved Johnny.

Directors loved him, too, especially Tim Burton, of course, but also Waters and Jarmusch. When I tried to talk to people he worked with for this piece before the judgment, they all said no because they wanted to protect him. Until very recently, he had a reputation for being one of the easier actors to work with, praised by the cast and crew of his movies for his professionalism and friendliness.

After he and Moss broke up, he got together with Vanessa Paradis, and they had two children, Lily-Rose and Jack. During their 14-year relationship, Depp, true to form, was positively uxorious about Paradis, praising her beauty and becoming a Francophile, giving interviews in French magazines about how much he loved the country. France, he said to the magazine *VSD* in 2010, 'has given me everything. A marvellous family and also an equilibrium which I missed enormously.' For a while, it looked as if Depp had gamed the celebrity system: he had found a way to be entirely true to himself while still being an A-lister and living a life of peace and contentment.

Depp had always approached fame with a very clear template. Among his 90s cohort, Phoenix struggled to match up his personal values with being a Hollywood actor, and Reeves didn't appear to give the matter an enormous amount of thought beyond just doing what he wanted to do. But as early as 1990, Depp had settled on heroes he would namecheck in interviews: Iggy Pop, Marlon Brando, Keith Richards, Hunter S Thompson.

Thirty years later he would still be talking about all of them; he is, really, the ultimate fanboy. His Captain Jack Sparrow in *The Pirates of the Caribbean* is a pastiche of Richards, while Depp has made himself the keeper of Thompson's flame, playing him in 1998's *Fear and Loathing in Las Vegas*, and then posthumously bringing Thompson's novel *The Rum Diary* to screen in 2011. It was on this film that he met Heard. Richards even had a small role in Depp's court case. In a photo taken by Heard to show the extent of Depp's drug use, the court saw cocaine lines laid out on the table, pirate-themed box of drugs nearby with the initials 'JD' engraved on it, and there, in the background, a solo CD by Richards. If this had been an episode of *Through the Keyhole*, the mystery of to whom this table belonged would have been solved in the opening credits.

On the one hand, for a man to have the same heroes at 57 as he did at 21 would seem to prove the old adage that the age you become famous is the age you stop growing. (Depp also proves another old adage: never trust a man over 30 who reveres Hunter S Thompson.) On the other, it could also be seen as a testament to Depp's consistency, even his authenticity. Whereas most actors pick up causes and side interests the way other people go through takeaway sandwiches, Depp has been enduringly faithful to his original loves.

Throughout his career, he sought out friendships with Richards, Thompson, Brando and Allen Ginsberg, which gave him a reflected retro sheen. He seemed to be from the past, his LA a grubby 50s version, as opposed to the glitzy 90s one in which he lived. In a 2011 interview with Patti Smith in *Vanity Fair*, she asked him about his 'mentors', and he described them, enviously, as coming from 'a radically different era ... I really believe that, at a certain point, if you're born in 60-something or whatever, you got ripped off – you know what I mean? I always felt like I was meant to have been born in another era, another time.'

Depp tried to bring the spirit of that era to his world, opening The Viper Room nightclub on Sunset Boulevard in 1993. That year, Phoenix collapsed and died outside it from an overdose.

In 2012, Depp announced he and Paradis were separating, and he was now dating Heard. Within a year, the once most famously romantic of Hollywood stars was sending text messages to his friend, the actor Paul Bettany, about Heard in which he said: 'Let's drown her before we burn her!!! I will fuck her burnt corpse afterwards to make sure she is dead.' When asked about the message in court, Depp said it was regarding a fight he had recently had with Heard: 'She didn't like me using alcohol and drugs because she had some delusional idea that they turned me into this sad monster.'

His reputation for professionalism started to crack. He delayed the shooting of the fifth *Pirates of the Caribbean* film because of what he said was a hand injury, which Heard claimed in court occurred when he punched a wall during one of their fights, and there were reports from that set that Depp was drinking heavily and needed to have his lines fed to him through an earpiece. Depp did not deny needing an earpiece, saying it helped him 'to act with his eyes'.

There has already been much discussion about how all of this will affect Depp's career, and the answer depends on whom you ask. But probably one of the better clues came from Jerry Bruckheimer, who produces the *Pirates* franchise. When asked in an interview in May if Depp would be in the next *Pirates* film he replied: 'We're not quite sure what Johnny's role is going to be. So, we're going to have to wait and see.'

It has been a long time now since Depp was cool. The photos of him in London during the case, wearing a Rasta hat and matching striped T-shirt, brought a sad pang for those old enough to remember when he was the most stylish man in the world. His last genuinely good film was *Sweeney Todd* in 2007, and he has spent the past few years making turkeys such as *Lone Ranger*, *The Tourist* and a genuinely unbearable cologne advert. His loyal fans would say that it all went wrong when he left Paradis for Heard in 2012. And it's true, leaving the mother of his children for a younger woman would have once, long ago, been beneath him. But it feels as though the rot started before that.

According to his former management company, he was spending more than $2 million a month, aided in no small part by the fact he cashed out to star in the *Pirates* franchise and was, for a time, earning more than $50 million per role. Even he called it 'stupid money', but insisted he was only demanding that price tag for the sake of his kids. His life quickly became absurd. In 2009, *Vanity Fair* ran what, in retrospect, looks like the tipping point piece, in which the writer described what it was like travelling on Depp's carefully designed boat ('Orient Express by way of Parisian brothel') to his private Caribbean island. The whole thing is grotesquely over the top and crassly predictable, with Depp wanging on (and on and on) about Thompson and Richards, and sharing the advice Brando gave him about how to buy an island. 'Money doesn't buy you happiness. But it buys you a big enough yacht to sail right up to it,' he declares.

But if he was merely working to earn money for his children, that has all come to naught: in 2018 he told journalists that his fortune of $650 million was gone. He insisted that his former managers had stolen millions from him; they claimed he had spent it. A $25 million lawsuit between them was settled – the terms of the agreement were confidential – but that he had $650 million to steal tells its own story. Who, really, can maintain any sense of reality when they are dealing with those sums of money? Maybe some people, but not fiftysomethings who idolise Hunter S Thompson.

Depp made the classic fanboy mistake of focusing only on the glamorous, external trappings of his heroes. He views Richards et al as eternal rock'n'roll figures, and constantly retells anecdotes from their hellraiser years. But all of them wrestled with the question of how hellraisers deal with getting older in a way that Depp, apparently, has not. Richards quit hard drugs in 1977 and Iggy Pop also cleaned up long ago. Thompson killed himself at 67, ground down by poor health and depression; Brando ended up a bloated mess. Depp could easily have grown into a figure like Richards or Iggy Pop: clean, cool, critically acclaimed, a revered cultural figure. Instead, in the past few years, he seems to have chosen the other option.

It's sad, and it didn't have to be this way. Of course, that's true of any celebrity downfall – any personal downfall – but with Depp, it felt like a different path was always there in front of him, in touching distance. That now feels like an alternative universe. It would be easy to dismiss this as yet another spoilt, obnoxious celebrity shown up for being spoilt and obnoxious – easy but wrong, because that would miss why Depp was so compelling for so long. Until the allegations of abuse emerged, the stories that came out about Depp were, by and large, notably nice. Kind, even.

There was the time he donated £1 million to Great Ormond Street hospital after his daughter had been treated there, and then afterwards visited the sick children still in there and read them stories. Even when his life started to be excessive, his good friends stayed loyal. But over the past decade, things started to change. Where once he drove journalists around LA and France and regaled them with loquacious thoughts about life, his more recent encounters with the press have had the feeling of Kurtz barricading himself in the jungle. In 2018, he gave an interview to *Rolling Stone*, ostensibly about how he lost all his money, and ended up keeping the journalist, Stephen Rodrick, with him for three days. Rodrick described him as 'alternately hilarious, sly and incoherent', with a 'scared, hunted look about him'. 'If his current life isn't a perfect copy of Elvis Presley's last days, it is a decent facsimile,' Rodrick wrote.

The real connection between Depp, Phoenix and Reeves was that they were all hyperconscious of not doing the predictable thing. But with Phoenix dead at 23 from an overdose, and Depp mired in divorce, drugs and legal hell, his reputation now destroyed, only Reeves, of all unlikely people, has avoided the wearily familiar templates. Only fools expect consistency from celebrities (from anyone, really), but what feels so strange about Depp to fans is how much he seemed to change, and how quickly, when he had been so consistent for so long. Or maybe he was the consistent one, with his eternal reverence for Thompson and Brando, and we're the fools for being surprised.

In any case, the photos shown in court of Depp passed out on hotel-room floors confirmed what most of us already knew, and the judge's verdict has carved it in stone: Depp has become a spent cliche. That was the one thing we thought he would never be. But once again, he complicated the narrative.

15 NOVEMBER

Small Axe review – Steve McQueen triumphs with tales of Britain's Caribbean history

ELLEN E JONES

Steve McQueen, the west London-raised son of a Trinidadian mother and a Grenadian father, has already secured his place in cinema history. In 2014, he became the first black director of an Academy Award-winning best picture with *12 Years a Slave*, a film set in the 19th-century United States. An equivalent epic about black people's history in Britain had never been made, until now.

McQueen's five-part anthology series tells four true stories and one imagined, set between the late 60s and mid-80s. The fact that it is airing on television, on the national broadcaster's flagship channel, is significant. Watching *Small Axe* provides viewers of Caribbean descent with the rare thrill of representation, but these histories are national histories – they are for everyone.

Small Axe begins with the story of the Mangrove Nine's landmark Old Bailey trial, which, given British telly's fondness for a Sunday evening period drama, has remarkably never been dramatised. Here we have a true story, featuring courtroom drama and inspiring heroism with a thrilling twist, and yet it's been overlooked? Apparently, every last Jane Austen scribble had to be adapted five times over and every serial killer needed his own three-part character study before we got around to it.

The basic story, if you aren't familiar (and most aren't), is this: in 1968, the same year that Enoch Powell delivered his 'Rivers of Blood' speech, Frank Crichlow (Shaun Parkes) opened a Caribbean restaurant in Notting Hill and called it the Mangrove. Crichlow's place soon became a hub for the immigrant community that had grown up in west London since the Windrush era, and Bob Marley was known to drop by when in town. It was also where the young Darcus Howe (Malachi Kirby) and the British Black Panther leader Altheia Jones-LeCointe (Letitia Wright) went to write pamphlets and hold meetings.

This was more than enough to make the Mangrove a target for police harassment, and between January 1969 and July 1970, the premises were raided 12 times on spurious grounds. In response, on 9 August 1970, 150 people marched to the local police station, resulting in arrests for 'inciting a riot' and the subsequent history-making trial of nine people.

Kirby and Wright are luminous as two of the nine. To see *Black Panther*'s Shuri embodying a real-life Black Panther hero is one part of this glow; to see them coming together with other leading lights of Black Hollywood such as McQueen and John Boyega (he stars as the senior Met officer Leroy Logan in a later episode), to tell a British story, is another. *Mangrove* also succeeds where 2017's *Guerrilla*, a more heavily fictionalised account of the British Black Panther movement, failed, by truthfully representing the shared struggle of London's black and south Asian communities at the time, without erasing the central role of black women. Our neatly intersectional introduction to Jones-LeCointe, for instance, is on the factory floor where she is attempting to unionise a group of south Asian men.

When people of colour are the story and not the set-dressing, there is suddenly room to explore. One of the most compelling of these struggles-within-The-Struggle is played out in Parkes' performance as Crichlow. Not a natural-born activist like Howe and Jones-LeCointe, he is just an ordinary bloke who wants to lead an ordinary life. But as *Mangrove*'s slow, tense build-up illustrates, even this simple ambition is denied by a racist police force.

Why hasn't the charismatic Parkes already had a string of lead roles? Why isn't *The Real McCoy* alumna Llewella Gideon (who plays Aunt Betty) hosting her own BBC Two panel show? These are questions for the British television industry to ask itself. In the meantime, McQueen ably shoulders the burden of representation, tells the untold stories and offers framed portraits of Caribbean heroes on the Mangrove's walls, as a reminder of how much more there is where this came from. (I look forward to a biopic of Paul Bogle, Jamaican hero and namesake of the 90s dance craze.)

But that's not all. With its meticulous recreation of the texture of life, *Small Axe* opens up a Mangrove-like space on television for the celebration and sheer enjoyment of British-Caribbean culture. The party really gets going in episode two, *Lovers Rock*, but there is also music and merriment here, including an extended steel pan street party. In this difficult year, the first without a Notting Hill carnival since its 60s inception, it's a scene that hits particularly hard.

16 NOVEMBER

A recipe for life – and for pasta

RACHEL RODDY

One of our many neighbours spends a fair bit of his day just outside the main gate of the building, or on the nearby corner of the piazza. He is 84, although he seems younger, and is always immaculately dressed: his trouser pleats sharp, his shirt collar firm, his suede jacket brushed in the right direction.

On the corner, he is part of a group of men – most of whom were born in one of the four buildings that box the piazza – who stand and chat in the Roman sunshine. At the gate, he is often waiting for his wife, also in her mid-eighties (and, in my opinion, the best-dressed *signora* in our neighbourhood).

It is a good day if, when coming round the corner from my part of the building, I coincide with her coming down the stairs from hers, so we can walk to the gate together, and therefore meet her husband, with his performed exasperation and obvious pride. Meeting her is rare, though. Usually, I see just him, waiting, and he always asks, '*Vai a spasso?*' ('Going for a saunter?'), and I always reply yes, even when I am rushing to the optician. And because trips out these days are short and masked, I might also see him on my way back, still waiting. And if it is lunchtime, which it often is, he always asks the same thing: '*Vai a cucinare la pasta?*' ('Going to cook pasta?'), and I always reply yes, mostly because I probably am, again.

'Again': usually, that's such a reassuring word in relation to cooking, suggesting often-made, much-loved dishes. Even 'not again', which makes me think of my grandfather, who complained about having the same thing again and again, but wouldn't have had it any other way, is a sort of reassurance. This November, however, 'again' is different, filled with uncertainty and a sense of being suspended, which ripples out like sound waves. I, for one, keep feeling stuck in life, work, writing and lunch.

I am helped by Anne Lamott's book *Bird by Bird: Some Instructions on Writing and Life*. The title comes from a piece of advice that her father gave to her brother when he was feeling rather overwhelmed by a school project about birds: don't get swamped by the immensity of the whole task. Rather, start by learning the bird names one by one.

Lamott's whole book is a treasure, a helpful approach to writing, but also to life and to cooking. So, bird by bird – or, in my case, pan by pan – I break it down. I get out the pan, fill it with water, put it on the stove and bring it to a boil.

Putting water on for pasta is a sort of switch that propels you to action. What have you got? Tinned plum tomatoes that can be chopped and simmered with olive oil, sliced garlic and chopped dried or fresh chilli. Or tuna, sardines or anchovies, to add to sliced, sautéed onion with a handful of olives and a sunny amount of lemon zest.

Do you have something green, maybe? Broccoli, courgettes or cabbage can be sliced and boiled along with the spaghetti, and then the whole lot finished with olive oil and grated cheese. Or something white? Ricotta or mascarpone can be loosened with a little of the pasta cooking water and seasoned with lemon zest. Or butter? Melt a slice as thick as a thumb, add a few anchovies for a deep, salty sauce, a spoonful of Marmite for a yeasty one, or mushrooms for a more substantial one. Or, simpler still, toss the hot spaghetti with diced butter, parmesan and lots of black pepper.

Unlike writing, where there is never any guarantee that what you put on paper will actually be any good, lunchtime pasta tossed with tomatoes, an umami sludge of anchovy and chopped onion, or butter and cheese is invariably good. As is a neighbour with sharp pleats, a firm collar and suede brushed in the right direction, standing on a sunny corner, asking if you are going for a saunter.

25 NOVEMBER

Shivering Dublin Bay swimmers slighted for their 'fancy fleeces'

RORY CARROLL

James Joyce opened *Ulysses* with a reference to the 'scrotum-tightening' effect of swimming in Dublin Bay but these days there is a secondary, somewhat more visible effect: dryrobe bashing.

A boom in sea swimming in Ireland has filled Dublin's bathing spots with people wrapped in fleece-lined hooded robes – and for some of the old-timers it feels like an invasion.

'By order: no Dryrobes or Dryrobe types!!!' said a sign erected by the Forty Foot swimming site in Sandycove, Dublin Bay, with a red line across an image of three people in robes. It referred to the dryrobe, a brand of UK clothing designed to keep sports-people warm.

'Warning: beware of dryrobe wankers,' said a poster in Blackrock. It complained about the 'grim reaper silhouette' and accused wearers of taking up too much space and using GoPro cameras, selfie sticks and other devices to document fleeting swims.

The critiques have sparked debate on social media and radio shows about tribalism, snobbery and social etiquette in the Covid-19 era.

Year-round sea swimming used to be the preserve of a few people, known as 'hardies', deemed brave or mad. That changed several years ago when sea swimming became trendy. The throngs multiplied this year after pandemic restrictions shut gyms and other amenities.

As defence against the post-swim chill identified in Joyce's masterpiece many bathers bought robes costing about €150 (£135). Some robes have been spotted inland, and dog walkers, outdoor drinkers and gardeners swear by them. But some hardies associate the robes with arrivistes who snaffle parking spaces, hog benches with their fleeces, call sea swimming 'wild swimming' and try to undo the Irish Sea's effects on the human body.

'The hardy guys wouldn't wear one if you gave it to them but I think they're great – warm, comfortable, practical,' Storme Delaney, 40, wearing a black dryrobe at the Forty Foot promontory, said yesterday. 'The real issue is that the hardies feel they're being taken over by the newbies.'

Fresh from a dip, David Mitchell, 63, said: 'I'm traditional. I wouldn't be into them myself. I'd be too warm in it.' He was wearing shorts.

Kay Wallace, 74, a lifelong Forty Footer, said robes took up bench space. 'People just feck them everywhere.' However, she was open to conversion. 'They look great. I might get one.'

Bathers, those with and without robes, laughed off the posters. 'It's funny, it's just teasing,' said Susan Ledwidge, 58, who received a robe as a birthday present last month and said she loved it. 'It's so nice and warm.'

Ian O'Meara, owner of the Viking Marine store in Dun Laoghaire, said he could barely keep up with the demand for robes. He lamented a 'sinister' tinge to the mockery. In an effort to restore harmony he has recorded a video on how to fold and store them.

27 NOVEMBER

One in four Britons don't shower every day. And the rest aren't doing it right

ZOE WILLIAMS

I am fed up with pretending we are all equally novices in the face of this novel virus, all just feeling our way through it. Particularly on the matter of working from home, I have been at this for 20 years and am much better at it than you. I knew that already and had it confirmed the other morning when Mr Z read in the *Daily Mail* that 25 per cent of people have stopped having a shower every day, and 14 per cent have stopped using deodorant. Guys, you have to have a shower. You just don't have to have a Shower with a capital S.

Like taking your shoes off when you enter a home, daily washing is an imported habit. When I was a kid, we had a bath once a week, and when I was at university, I lived a whole year in a building and never found out where the bath was. Perhaps that was extreme, but washing every day was considered much more so: I always thought it conveyed some minor but problematic self-hatred, and felt quite sympathetic to people who always smelled so good, though, truthfully, there weren't that many of them.

Then I went out with an Australian (like I said, imported) and we had a conversation like two people splitting up in a Gillian Welch song (you can't really remember what happened, you just wake up feeling shaky) except we weren't splitting up (yet), he was just telling me I had to wash every day.

'Seriously?' I said. 'What if I haven't done anything?'

'If you've *done* something, you have to shower *twice*.'

'Back to back? Isn't that just a long shower?'

'Not back to back! Once when you wake up, another time after the thing you did!'

(Huh, turns out I actually remember this quite well.)

It's actually a damn fool thing to wash every day, because your body gets used to it, then demands it, like giving a cat lunch. But after a period of time, it becomes the transition point between being in bed and being up, without which there is a real danger that you won't get up at all. It is said that people can tell even if something has been written in bed. I don't know if that's true, but you can definitely tell if someone over the phone is in bed: the duvet does something to the acoustics.

So, for those of you who have spent less time studying such things: a Shower is where you get completely into the shower and also wash your hair. A man shower is where you get your hair wet but don't wash it. And a shower (lower case, no stated gender) is where you just stand at the sink, splashing yourself. This used to be called a French wash, but then young people repurposed the term to mean something much ruder, while simultaneously becoming much more careful about using gross generalisations around nationality on the grounds of – you know, boomer – *racism*.

If you spray deodorant on and call that a shower, that's a Sure-er (you have to say it, not spell it). If you spray deodorant on and spray dry shampoo into your hair, you've had a Febreze. If you can't be bothered to shower and instead get into the sea because you are near it, you've had a Sea Febreze.

A bath, by the way, is not an alternative to a shower: it is a hot lie-down. If you choose it, you are probably unwell, and then you don't have to wash at all until you have recovered.

What I loved about the original survey was that it was a flash-back to a pre-pandemic, even pre-Brexit time, when not much had happened and people would have to produce news in the old-fashioned way, by asking each other lifestyle questions, like lighting a fire with sticks. In the 90s, a truly carefree decade, an enterprising dry-cleaning firm made the front pages when it discovered that 18- to 24-year-olds changed their romantic part-ners four times more often than they dry cleaned their duvets. There was a wildly hot debate around whether or not it was just good manners to get your duvet dry cleaned to mark the start of a new relationship and, if so, how this etiquette had failed to percolate down to the younger generation.

Plus, if you just look at these statistics from a slightly different angle, 75 per cent of people are still showering – presumably most of them Showering – and a landslide of people, 86 per cent, are still using deodorant. We talk a lot about when we will return to normal, often concluding that normal is over, yet all around you, there are people sitting in their homes, clean enough that they could walk into an office right now. This is about as normal as it gets.

3 December

The rock star of retail: how Topshop changed the face of fashion

JESS CARTNER-MORLEY

'What's this I'm reading in the paper? It's a load of absolute shit, that's what it is. What's the matter with you? Are you stupid or what? I've never read so much rubbish in my life.'

It was February 2010, and I was at my desk in the *Guardian* office. Philip Green didn't need to introduce himself. His habit of bellowing down the phone was unmistakable, and I had just written an article about how I was falling out of love with Topshop after a decade being in its thrall. Green never did take kindly to criticism of the golden child of his Arcadia empire.

Of the thousands of businesses that have been brought to their knees by the pandemic, Topshop is the most high-profile scalp; Arcadia Group collapsed into administration on Monday. Topshop in its prime was the most glamorous store the British high street has ever had. From late 1990 until a few years ago, it was the rock star of retail. Topshop dresses regularly featured on the pages of *Vogue*. Every Saturday, the 90,000 square feet of its flagship store on Oxford Circus were packed with shoppers high on catwalk-adjacent clothes at accessible prices. When Beyoncé flew into London, the store opened an hour early so that she could shop privately on her way to rehearsals. At London fashion week, where the brand staged a twice-yearly show from 2005 until 2018, the Topshop front row regularly outshone designer labels with the glossiest celebrities, the sharpest new trends, the most copious champagne. Green would position himself in the place of honour, with Anna Wintour on one side and Kate Moss on the other. He was the uncontested king of the high street.

The story of Topshop's glory years – and of its fall – is closely tied to Green, but the story of its rise belongs to someone else. Topshop's ascendancy was a phenomenon under the stewardship of Jane Shepherdson, several years before Green arrived. As brand director, Shepherdson created at Topshop the kind of brand that had never before existed. Until then, high-street fashion had tended to fall into two camps. There were sensible skirts-and-blouses for grownups, and then there was 'youth' fashion – basic denim, brightly coloured T-shirts, generically skimpy party dresses, cheap rip-offs of catwalk silhouettes. Topshop changed this, thanks to Shepherdson's unerring taste and her eye for the best fashion-school graduate talent with which to fill the design studio. Topshop offered high-fashion sophistication at a high-street price. In 2006, Paolo Roversi shot a Topshop advertising campaign between shooting covers for Italian *Vogue*.

Fashion is never just about clothes, and Topshop on a Saturday in the noughties was a playground. The democratisation of style that it represented felt like a progressive and cheering development, and the loud music and video screens lent the stores a festival mood. There were on-floor stylists and walk-up nail bars. Green, who bought Arcadia in 2002, had little time for the nuance of design but he immediately grasped the value of the shop floor experience that Shepherdson had created at Topshop ('Fashion Disney,' she once called it). There are not many points on which Green and I agree, but he was right about one thing: he knew that the business of fashion is about emotion. A man ruled by ego, he instinctively knew the power that clothes have to make you feel good about yourself. For a certain type of consumer, a

Savile Row suit signals status to everyone who matters; Green understood that the same principle could be rolled out for a £50 leather biker jacket that could be sold by the lorryload.

The rise of Topshop is a tale of how fashion reached its zenith. In the first decade of the 21st century, culture shifted away from words and towards pictures. The world's operating systems became ever more visual on a granular level, as mobile phones segued from being about the spoken or typed word to being about images. As a result, fashion became ever more visible. The luxury industry grew, so fashion brands became wealthier and more powerful. Fashion weeks evolved from being industry-facing show-rooms for clothing into major media events. At the Oscars, the red carpet became as high-profile as the awards themselves. Fashion, the arena where visual messaging meets identity politics, found itself in the spotlight, and Topshop rode the crest of this wave. In May 2007, just a few months after the arrival of the first touch-screen iPhone, the first Kate Moss for Topshop collection went on sale. Launch night brought Oxford Circus to a standstill. Moss, dressed in a long ketchup-red dress from the collection, struck mannequin poses in the shop window to entertain the waiting crowds, before being escorted by a beaming Green to a cordoned-off VIP area, where friends including Meg Matthews and Sadie Frost joined her. This was a world of supermodels, champagne and rock'n'roll, and the name above the door was Topshop.

Retail theatre has always existed among the highest echelons of fashion, and among its lowest, but until the 21st century it was missing from the high street. At its best, a visit to an expen-sive boutique is performance art, from the elaborate courtesy of a doorman that marks your arrival to the lavish rustle of tissue and ribbon that accompanies your exit. Shopping at a street market, in a different way, is an equally immersive experience: a world of larger-than-life personalities, drama and banter. A department store womenswear floor, however, was once a dry and dreary world where a half-hour wait for an assistant to check the stockroom for a size passed in a torpor of lift music and the desultory rustle of plastic hangers. Then came noughties Topshop, which, along with H&M, brought event fashion to the high street with designer collaborations that turbocharged the shopping experience into a hot-ticket moment. Topshop's collaborations were an intoxicating mix of fun and genuine bargains – I still have, and still wear, a sundress from that first Kate Moss collection, and a velvet and lace party dress from a Christopher Kane for Topshop collaboration bought the same year.

It is no secret that Shepherdson and Green never saw eye to eye – when, after several years overseeing from a distance, Green moved to take closer creative control at Topshop, Shepherdson made a swift exit – but the combination of her passion for fashion and vision for the possibilities of customer experience with his appetite for grandstanding made for a great show.

For Green, Topshop was always personal. Once, when my *Guardian* fashion-desk colleagues and I were being talked through a new collection in the brand's showroom, he marched in, unhappy about something we had written, and demanded an apology. When none was forthcoming, the conversation deteriorated until he insulted, in my recollection, the size or shape of someone's nose. By now we all know that this was nothing compared with the bullying and abuse reported by some employees. Green denies any 'unlawful ... racist or sexual behaviour'. But even before allegations about serious misconduct came to light, his behaviour was coming to seem increasingly out of step with the expectations and values of his target market. Generation Z have changed culture for all of us. They have no time for a billionaire who expects to stand on the deck of his yacht and shout into a mobile phone, rather than listen to what they have to say.

First, Topshop found itself threatened by cheaper brands such as Primark. This was perhaps less a business failing on the part of Topshop than a symptom of the structural catastrophe of a cycle of ever-cheaper fast fashion. (If Topshop had slashed its production costs to compete in a marketplace of £10 jeans, it would have been nothing to cheer.) What happened after that, though, is a bit more complicated. With the rise of Boohoo and Missguided, Topshop was overtaken by brands that, like its target market, saw shopping as oriented around phone screens and the young influencers who hold the power in that magical world, not shop floors and their middle-aged bosses. That it would be overtaken by a new generation of brands was perhaps the price that Topshop paid for becoming a high-street rock star. No teenager wants to listen to her mum's music once she can assert her independence, after all. Why would she want to wear her mum's fashion brands?

Yet of all the Arcadia brands, Topshop has the best chance of a second act. In a crowded marketplace, a globally recognised brand that was at one time synonymous with the giddy thrill of shopping remains a valuable commodity. But to reclaim the potency it once had, it will need to look very different.

For a brand to seize the imagination today in the way that Topshop once did, it has to embrace a serious commitment to sustainability. It is no coincidence that Shepherdson, a woman who has been on the front foot of the zeitgeist since the 1990s, has now shifted out of retail into rental, as the chair of My Wardrobe HQ, the UK's largest fashion-rental platform.

For the past four years, Green has ruled the headlines as the villain of the Topshop piece – but the fast-fashion industry had a deeper, more poisonous dark side all along, with the long tail of environmental damage wreaked by clothes that have a six-week shelf life. Topshop was once about the future. To get back there it will need more than just a few new clothes.

8 December

Steve Thompson:
'I can't remember
winning the World Cup'

ANDY BULL

After Steve Thompson won the World Cup in 2003, he took part in the victory parade through the West End, was picked as one of the three best players in the world and went to Buckingham Palace, where they gave him an MBE. Thompson won a grand slam too, as well as a European Cup with Northampton Saints, and he played for the British and Irish Lions.

Now, at the age of 42, he has been diagnosed with early-onset dementia and probable chronic traumatic encephalopathy. 'It's the rugby that's put me through this,' he says. And that's why, if he could, he would undo all of it. 'Some people go for the big lights, whereas I don't want that. I never wanted that. I'd rather just have had a normal life.'

Thompson was on a job in Kendal not long ago, living away from home while he was repairing a burst water main. While he was there, they were showing some of the England games from the 2003 World Cup on TV. He had never watched them back before, except for little bits and pieces when they were doing their post-match analysis during the tournament. But he did now.

'And it was as if I was watching England play now. Except I was there. But I can't remember at all being there. Honestly, I don't know scores from any of the games.' A lot of his career is like that, patchy and full of gaps. He used to pride himself on his memory and have a head full of complicated lineout calls. 'If you put them in now, not a chance. Not a chance.'

These days, he forgets. He forgets directions, which bits of a book he has read and what TV shows he's watched. Sometimes he even forgets his wife's name. 'I could look at Steph sometimes. And she says it's like I'm a complete blank. And she'll go: "I'm Steph." The name's gone. Gone.' He suffers from anxiety, too, and has started having panic attacks. Sometimes he finds he gets aggressive for no good reason. 'It's weird. It's a bit like an out-of-body experience, to be honest, and it happens a lot more now.'

And he wonders what the point of it all was, why he spent all those years playing a game that, he believes, has led him here. 'I finished up with nothing really at the end of it.' Not even memories. 'I can't remember it. I've got no memorabilia. I've got no feelings about it. You see us lifting the World Cup and I can see me there jumping around. But I can't remember it.' The money is gone, too. 'No one could ever say that I'm money-orientated, because that's the one thing I'm not. I just wanted a simple life. I would have liked to be able to work outside and use my body and my mind. That's not going to happen now.'

What he does have is guilt. Steph is younger than him 'and I'm thinking, what have I done to her? She doesn't deserve this.' She has taken the diagnosis in her stride. 'She just went: "I'll just have to care for you, won't I?"' But he worries how she will cope. 'I'm not a small bloke, I'm six foot three, 120 kilos. So if you've got to care for me, it's quite a bit of meat to carry around.'

Thompson started playing when he was 15. 'Was it a massive love of my life? No, no, not really. But it was a job. I happened to be good at it in those times. I enjoyed the company of the lads and things like that. But then, would I do it again? No, I wouldn't.' He has four kids, the youngest of them a one-year-old boy. They still go down to the local rugby club, for the social side. 'But I don't really want my boy playing rugby, the way it is at the moment.' He watches the players 'knocking the hell out of each other' and he worries. 'You know, when you're younger, you feel a bit macho, and you feel like you can't be broken.'

That's how he was. Thompson was one of the first generation of professional players. When he started, he was training two nights a week. He remembers the switch to full-time training. 'It was like: "So what do we do now then?" It felt like the coaches were thinking: "We'll just knock the hell out of each other. That's what we'll do." And we did.' It was worse when he got called up to play for England. 'It was so brutal during the week that you'd come home on the Thursday for your day off and I'd just be like: "I don't think I can play, I feel utterly battered."'

The game in those early professional years had a brutal culture, Thompson says. 'They had us for that Six Nations period, and the autumn internationals, and they literally just beasted you until you fell apart.' They were back in training two days after they won the World Cup. A lot of them played for their clubs the next weekend. It made him feel like 'a bit of meat'. But he was so anxious about being dropped that he got on with it.

He guesses a lot of players from that era may end up having similar problems. 'I can see the numbers being high, especially for the first players to come through, what, '96–97 up to the mid-2000s, really.' He could see attitudes were changing by the end of his career. 'The 2011 World Cup camp was completely different to the 2003 World Cup camp. In 2011 it was a lot more technical, whereas in 2003 you just had to beast yourself.'

He didn't worry about it, because he didn't think he had to. 'I don't service my own car. Someone else does that, because that's what they do. I was there to play rugby. And then you've got people there that look after you.' But the players, in that culture, with the absence of regulation, were not protected. 'You think how many specialists were out there watching that and not saying anything,' he says.

'They knew what was happening. And nothing was done about it. People were getting knocked on the head and it was not being recorded. I'm knocked out in training and it was always: "It's just a knock on the head, he'll be fine."

'In the old days it was a bit of a laugh. If someone got whacked in the head, it was: "Oh, look at him, he's had a belt. He'll be up in a minute."' One of his doctors asked him how many concussions he had had. Thompson asked him back what counted as a concussion. 'Is it when you're totally out? And he said: "No, that's not true any more." And I'm like: "Well, I was doing it every training session then, really, when you look at it."

'The amount of head bangs I had in training. I was known for it. "Oh, he's having a little sleep, he'll get up in a minute."' He remembers all the gruelling sessions on the scrum machines. 'There's so much pressure. They aren't moving, they've got pegs in it, they've got people stood on it, and you drive into it, all that weight coming through.' He'd push until the point when his head started to go. 'And suddenly, as the pressure comes off, you start getting the light, the little white dots, and you don't know where you are for a few seconds.'

He is angry with the clubs, who he feels haven't provided proper aftercare, angry with the Rugby Football Union, and angry with the Rugby Players' Association, which he believes should be fighting harder for the players. 'I don't want to kill the game. I want it regulated.' He thinks professional players should be allowed to play only if they have a brain scan at the start of every season. 'Every year you drive your car you get an MOT. The body's exactly the same thing. If it's not working, you shouldn't be doing your job. It sounds awful, because lads are going to have to retire at 22 or 23. But trust me, it's better finishing then than to be where I am now.'

8 December

'It has given people hope': patients and NHS staff on day one of Covid vaccination

AAMNA MOHDIN

It was 6.31am when Margaret Keenan, an early riser, rolled up her sleeve in her local hospital in Coventry and became the first person in the world to receive the Pfizer/BioNTech Covid-19 vaccine as part of a mass vaccination programme. The 90-year-old made history while wearing a penguin Christmas sweater.

The sun had yet to rise, but a new dawn had broken in the UK's battle against this coronavirus.

It only took a few seconds for Keenan, known to friends and family as Maggie, to be vaccinated. She was met with applause from hospital staff as she was pushed down a corridor in a wheelchair. Keenan's injection marked the beginning of the largest vaccination programme the UK will ever see. Keenan turns 91 next week. She has four grandchildren. She said: 'I feel so privileged to be the first person vaccinated against Covid-19. It's the best early birthday present I could wish for because it means I can finally look forward to spending time with my family and friends in the new year after being on my own for most of the year.'

The last week has been a rollercoaster for the Keenans. Maggie's son, Philip, 61, said they were preparing for the worst when his mother was admitted to hospital last Thursday with an infection. She was placed in intensive care.

'We're all completely shocked,' he said from his home in Hertfordshire. 'Four days ago my mum was dying. She had a medical emergency and we had to get an ambulance to get her to Coventry hospital. My sister and I thought we were going to lose her, so I got ready to go up and say goodbye.'

But Keenan, who has been self-isolating for much of the year, made a remarkable recovery. 'Two days later, my mum is talking to me on the phone and she sounds like she's completely normal. She's got a voice back, her breath back, and it's like a miracle, to be honest.'

Originally from Enniskillen, Northern Ireland, Keenan has lived in Coventry for more than 60 years. She trained as a seamstress and window dresser, and worked for the C&A department store in Belfast and, later, Coventry. She was a hard worker, her son said, who always spent Christmas Day serving meals to those in need.

And this isn't the first time Keenan has made British medical history. After contracting tuberculosis in the early 1950s, aged 19, she was one of the first people in the UK to receive *Streptomyces* to treat her TB. She was treated for almost a year in Queen's hospital, Belfast. The nurse who administered Keenan's vaccine, May Parson, said it was a huge honour to be the first in the country to deliver the vaccine to a patient. 'The last few months have been tough for all of us working in the NHS, but now it feels like there is light at the end of the tunnel,' said Parson, who is from the Philippines but has worked in the NHS for the last 24 years.

The second person to be vaccinated was 81-year-old William Shakespeare, known as Bill, from Warwickshire, who said he was pleased to have received it. Shakespeare, whose name sparked a flurry of puns online, said: 'It could make a difference to our lives from now on.'

After watching Shakespeare's vaccination, the health secretary, Matt Hancock, told *Good Morning Britain*: 'It's been such a tough year for so many people. There's William Shakespeare putting it simply for everybody: that we can get on with our lives.' Shakespeare's niece, Emily, 47, who lives in Tramore, in Ireland, said that, like his famous namesake, her uncle's last claim to fame lay in Stratford-upon-Avon.

'He was caught speeding in Stratford in the 60s. It was the 60s version of going viral,' she said before laughing. 'He would have only been young and he had this old banger of a car. He was going downwards on a hill and he was caught. It was in the local press and everything. The story follows him around wherever he goes.'

And was there any connection to the playwright? Emily said she was 86 per cent sure there was, but planned to do more research when she retired.

The day has also been emotional for NHS staff. Claire Hobbs, a health and wellbeing practitioner and flu lead at Milton Keynes university hospital trust, was vaccinating patients yesterday. 'It's been a really good feeling knowing that there is something now that might give us that sense of normality back. It might give families the chance to get together with the rest of their family, without having to worry about bubbles. It has given a lot of people around the country hope,' she said.

Back in Hertfordshire, Philip Keenan was preparing to pick up his mother from the hospital. He described her as a 'pretty strong' woman: 'She was only decorating my house last year. She was decorating my bathroom. She was 89 then.'

The day has been a whirlwind for both of them. Neither expected her to become an international media star, appearing in the *Washington Post* and *Japan Times*. 'I just keep staring at the TV thinking, "This is my mum",' he said.

13 DECEMBER

Has a year of living with Covid-19 rewired our brains?

PAULA COCOZZA

When the bubonic plague spread through England in the 17th century, Sir Isaac Newton fled Cambridge, where he was studying, for the safety of his family home in Lincolnshire. The Newtons did not live in a cramped apartment; they enjoyed a large garden with many fruit trees. In these uncertain times, out of step with ordinary life, his mind roamed free of routines and social distractions. And it was in this context that a single apple falling from a tree struck him as more intriguing than any of the apples he had previously seen fall. Gravity was a gift of the plague. So, how is this pandemic going for you?

In different ways, this is likely a question we are all asking ourselves. Whether you have experienced illness, relocated, lost a loved one or a job, got a kitten or got divorced, eaten more or exercised more, spent longer showering each morning or reached every day for the same clothes, it is an inescapable truth that the pandemic alters us all. But how? And when will we have answers to these questions – because surely there will be a time when we can scan our personal balance sheets and see in the credit column something more than grey hairs, a thicker waist and a kitten? (Actually, the kitten is pretty rewarding.) What might be the psychological impact of living through a pandemic? Will it change us for ever?

'People talk about the return to normality, and I don't think that is going to happen,' says Frank Snowden, a historian of pandemics at Yale, and the author of *Epidemics and Society: From the Black Death to the Present*. Snowden has spent 40 years studying pandemics. Then last spring, just as his phone was going crazy with people wanting to know if history could shed light on Covid-19, his life's work landed in his lap. He caught the coronavirus.

Snowden believes that Covid-19 was not a random event. All pandemics 'afflict societies through the specific vulnerabilities people have created by their relationships with the environment, other species, and each other,' he says. Each pandemic has its own properties, and this one – a bit like the bubonic plague – affects mental health. Snowden sees a second pandemic coming 'in the train of the Covid-19 first pandemic … [a] psychological pandemic'.

Aoife O'Donovan, an associate professor of psychiatry at the UCSF Weill Institute for Neurosciences in California, who specialises in trauma, agrees. 'We are dealing with so many layers of uncertainty,' she says. 'Truly horrible things have happened and they will happen to others and we don't know when or to whom or how, and it is really demanding cognitively and physiologically.'

The impact is experienced throughout the body, she says, because when people perceive a threat, abstract or actual, they activate a biological stress response. Cortisol mobilises glucose. The immune system is triggered, increasing levels of inflammation. This affects the function of the brain, making people more sensitive to threats and less sensitive to rewards.

In practice, this means that your immune system may be activated simply by hearing someone next to you cough, or by the sight of all those face masks and the proliferation of a colour that surely Pantone should rename 'surgical blue', or by a stranger walking towards you, or even, as O'Donovan found, seeing a friend's cleaner in the background of a Zoom call, maskless. And because, O'Donovan points out, government regulations are by necessity broad and changeable, 'as individuals we have to make lots of choices. This is uncertainty on a really intense scale.'

The unique characteristics of Covid-19 play into this sense of uncertainty. The illness 'is much more complex than anyone imagined in the beginning', Snowden says: a sort of shapeshifting adversary. In some it is a respiratory disease, in others gastrointestinal, in others it can cause delirium and cognitive impairment, in some it has a very long tail, while many experience it as asymptomatic. Most of us will never know if we have had it, and not knowing spurs a constant self-scrutiny. Symptom checkers raise questions more than they allay fears: when does tiredness become fatigue? When does a cough become 'continuous'?

O'Donovan sighs. She sounds tired; this is a busy time to be a threat researcher and her whole life is work now. She finds the body's response to uncertainty 'beautiful' – its ability to mobilise to see off danger – but she's concerned that it is ill-suited to frequent and prolonged threats. 'This chronic activation can be harmful in the long term. It accelerates biological ageing and increases risk for diseases of ageing,' she says.

In daily life, uncertainty has played out in countless tiny ways as we try to reorient ourselves in a crisis, in the absence of the usual landmarks – schools, families, friendships, routines and rituals. Previously habitual rhythms, of time alone and time with others, the commute and even postal deliveries, are askew.

There is no new normal – just an evolving estrangement. Even a simple 'how are you?' is heavy with hidden questions (are you infectious?), and rarely brings a straightforward answer; more likely a hypervigilant account of a mysterious high temperature experienced back in February.

Thomas Dixon, a historian of emotions at Queen Mary University of London, says that when the pandemic hit, he stopped opening his emails with the phrase 'I hope this finds you well'.

The old 'social dances' – as the psychotherapist Philippa Perry calls them – of finding a seat in a cafe or on the bus have not only vanished, taking with them opportunities to experience a sense of belonging, but have been replaced with dances of rejection. Perry thinks that's why she misses the Pret a Manger queue. 'We were all waiting to pay for our sandwiches that we were all taking back to our desks. It was a sort of group activity even if I didn't know the other people in the group.'

In contrast, pandemic queues are not organic; they are a series of regularly spaced people being processed by a wayfinding system. Further rejection occurs if a pedestrian steps into the gutter to avoid you, or when the delivery person you used to enjoy greeting sees you at the door and lunges backwards. It provides no consolation, Perry says, to understand cognitively why we repel others. The sense of rejection remains.

The word 'contagion' comes from the Latin for 'with' and 'touch', so it is no wonder that social touch is demonised in a pandemic. But at what cost? The neuroscientists Francis McGlone and Merle Fairhurst study nerve fibres called C-tactile afferents, which are concentrated in hard-to-reach places such as the back and shoulders. They wire social touch into a complex reward system, so that when we are stroked, touched, hugged or patted, oxytocin is released, lowering the heart rate and inhibiting the production of cortisol. 'Very subtle requirements,' says McGlone, 'to keep you on an even plane.'

But McGlone is worried. 'Everywhere I look at changes of behaviour during the pandemic, this little flag is flying, this nerve fibre – touch, touch, touch!' While some people – especially those locked down with young children – might be experiencing more touch, others are going entirely without. Fairhurst is examining the data collected from a large survey she and McGlone launched in May, and she is finding those most at risk from the negative emotional impact of loss of touch are young people. 'Age is a significant indicator of loneliness and depression,' she says. The loss of the connecting power of touch triggers 'factors that contribute to depression – sadness, lower energy levels, lethargy'.

'We are becoming a sort of non-person,' says Perry. Masks render us mostly faceless. Hand sanitiser is a physical screen. Fairhurst sees it as 'a barrier, like not speaking somebody's language'. And Perry is not the only one to favour the 'non-person clothes' of pyjamas and tracksuits. Somehow, the repeat-wearing of clothes makes all clothing feel like fatigues. They suit our weariness, and add an extra layer to it.

Cultural losses feed this sense of dehumanisation. Eric Clarke, a professor at Wadham College, Oxford, with a research interest in the psychology of music, led street singing in his cul-de-sac during the first lockdown, which 'felt almost like a lifeline', but he has missed going to live music events. 'The impact on me has been one of a feeling of degradation or erosion of my aesthetic self,' he says. 'I feel less excited by the world around me than I do when I'm going to music.' And the street music, like the street clapping, stopped months ago. Now 'we are all living like boil-in-a-bag rice, closed off from the world in a plastic envelope of one sort or another'.

No element of Covid-19 has dehumanised people more than the way it has led us to experience death. Individuals become single units in a very long and horribly growing number, of course. But before they become statistics, the dying are condemned to isolation. 'They are literally depersonalised,' Snowden says. He lost his sister during the pandemic. 'I didn't see her, and nor was she with her family ... It breaks bonds and estranges people.'

For a short while, the pandemic may have made people feel as if they were somehow together in those plastic envelopes that Clarke describes; literally so for those who posted YouTube videos of homemade plastic 'cuddle curtains' through which to hug loved ones. 'If you know the literature on disasters, immediately afterwards you get this altruistic community thing where you all have this sense of common fate,' says John Drury, a professor at the University of Sussex who specialises in crowd psychology. 'But you can't sustain that.'

Now, allied to the depersonalisation is a heightened sense of individualism – it's a tough combination to feel both more of an individual and less of a person. 'We are no longer in it together in the same way,' says Clarke, the musician.

Greater individualism can be seen at international and political level too, as when Donald Trump moved to withdraw the US from the World Health Organization. His description of Covid-19 as the 'Wuhan virus' or 'kung flu' melded the fear of an other – which a pandemic is likely to generate – to racism. From the UK and Germany to the US, there has been a rise in the incidence of racist hate crimes towards some Asian communities.

What you can do, and probably have done, is adopt compensatory behaviours. The maladaptive of these will add to that lengthening second pandemic, the psychological aftermath of the first. In Scotland, for instance, substance abuse deaths have risen by a third; the British Liver Trust has reported a 500 per cent rise in calls to its helpline; domestic violence has surged worldwide.

But even the tiniest positive alterations to habit can be hugely effective. Fairhurst, for instance, wears more perfume and spends longer washing her hair – 'a direct activation' of her C-tactile afferent nerves, she thinks. Her research data has shown that 'people who are less lonely are those who are grooming more'. Snowden survived his isolation intact partly thanks to a Zoom group of school friends who meet online each week despite not having got together for 56 years previously. Dixon did art with his children. Drury, 'a very functional person' who would walk only if he needed something, now walks 'for emotional and mental health'.

'We had pandemics in the past and we are still here,' says Fairhurst. To adapt is to survive. To notice the adaptations, however small, is to appreciate humanity.

So will the pandemic alter us for the long term?

O'Donovan, in San Francisco, who has for years studied post-traumatic stress disorder, believes an increase in the incidence of PTSD will probably follow Covid-19. It is also likely that Covid19 will challenge the criteria for diagnosing PTSD. While 20 to 30 per cent of those who go into intensive care units will later experience PTSD, what of those who fear for their lives in previously innocuous situations – such as in the grocery store or on public transport? Might PTSD be triggered by a close stranger's uninhibited cough? There are people who recovered from Sars in 2003 and were still being treated for PTSD more than a decade later. 'We have a lot of work to do,' O'Donovan says.

And then there is the possibility that the fear of Covid-19 may outlive the worst of the disease itself. Drury thinks people will easily relearn how to behave in a crowd. The big question is for how long will they fear crowds. After the London bombings of 2005, the terror threat level was lowered and people resumed their travel habits, he points out. But this summer, when the British government urged a mass return to work, many resisted. 'They believed ... that there was still danger.' What follows the pandemic will depend on how safe people feel. And all the while, the more 'systemic inflammation' people have, because their biological response to stressors is activated, the more sensitive they will be to perceived social threats.

No wonder, then, that for Thomas Dixon, the emotional historian, the pandemic is 'akin to a world war' in its emotional fallout. 'We will have, I assume, a global recession. There is going to be serious suffering and inequality and poverty. It is a world event with big emotional consequences, and it seems to me that in times of adversity people's emotional repertoire changes,' he says. He thinks that 'a more resilient, and perhaps more reserved, emotional style' might evolve out of the pandemic and its aftermath.

Snowden says: 'There are silver linings in something uniquely bad and dark. Maybe as a result of this we will transform our healthcare system so that it pays proper attention to mental as well as physical health. Maybe [the pandemic] will help us rethink what medicine is for.'

And maybe, a little like Newton's orchard, the pandemic will give us a chance to see things we have seen many times before, but with new clarity. It would seem unlikely that every person who worked solely in an office will spend every working day in one post-vaccination. Changes to road layouts and car exclusions are under way in many cities, with Carlos Moreno's '15-minute city' concept gaining critical airtime from Paris to Buenos Aires. In late 19th-century England the telephone was introduced in hospitals to help people with scarlet fever communicate with their loved ones; it caught on. With coronavirus, FaceTime and Zoom have offered the same solace of remote connection (though when some meetings shift back offline, and Zoom is no longer there to arbitrate on conversational turn-taking, and remind us of people's names, we may have to relearn some communication skills).

'We can use this pandemic as a galvanising force for change,' says Alexandre White of Johns Hopkins University, who would like to see a universal healthcare act in the US 'to prevent a lot of the worst healthcare outcomes that come from inequality but also to minimise the economic, social and health inequality in the first place. The conditions of possibility are there.'

And maybe that is the point – to see these times as creating the conditions for new opportunities. The challenges will be many; the fallout painful. But there is an opening for previously unthinkable change, not only to the structures of societies, but also in countless small ways – privately, personally. We have lived for months at close quarters with ourselves. We will deepen our appreciation of some of the simple things we have missed, and some of the pleasures that have helped us through, even if it is only the taste of a new-season apple. And, in some measure, we will know ourselves better.

16 DECEMBER

'There are plenty of schlongs in art' – Maggi Hambling defends her nude sculpture of Mary Wollstonecraft

STUART JEFFRIES

Maggi Hambling is listing her favourite sculpted penises. 'The Elgin marbles,' she says. 'Michelangelo's *David*. And Shelley's, though it is rather small.' She means the Shelley memorial, Edward Onslow Ford's attempt to depict the sea-shrunken corpse of the drowned poet. She takes a drag on her cigarette, exhales and giggles.

We're sitting on the pavement outside the Marlborough Gallery in Mayfair so Hambling can have a cigarette. It's stupidly cold but this is the only place we can do the interview, unless the artist quits. And that's not going to happen. She is an incorrigible smoker, refusing to be photographed without a cigarette in hand. Until recently, the gallery made an exception, allowing

Hambling to light up inside. 'But the people in the offices above objected to the smell,' she says. 'They threatened to close down my show.' So she has evicted herself from her own exhibition for four cigarettes and a coffee.

Why are we talking penises? Because I asked Hambling to address the critics of her statue of Mary Wollstonecraft, the feminist icon and mother-in-law of Shelley. It was unveiled last month in Newington Green, north London, sparking an instant furore. The hostile response, which came in no small part from feminists who had waited a long time to see their heroine honoured, was provoked by the tiny, naked and luxuriantly bushed figure of Wollstonecraft crowning Hambling's sculpture. A piece in the *Guardian* was headlined: 'Why I hate the Mary Wollstonecraft statue: would a man be "honoured" with his schlong out?' Hambling replies: 'Oh, but there are plenty of schlongs honouring men in art.' This is true. But not far from this spot, on the facade of the Royal Academy, four male philosophers – Francis Bacon, Gottfried Wilhelm Leibniz, John Locke and Adam Smith – are all honoured fully clothed. The feeling was that the work played to the male gaze, offering yet another obligingly passive and implausibly perky female nude. So shouldn't Hambling have honoured the author of *A Vindication of the Rights of Woman* with her clothes on? 'The figure had to be nude because clothes define people,' she says. 'Put someone in tweeds and they become horsey. Put someone in period dress and they become part of history. I didn't want to do that to her.'

She adds: 'I wanted to capture the spirit of Mary Wollstonecraft and the struggle for the rights of women. It's a struggle that goes on – and so the figure is a challenge to our world.'

The controversy doubtless helped make Wollstonecraft better known. Bee Rowlatt, author of *In Search of Mary*, was among the women who had campaigned for a statue. She pointed out that millions read about Wollstonecraft because of the outcry.

Hambling knows from experience that anything can happen once her art leaves her studio. 'It goes out into the world and I'm not in charge of it any more.' Yet she feels that a lot of the commentary missed the point. The idea, as Rowlatt explained, was to represent the birth of a movement, rather than Wollstonecraft herself. The hope, too, was to get away from putting people on pedestals.

But if that were true, shouldn't Hambling have done something more akin to, say, Kathryn Gustafson's Hyde Park memorial to Princess Diana, a fountain deliberately conceived as anti-phallic and anti-representational, albeit one that Britons swiftly diminished by washing their dogs in? 'Well, I suppose you could say my sculpture is phallic. Somebody said to me, "It's like a skyrocket going up." I like that.'

Certainly, Hambling's sculpture is not so much resting on a pedestal as rushing skywards on a froth of mysterious matter. That matter, Hambling explains, represents the fight against the patriarchy. 'The tower the figure rests upon refers to the struggle of women. They are mingling female forms.' As she points out, many of the articles damning her sculpture cropped out that context to focus on the nude figure. Would she have done Wollstonecraft differently had she known the uproar it would cause? 'No,' says the artist. 'I couldn't. I'm not in control of what I do. The subject speaks through me when I work.'

18 December

Le Carré's death touched me. It feels like the grownups are leaving the room

JONATHAN FREEDLAND

This week I've been hearing the call of the dead. It's been loud, following the death of David Cornwell, the writer known to the world as John le Carré. Ever since the news broke last Sunday, I've been devouring every obituary, reading every appreciation. And that's prompted a question. What is it exactly that we mourn when we mourn a public figure?

In the case of Le Carré, I can claim only the smallest personal connection. One weekday morning around a decade ago, he called entirely out of the blue and asked me to lunch – in two hours' time. Whatever plans that I might have had, I dropped. We met at a London restaurant so crowded that they couldn't give him a table. So we sat side by side at the bar. He asked me a few questions, listened intently, then, once the main course had arrived, he changed gear, delivering a string of anecdotes and witty, shrewd and entertaining observations.

At no point did he explain why he had wanted to have lunch with someone he'd never spoken to or met before, or why so urgently.

Only a year later, with the publication of *A Delicate Truth*, set in the New Labour era, did I realise that I had, unwittingly, experienced something halfway between an interrogation and the debriefing of an asset.

I cherished that encounter and a couple of later ones, but that's not why I'm feeling Le Carré's loss so keenly. Part of it is simple admiration. 'Writer of spy novels' doesn't capture it: Le Carré was one of the giants of postwar English literature, a master of his chosen form and an exceptional prose stylist. He had an ear for the dialect of the governing classes of this country, perfectly tuned to their evasions, their deceits, their melancholy.

Still, that's not wholly it either. I also respected his deep moral sense: he was fiercely against Brexit, for example, because he saw European cooperation as the only possible weapon against the murderous furies that had been unleashed in the 1930s, the decade of his birth. And I admired his ability to walk moral high wires. In the cold war era that his novels came to define, he exposed the hypocrisies of the west without ever overlooking the cruelties of the Soviet east. He was an unforgiving critic of Israeli militarism, yet was the first to sign a 2019 letter denouncing Labour antisemitism. It sounds straightforward, but few manage to tread those lines without losing their balance.

Perhaps it's also worth mentioning that Cornwell was close to the age of my father, who died two years ago. That inches closer to the heart of the matter. For the way we experience the death of public figures is private, even intimate.

Part of it is that the death of one person revives the memory of the death of another. Loss is like that – cumulative, each new bereavement containing those that went before. I remember how many of those who filled the streets in the strange, intense week that followed the death of Diana in 1997 confessed to grieving for someone other than a lost princess. On TV they looked like they were sobbing for an estranged royal, but for many there were tears within those tears – for a husband, a mother, a son.

Part of it is nostalgia. The death of Sean Connery in October, for instance, evoked the optimism and confidence of the 1960s, when a British hero could cut a dash. But the more intense nostalgia is personal – the life of a famous person, rewound and replayed when they die, prompting reminiscences of your own past. That's particularly true of actors and, perhaps even more so, musicians. When David Bowie died in 2016, many mourned the man who they said had supplied the soundtrack of their lives, their young lives especially. They could measure out their memories in his songs: where they were, how they felt, who they loved.

Of course, those songs are still there, just as Le Carré's books will be no less available to read this week than they were last. So what's the problem? It might be the knowledge that there will be nothing more, nothing new. After 2020, you'll never see a new Diana Rigg performance you haven't seen before. For a different generation, it might be Chadwick Boseman or Kobe Bryant, but the sentiment will be the same. Those people who, in your teens, struck you as the incarnation of vitality or beauty are now part of the past – and so, therefore, is your youth.

Even those who were never our idols, who were just around, prompt a pang when they go. I might not have thought of Des O'Connor, Barbara Windsor or Geoffrey Palmer in years, but their deaths register all the same. A small piece of mental furniture, a memento of childhood, has been removed. Anyone who has packed up their parents' home, sorting into piles and boxes the tiny, trivial items – a biscuit tin, a holiday trinket – that were once so familiar but will never be seen again, knows the feeling.

With those we greatly admired, it goes deeper. Those who used to guide us can guide us no longer. In 2021 US campaigners for equality and civil rights will not be able to rely on the inspiration and counsel of John Lewis or Ruth Bader Ginsburg. They'll have to push ahead without them. In my own life, I found it comforting to know that, say, the former chief rabbi Jonathan Sacks or the legendary newspaper editor Harold Evans were still around – able to offer sage advice to Jewish people or journalists on how we should approach whatever new challenge arose. But now they too are gone.

Sometimes, and irrationally, I've wondered if the timing is deliberate. Leonard Cohen died the day before Donald Trump was elected in 2016, as if he was exiting the stage so he wouldn't have to witness the monstrous clown taking the spotlight. An ardent European, Le Carré departed just days before Britain's last ties to the European Union will be severed.

It means we will have to face the future alone, without these older, wiser minds around to light the way. It can feel lonely, similar to the day you realise your parents – or an older sibling – are no longer there to place a gentle, restraining hand on yours.

The grownups are leaving, one by one. From now on, it's only us – guided by the lessons they taught us and the memories they left behind. And comforted by the thought that, perhaps, they once felt exactly the same way.

Winter

Barbara Blake-Hannah: how Britain's first black female TV reporter was forced off our screens

ELLEN E JONES

In 2008, Barbara Blake-Hannah wrote a letter of admonishment to the *Guardian*. 'I must put history right,' she wrote, explaining that a poster issued by the paper was incorrect. It contained, she noted, the common misconception that Trevor McDonald was the first Black person to report the news on British TV after he joined ITN in 1973 and that Moira Stuart, on BBC News from 1981, was the first Black woman. In fact, said Blake-Hannah – an author, filmmaker and former Jamaican senator – in 1968 she was one of three Thames Television on-camera reporters for the current affairs programme *Today*. (The BBC had hired a Black trainee reporter, Eric Anthony Abrahams, a few years earlier.)

Her appointment made every daily newspaper, bar the *Daily Express*. Blake-Hannah claims the *Express* held out only because 'they had a rule: no Black people on the front page'. 'Shirley Bassey sang regularly and there were comedians, but we were allowed in an entertainment capacity, not as serious news people, delivering serious stories.'

She reported five days a week, on everything from the closing-down sale of the Beatles' Baker Street shop to gang crime in the East End of London. But, after nine months, the producers told her abruptly that they would not be renewing her contract. Why?

Because of the numerous calls and letters from viewers objecting to a Black person on TV. 'It broke my heart,' she says.

Blake-Hannah is speaking to me from her home in Kingston, Jamaica, where she settled in 1972. She embraced Rastafari. The straightened, Vidal Sassoon-style bob of her 60s TV appearances has long been replaced by a leopard-print headwrap. Her only child, Makonnen Hannah, is nearby – he made headlines globally in 1998 when, as a 13-year-old, he was appointed the youngest-ever adviser to Jamaica's Ministry of Commerce and Technology.

Blake-Hannah was raised in an affluent part of the Jamaican capital by her father, Evon Blake, a prominent magazine editor. She says he is best remembered as the man who desegregated the swimming pool of the upmarket Myrtle Bank hotel, a favourite haunt of one of his employees. 'This accountant would go and swim there every midday, but my father, his boss, couldn't. So one day my father put on his swimsuit and dived in. The horror! The manager came and said: "Mr Blake, you have to get out of the pool." He said: "No. Call the manager, call the prime minister, call God!" And that was it: he liberated that pool, and he liberated Jamaican tourism.'

It was never about the pool. The family had access to a pool and Blake-Hannah and her sister swam every morning. They were attended to by a cook, a gardener and a nursemaid and had places at the prestigious boarding school Hampton, alongside the daughters of the Caribbean elite. 'There were 100 girls, only 10 of whom were Black, of whom my sister and I were the "blackest",' she says.

The young Blake-Hannah's expensive education ended prematurely, however, just after her O-levels. 'By then, my father's finances had collapsed. He took me out and put me in secretarial school. I wept bitter tears, but it really turned out to be most useful.' By the time Blake-Hannah accepted a job offer in Britain – a bit-part in the 1965 film *A High Wind in Jamaica*, starring Anthony Quinn – her work experience already included journalism, copywriting for an advertising agency, hosting a TV quizshow, appearing in a pantomime and a spot of modelling.

It was a good life, but she felt drawn to the 'mother country'. 'I'd been educated to be a Black Englishwoman. I could tell you the average rain rate for all of the Lake District and recite Wordsworth's poem to daffodils. I spoke and wrote perfect English and I thought: "Well, apart from the disadvantage of brown skin, kinky hair and a broad nose, I would be quite OK, y'know?"'

Britain did not offer the warm Commonwealth welcome she had hoped for. 'The contempt was so visible all the time; that was a real shock,' she says. A shock, but hardly a surprise. 'Slavery already taught us that, y'know? The white man will have contempt: you are his inferior and he doesn't have to like you. So you're kind of prepared. At that time in the development of Black people in the world, that was our attitude.'

The practical difficulties, however, were a shock. 'Trying to get accommodation is really where it hit home,' she says. 'No one would rent you anywhere decent. You had to be prepared to have the worst accommodation, in the worst parts of town.' In the end, she could find only a room in a house where she had to share the single bathroom with two families from India. 'It was really awful to have to put up with life under those conditions,' she says.

Work was easier to come by, although she had to start at the bottom. After a succession of temporary secretarial jobs, Blake-Hannah got a position at the PR company employed in the UK by Jamaica. In time, she began writing for the *Sunday Times* and felt herself embraced by a community, alongside the expat West Indian one.

'I had a very good girlfriend – Celia Brayfield, who became a bestselling author – and we'd go to the parties that the *Sunday*

Times and other journalists would give,' she says. Was she the only person of colour within that media circle? Probably, but the thought never occurred to her. 'It was an artistic community that was colourless, y'know? It didn't matter. The Beatles had just gone to India, good heavens! So everybody was dressing in Indian clothes. It was a multicultural melting pot.' It offered respite from discrimination elsewhere. 'You were aware of racism at all times. I think it was just this circle of people who had no hang-ups, no prejudices, that made life not too difficult.'

By the mid-60s, the Black liberation movement was well under way, yet it felt far removed from Blake-Hannah's life in London. 'The revolution was something that was happening in America,' she says. '"Black is beautiful", Black Power, Malcolm X, Stokely Carmichael; our Black brains started ticking over because of them, but the Black community on Ladbroke Grove was a place you tried your best to get away from, because it was really the bottom and you weren't accustomed to that; I certainly wasn't.'

It would take several more years – and a Rastafari awakening – before Blake-Hannah began to consider her place in this revolution. She moved in different circles to the activists such as the Mangrove Nine, who were arrested for protesting against police harassment of the Mangrove restaurant in Notting Hill and then fought a landmark legal battle to highlight racism in the criminal justice system. 'Mangrove was happening at the same time as I had my PR job. I took people to lunch, y'know, at restaurants on Kings Road. I didn't take clients to lunch at the Mangrove.'

When conducting interviews in public, she was shielded from much of the prejudice, if only because most people were flattered by the presence of a camera. 'I put that down to the fact that people like to be on television. It doesn't matter who's asking them the questions,' she says. But being a journalist couldn't protect her from racism within the media. 'I remember a job in Birmingham; they asked me one morning: "Well, Barbara, if Black people are so great, how come they didn't paint the *Mona Lisa*?"' She was speechless. 'I didn't have an answer. I didn't know there was anything to compare to the *Mona Lisa*. I thought that Egypt was Elizabeth Taylor in *Cleopatra*, y'know? I didn't know anything about Africa. Except that we had come from there as slaves. That's all I knew.'

One day in 1968, she was sent to report at the Houses of Parliament. 'I remember being on a bus and passing by South Africa House in Trafalgar Square and white people using the N-word and shouting up at my face in the bus: 'Go back home.' This was the year of the bill proposing amendments to the Race Relations Act 1965, making it illegal to refuse housing, employment or public services on the grounds of race. In March, Enoch Powell had delivered his infamous 'Rivers of Blood' speech in objection to the bill. For Blake-Hannah, the timing of her dismissal from *Today* that year is significant. 'Thames Television had a good opportunity to act on the Race Relations Act and they didn't. They decided to continue the racism. I didn't know it at the time – I couldn't say anything – but, looking at it now, it was really wrong. They could easily have said [of the racist complaints]: "We don't care."' After being let go in such a manner, she says: 'I realised there was no space for me in Britain.'

She did find another job in TV, at Associated Television in Birmingham, but unrelenting racism interfered again. No accommodation near her job would accept a Black tenant, so she was forced to undertake an exhausting daily commute from London. In her 2008 letter to the *Guardian*, she recalled how she had to 'listen without reacting when the production staff asked: "What 'wog' story are we doing today?"' On another occasion, she wrote, Powell agreed to an interview 'on condition that "the Black girl" was not there'.

A few years later, she was asked to do PR for the Jamaican film *The Harder They Come*. She decided to leave the UK. 'The entire population of Jamaica tried to get into the cinema that premiere night. When the show was over, the best party I've ever been to in my life was held by the Jamaicans. I couldn't wait to get back home ... I did not look back.'

What she did on her return was enough to fill many books – and illustrates just how much Britain lost. She produced several films, including the 1982 Channel 4 documentary *Race, Rhetoric, Rastafari*, and several books, including a 2010 memoir covering her time in Britain and an influential manual on home schooling. In 1984, she was elected as an independent senator, becoming the first Rastafarian to serve in the Jamaican parliament. She has always kept abreast of British news and now campaigns against what she calls 'heartless' Home Office deportations to Jamaica – which Priti Patel, the home secretary, last week promised to make a 'regular drumbeat' of British life.

Blake-Hannah tells the story of Treymane Brown, a 25-year-old who left Jamaica for the UK as a six-year-old and was separated from his own six-year-old son when he was deported in 2017. While homeless in Jamaica, Brown saved a young boy from drowning in a gully. 'All they could do was give him a hero's award. He still has no job, no money and nowhere to live. None of them do. None of them have any connection with Jamaica except their genes.'

What shocks her most, however, is how little the British media have changed in the 50 years since she was sacked, lest the shade of her skin offend racists. 'When Meghan [the Duchess of Sussex] was still in Britain, you'd see a story and go into the comments section ... I could see into the minds of the people who would call in [to *Today*] and say: "Get that N-word off our screens!" Those people still exist in Britain today.'

Whether it is supermarkets' TV adverts, Black Lives Matter-themed dance performances or breakfast news presenters being disciplined, it often seems the racists in the audience have their feelings considered more than the non-racist majority. 'You know why? British people have never been taught the full story of their history ... the Queen of England is a nice old lady, nuff respect, but when I see Colston's statue toppled and I read the history of the Royal African Company ... You all need to know your history! That will stop the arrogance and that will stop the racism.'

Her own place in that history is being reclaimed. This year, the annual British Journalism Awards awarded the inaugural Barbara Blake-Hannah prize to the *Independent*'s Kuba Shand-Baptiste. The award for up-and-coming minority ethnic journalist also had the coolest prize – to fly out to Jamaica to meet Blake-Hannah. She is also part of Britain's Black History Month curriculum and has received an Order of Distinction from the Jamaican government. But the journalism award is, she says, particularly meaningful: 'Every year, I will be remembered by all these beautiful Black, brown, Asian journalists. I am so honoured.'

The advice she has for the recipients is the same as that for all who follow in her footsteps: 'Learn your history. Don't be like Barbara Blake when they said: "If Black people are so great, how come they never painted the *Mona Lisa*?" Have an answer, because somebody's gonna ask you. And then teach them something. Come into work one morning and say: "Hey, do you know that it's Usain Bolt's birthday today?" Just once in a while, say something Black.'

7 JANUARY

The *Guardian* view on the storming of the US Capitol: democracy in danger

GUARDIAN EDITORIAL

What took so long? 'When someone shows you who they are, believe them the first time,' Maya Angelou counselled. Donald Trump's keenest supporters believed him. But too many others, even among those who reviled him, nonetheless assumed that there were limits. They can no longer be complacent. The American carnage of Wednesday night – the storming of the Capitol by an armed and violent mob, incited by the president, in an attempt to terrorise Congress and stop the peaceful transfer of power – marked an extraordinary moment in US history. 'If the post-American era has a start date, it is almost certainly today,' wrote Richard Haass, president of the Council on Foreign Relations.

Yet this was merely the ultimate and undeniable proof of what was always evident: that this man is not only unfit for his office, he is also a danger to democracy while he retains it. He built his political success on lies, contempt for democratic standards, the stoking of divisions – most of all racial – and the glamorising of force. They were evident when he campaigned for the presidency, and more blatant when he talked of 'very fine people' among the white supremacists of Charlottesville. When the House impeached him for abusing power for electoral purposes. When he lied that the election would be stolen, and then lied that it had been. When he called supporters to Washington. When he told them that they would 'never take back our country with weakness' and urged them on to the Capitol.

The Senate majority leader, Mitch McConnell, and others deserve no credit for belated pieties about the state of the republic. All those who helped or 'humoured' Mr Trump's election-stealing attempts are culpable. Already expert in more genteel endeavours, such as voter suppression and gerrymandering, the Republican elites have enabled and encouraged Trumpism: standing at his side, acquitting him when impeached, staying silent, or amplifying his lies. Having invited in an arsonist and supplied him with accelerant, they offer a cup of water to douse the inferno.

The urgent issue is how to deal with Mr Trump. No faith can be put in his last-minute promise of an orderly transition when he continues to foment rage. The Democratic leader in the Senate, Chuck Schumer, has called for his immediate removal. Cabinet members are reportedly now discussing the use of the 25th amendment, which allows the replacement of an 'unfit' president. But this is not about mere failings or incapacity: a better choice would be to begin impeachment proceedings. Action must be taken against Mr Trump, as it must against those he incited, to prevent him from running again and send a clear message to anyone tempted to follow.

For the truly important issue is how to salvage democracy in America. While Wednesday may prove a wake-up call for some Trump voters, many are already explaining away events, or excusing them through false equivalences with the Black Lives Matter movement. Divisions run deep through American society and even its institutions. A full investigation is needed of the failure to protect the Capitol when extremists had openly talked of such a plan – in stark contrast to the intense security and aggressive treatment that greeted peaceful BLM protesters. Tens of millions of Americans now believe that the election was stolen: one report suggests that only a quarter of Republicans trust the result. Rightwing media have fostered lies, and social media allowed people to dwell in alternative political universes. Though Facebook has finally suspended the president's account, the stable door is shutting long after disinformation galloped off into the distance. None of this will end when Joe Biden is inaugurated on 20 January.

Democracy exists not in the provisions written down on paper, but so long as it is practised, which is to say, defended. The remarkable twin victories in the Georgia runoffs on Wednesday, giving the Democrats control of the Senate via the vice-president's casting vote, were a welcome testimony to what is possible. But their importance is dwarfed by the threat looming over the system itself. The struggle is only just beginning. America has shown its people what it is. They should believe it – and act accordingly.

9 JANUARY

It's a Sin: 'If Covid was an STD it would be hidden too'

LOUIS WISE

Russell T Davies's drama *It's a Sin*, charting the early years of the Aids epidemic in the UK, arrives on our screens with a pep in its step that may at first seem at odds with the subject. It is difficult, after all, to think cheerfully about an epidemic that has taken thousands of lives in Britain alone, and a virus that an estimated 100,000 people in the country still live with. Its title is particularly apt: the 1987 Pet Shop Boys track it's borrowed from summons both the decadent pleasures of the era and that all-pervading sense of shame: the shame of the illness itself, so vicious and mysterious at first, and the fact that it often came from gay sex, perceived for so long as shameful, too.

And yet – it *is* a Russell T Davies show. This is the man who gave us *Queer as Folk*, *Cucumber* and an enjoyably queered *Doctor Who*. As we follow a ragtag bunch of young friends in London in the early 80s, spearheaded by the effervescent Ritchie (played by Years & Years singer Olly Alexander), there are shags, gags and parties galore, plus the undeniable camp of Tracy-Ann Oberman as Ritchie's agent and a glorious Keeley Hawes as his mum. Ritchie's clan includes sweet Welsh lad Colin (Callum Scott Howells), the fiercely defiant Roscoe (Omari Douglas), the more sensitive Ash (Nathaniel Curtis) and Lydia West's Jill, unofficial mum to the group. We see them negotiate the usual stuff young adults have to face – sex, studies, jobs and litres of booze – against the slowly darkening backdrop of the HIV/Aids crisis. Some live, some die, but all resolve to have a hoot. If *It's a Sin* is about the horror of so many lights being snuffed out, it is still utterly flaming.

It is that mixture of innocent joy and growing dread that is the show's calling card, according to the cast, first interviewed early last year. 'It's not mainly about death,' promises Scott Howells, sitting alongside Alexander and West in a former school on the outskirts of Manchester, which has been turned, for the production, into the friends' den-cum-flat 'The Pink Palace', all 80s pop star posters and uncompromising wallpaper. 'It's about life: their vibrant, colourful, beautiful lives.'

'People hear: "It charts the progress of the Aids crisis," and they think: "God, this is gonna be real heavy,"' agrees Alexander, 30, making a welcome return to acting following his appearance in the final series of *Skins*. 'And there are some heavy moments, but it's more about the joy of these characters.' That's especially because, West adds, these youngsters had no idea what was happening. In an era characterised by disbelief and misinformation, they can't help but be blithe. 'You're not playing the tragedy, you're just living it,' she says.

There is a rich artistic canon documenting HIV/Aids, from *Angels in America* to *Pose* to the West End hit *The Inheritance*. But Davies, 57, feels that *It's a Sin* fills a new space. Watching 2017's vibrant French Aids activism film *120 BPM* confirmed he was right to take a new route. The characters in *It's a Sin*, he says, 'have moments ... but they are not a flat full of activists. They're ordinary people, and I'm interested in that because their stories aren't often told.' In fact, he sighs, so few people actually go on those marches that make history. 'The rest of us just sit there worrying.'

Although Davies drew on his experiences – at 18 he moved to a big city, Manchester, in 1981 – he himself has not contracted the virus. 'I can't believe my luck, because I had a good old time,' he says in his mile-a-minute Welsh chatter. 'We all had those nights where there was too much hot blood and alcohol, and it gets you carried away. We all wish we were safe all the time, and so few people are. I was lucky.'

Davies did lose plenty of friends to the disease, and it is clear he is partly writing the show for them. But grief of another sort hovers over the show: he lost his husband Andrew Smith to cancer in 2018 after a long illness. 'It's there enormously,' he says. 'There's no way you can sit there writing all day without that coming out. I think if I was sitting here writing *Fireman Sam*, something sad would have happened to his cat.' One of the deaths in the show echoes Andrew's almost stage by stage, but that is also, he says, just the writer in him scavenging for material. 'You can't help but use it.'

If *It's a Sin* is a period piece, its very creation now looks like another type of period piece, considering that filming was done before the pandemic hit. When I visited the set in January 2020, there was only one virus on our minds. Talking with Davies and Alexander months later, they shrink from glib comparisons.

'I definitely had many complicated feelings,' says Alexander. 'All the sensational headlines, all the rumours about where coronavirus came from and who was to blame ... The response in the 80s, when this disease first appeared, was just so lacking – and there are loads of reasons for that. But it took decades to get on top of it.'

Both agree that things have radically improved in terms of HIV acceptance; Alexander has educated himself hugely over the last decade, after shirking the topic, as many do, in his teens. But they emphasise that there is still an awful long way to go.

'We can get as embarrassed about sex now as we did then,' says Davies. 'If coronavirus was a sexually transmitted disease, it would be much more hidden, still.'

Is *It's a Sin* political? It does intersect with Westminster when Roscoe embarks on an affair with a Tory MP (Stephen Fry), and Margaret Thatcher makes a tiny cameo ('She gets her comeuppance!' cries Davies, delightedly). Yet he didn't want to make a 'corridors of power' drama; he doesn't believe in simply vilifying Thatcher's government for its broadly inadequate response. It's a nuanced situation this domestic drama couldn't make room for.

'It was a big decision I made early on,' he says. You could, he points out, write a drama where you are with the then health secretary Norman Fowler as he discusses the 1986 'Monolith' TV advert, a stark public announcement that advised viewers: 'Don't die of ignorance.' You could also, he says, show Princess Diana holding an Aids patient's hand at a time when fears about contagion were rife. 'That's a gorgeous moment and more pivotal, more epic, than we can even realise today,' he says. 'But the whole thing would have started to look like *Zelig*, if our characters had been at all these key moments in history.'

One area where the show is defiantly political, though, is in its casting. *It's a Sin* is not only racially diverse, but it also satisfies the current demand for gay actors to be cast in gay roles. Davies is still marked by someone coming up to him on a dancefloor in Manchester after 1999's *Queer as Folk* came out, and asking why he didn't cast gay people in the leads. 'I said: "I didn't know you existed, I'm sorry," and he said back: "Did you look?"' So now, Davies says, he looks. He estimates that *It's a Sin* cast 40 to 50 gay actors, even in straight roles, something else he is unapologetic about ('You're just correcting an imbalance that goes back thousands of years'). That said, he admits this is a very 2020 stance. 'It was different five years ago – and I might change my mind in five years.'

Speaking of 2020, did Davies have to watch his mouth for a more woke audience? 'I know what you mean,' he says. One of the chief characteristics of queer culture is saying the unsayable – vicious transgression soused in irony. But this can date, or just seem cruel. 'You could have written a bunch of gay boys in the 80s sitting round a table taking the piss out of lesbians,' says Davies. 'But in the 80s we were thicker about everything.' Being wildly un-PC would have 'overwhelmed the drama', he thinks. 'It's all we'd sit and talk about now.'

Still, no one could mistake *It's a Sin* for a sanitised version of the culture it portrays. It doesn't shy away from the less palatable sides of the story; for one thing, one character admits they have very probably infected others with HIV, shagging away in denial. This was something very important, and rare, to feature, says Davies. 'Those people who had HIV and who continued to sleep with people are always portrayed as villains – and they weren't. They were just boys. Just horny, stupid boys who couldn't believe what was happening to them.'

I also congratulate him on a scene in the first episode where Ritchie, still a virgin, is schooled on the importance of hygiene before sex. Davies honks with laughter, but gets serious again. He never puts those things in 'just for a laugh', he promises. 'That's a really important scene,' he says, 'the one where Ritchie washes his arse. Because it says: this is where we are; this drama is on the level of body fluids and fucking and good behaviour in bed – because, actually, this is where the virus happens.'

Fair play, I say: your next honorary Bafta is sorted. Another honk. 'A gold-plated douche!'

12 JANUARY

Now that he's been banned, we can say it: Donald Trump was a genius at Twitter

DAN BROOKS

On 8 January, Twitter indefinitely suspended the account of one Donald J Trump, president of the United States. Banning Trump from Twitter is a little like banning *E. coli* from your large intestine: even if he never comes back, the memories will be enough.

Trump used the social media platform in a way that no figure in American government has ever managed before. Between last November and 6 January, when a mob of his supporters briefly overran the US Capitol and interrupted the certification of the 2020 electoral college vote, he used it to whip his followers into a frenzy. The riot was the reprehensible end to an extraordinary online career. Over the course of his presidency, Trump did for Twitter what James Dean did for the open-top sports car, making a cultural touchstone of a vehicle that ultimately destroyed him.

In the wake of his suspension, some have suggested Trump was the greatest Twitter user – or 'poster' – of all time. I'm not sure that's true. It raises the question of what great posting is. The first criterion is intangible: great posters are very much themselves, not just communicating ideas but iterating with each tweet a character – one that offers both a candid presentation of their thoughts and a knowing, semi-ironic performance of them. The second criterion is that lots of people read it. By these metrics, the greatest Twitter user of all time is probably @dril, an anonymous account that has accumulated 1.6 million followers by posting stuff like this:

wint
@dril
issuing correction on a previous post of mine,
regarding the terror group ISIL. you do not, under any
circumstances, 'gotta hand it to them'

Dril's Isil tweet spawned a Twitter cliche: users now commonly remark that 'you do not, under any circumstances, gotta hand it to them' in situations where a public figure is forced to walk back a previous statement. If such influence is the measure of success as a poster, then you do, under these circumstances, gotta hand it to Trump: his Twitter account truly shaped the culture.

Consider the Trumpian Sad. Trump first concluded a tweet with the exclamation 'Sad!' in December 2011, in reference to his belief that former Walter Mondale campaign manager Bob Beckel should not appear on Fox News. His use of this odd affectation increased after he announced his candidacy for president. A classic example from 25 November 2015:

> The numbers at the @nytimes are so dismal, especially
> advertising revenue, that big help will be needed fast.
> A once great institution – SAD!

The key, here, is that he is not actually sad. The inherent humour of using 'Sad!' as an exclamation – a thing people simply do not blurt out when they are overcome – is compounded by the sense that Trump is in fact revelling in the (imagined/falsified) decline of the *New York Times*, a newspaper he makes no secret of despising. This crocodile-tears expression would become a motif of his posting during his presidency, and ending tweets with 'Sad!' became a platform-wide joke as a result. Trump similarly propagated countless other phrases, including the infamous 'haters and losers'.

This tweet from 2013 – 'I would like to extend my best wishes to all, even the haters and losers, on this special date, September 11th' – is as close to Dril as anyone else ever got, although, as with many of Trump's successes, it's impossible to say whether he did it on purpose. Trump made 'haters and losers' a kind of catchphrase of his Twitter activity during his presidency, despite the fact that it is a phrase more appropriate to the villain in a children's story than the president of the United States. This kind of off-tone communication, though, was the secret to Trump's Twitter success. Here is the president on 30 April 2020:

> Lyin' Brian Williams of MSDNC, a Concast Scam Company,
> wouldn't know the truth if it was nailed to his wooden
> forehead. Remember when he lied about his bravery in a
> helicopter? Totally made up story. He's a true dummy who
> was thrown off Network News like a dog. Stay tuned!

It is true that any dog who made it on to a network news broadcast would be thrown off immediately, but this message – full of

axe-grinding inaccuracies – still does not quite fit the comport-
ment one expects from a head of state. He often used arbitrary
capitalisation, adding to the jarring effect. As president, Trump
was criticised for routinely committing spelling and usage errors
in his tweets, but this criticism ignored the fact that such errors
were a feature, not a bug – as members of his staff admitted to
the *Boston Globe* in 2018. In the same way that getting a text from
your mother that uses 'u' in place of 'you' disrupts your image
of a lifelong figure of authority, seeing the president use Twitter
to talk about television, 'covfefe' and 'losers' shatters the aura of
the office. For much of the American public, this shattering was
a crisis, but for his supporters, it was a release.

For the most part, politicians' Twitter accounts are boring.
They lack the off-the-cuff quality that is the principal pleasure
of following a public figure on social media as opposed to in
the news. Trump's genius was to use Twitter the way ordinary
people use social media: poorly. His typos, his regular indulgence
in slander, his unthinking repetition of inaccurate news from
obviously unreliable websites: these are precisely the problems
official communications from public figures have historically
sought to avoid.

By embracing them – by calling a journalist a dummy and his
political opponents losers, by complaining about whatever was on
TV and apparently not bothering to read it over before he hit send
– Trump made his Twitter feed relatable in a way more calculated
communicators never could. He joined a time-honoured mode of
discourse that I call Just Sayin' Stuff: the practice of speaking as
an end in itself, with little regard for the truth of what one says
or how it might affect other people. Just Sayin' Stuff is the cate-
gory of behaviour that encompasses water-cooler banter and the
moment, just before the movie starts, when you lean over and tell
your date that the CIA runs Hollywood now. It is speech at its least

serious, and Trump indulged in it in a public forum, as president of the United States.

This behaviour was insanely irresponsible. It ended in a mob assault that interrupted the normal functioning of government and got several people killed. Trump succeeded on Twitter by treating what he said as though it didn't matter, and, in doing so, he ironically brought about the one outcome most users cannot imagine: what he said did matter, at a level that shaped not just online discourse but historical events. The argument for Trump as the greatest Twitter user of all time is that he made the platform relevant. The lesson, probably, is that Twitter should never be so relevant again.

16 JANUARY

Can Joe Biden make America great again?

FINTAN O'TOOLE

Every year after 1975, Joe Biden, his second wife Jill, his sons Beau and Hunter and their growing families, would gather for Thanksgiving on Nantucket island off Cape Cod. Part of the annual ritual was that the Bidens would take a photograph of themselves in front of a quaint old house in the traditional New England style that stood above the dunes on their favourite beach.

In November 2014, when Biden was serving as Barack Obama's vice-president, he found, where the house should have been, an empty space marked out by yellow police tape. The building, he wrote in his memoir *Promise Me, Dad*, had 'finally run out of safe ground and run out of time; it had been swept out into the Atlantic'.

This absence haunted him. On his return to Washington, Biden 'kept seeing the little ... house, undermined by the powerful indifference of nature and the inevitability of time, no longer able to hold its ground; I could almost hear the sharp crack as its moorings failed, could envisage the tide as it washed in and out, pulling at it relentlessly and remorselessly until it was adrift on the water, then swallowed up by the sea'.

If Biden were to write this now, it would read as a heavy-handed political metaphor. He is about to fulfil an ambition that has driven him for half a century by assuming the presidency of the United States.

But he arrives to find that great office a ruin, with police tape all around it. Donald Trump's demented last days have washed away the illusion of the US as a stable, settled democracy. On 6 January, a date that will live long in American infamy, all the entitled rage of the white nativism that Trump has channelled finally burst through the seawalls that protected the illusion of a healthy, functioning republic. The polity escaped complete inundation, but the breach is gaping.

Yet Biden, in 2014, was not thinking of the collapsing house as an image of American politics. It troubled him, rather, as a token of the fragility of human existence. Has there been, at least since Abraham Lincoln, an American president so melancholy? One so inclined to view the world through the lens, not just of history, but of eternity?

The impulse comes with the territory of Biden's Irish Catholicism, its fatalistic view of this earthly existence as, in the words of the rosary, a 'valley of tears'. This is, as Biden sees it, 'the Irishness of life'.

This rueful stoicism is, however, primarily shaped by intimate experience: the road crash that killed his first wife, Neilia, and their daughter, Naomi, in December 1972, shortly after Biden was elected to the Senate at the age of 29; Beau's death from cancer in 2015. When he was a young senator, the journalistic in-joke was to refer to him as 'Joe Biden (D-Del, TBPT)'. Those last four letters stood for 'touched by personal tragedy', a label that clung to him like a clammy mist of perpetual mourning.

The odd thing is that this tragic vision just might be what his country needs right now. Perhaps the way that the old house acts as both a political metaphor and a personal memory points to a confluence of the man and the moment. Perhaps the dark shadow of TBPT that walks beside the triumphantly ascendant Potus is not so much a ghost and more a guardian angel.

The culture wars that have racked America, and the flags waved during the assault on the Capitol that said 'Jesus is My Savior, Trump is My President', make it too easy to see the Republicans as religious zealots and the Democrats as rational secularists. Too easy, therefore, to miss the most obvious thing about Biden: his religious sense of mission.

In his speech accepting the Democratic party's nomination for the presidency he evoked 'a battle for the soul of this nation'. He conjured Trump as a malign demiurge who has 'cloaked America in darkness', plunged the country into 'this season of darkness', and written 'this chapter of American darkness'. He promised to be 'an ally of the light, not of the darkness'.

In normal times, this rhetoric would seem ludicrously over the top, all the more so coming from a garrulous, glad-handing old Irish pol, who spent 36 years in the Senate and eight as vice-president. Biden is not obvious casting for the role of apocalyptic warrior.

In fact, however, as 6 January made all too clear, Biden's oratory is understated. The darkness of Trump's presidency has not been a season or a chapter. Biden's own presidency cannot, therefore, be an American spring that naturally succeeds the Trumpian winter, or a happy resolution to a grim but temporary twist in America's narrative of democratic progress.

The darkness, as Trump's antics and the violence of his most loyal supporters have demonstrated, is not going to go away at the flick of a switch. Biden's great strength may be that, because of what life has done to him, he knows his way around in the dark.

There are, in effect, two Bidens: the politician and the person. The second is more interesting than the first. The paradox is that the more personal his presidency is, the more politically potent it can become.

Trump abolished the distinction between the private and public selves of the presidency, embodying the principle of personal rule, government by whim, instinct, gut feelings and above all by self-interest. The logic would seem to be that Biden has been elected to do the opposite. But it is a logic he has to resist.

There are, of course, many basic ways in which Biden must indeed restore the idea of a government of laws, not of men. The rule of law itself has to be re-established after Trump's flagrant delinquency, corruption and treachery. The commitment to competence and expertise, so wilfully trashed by Trump, has to be renewed. The tools of democratic deliberation – truthfulness and evidence-based rationality – have to be refashioned.

As the mob took control of the Capitol, Biden called for 'the restoration of democracy, of decency, of honour, of respect, the rule of law. Just plain, simple decency.' No doubt in that moment, these words resonated with the majority of Americans.

The danger, though, is that this idea of restoration slips too easily into Biden's instinct, forged over five decades of deal-making, for doing business as usual. It dismisses Trump as a wild, one-off deviation, a freakish fever after which the body politic can return to its natural, healthy condition of consensual bargaining.

What makes this temptation so attractive is sheer relief. After the relentless torrent of toxicity that has poured out from Trump, even the sound of silence would be a joy. Biden offers the chance to exhale. But the pleasure, however deep, will be brief. Consensus is not on offer.

Biden the Irish pol is a revenant from a dead era. His skills as an operator, a fixer, a problem-solver are finely honed – but they are redundant. He is a horse whisperer who has to deal with mad dogs. He is a nifty tango dancer with no possible partners. There is no reasonable, civilised Republican opposition with which he can compromise. There can be no such thing as a unilateral declaration of amity and concord.

If he did not know this already, the Republicans' support for the nullification of the November election, maintained by its leaders in the House of Representatives even after the storming of their citadel, has surely brought it home to him. The most basic rule of the old order – the acceptance of the result of an election – can no longer be taken for granted. There has been an open attempt to turn the US into an authoritarian regime in which elections exist merely to endorse the eternal strongman. What has happened once can happen again.

And this is not just about Trump. Nearly 75 million people voted for him knowing (because he repeatedly told them so) that he would never accept defeat. Almost the entire Republican party in Congress either explicitly supported his attempt to subvert democracy or sat silent for months while it unfolded. For Biden to pretend that he can restore a pre-Trump normality would be disastrous. Trump and the Republican base he still owns will simply exploit conciliation to make Biden look weak and foolish.

In that sense, the political Biden is not the man who can change America. It is that other, richer persona, the private self, shadowed by time and loss and a sense of tragedy, that must come into its own. His supporters understood this in November – they voted for him in unprecedented numbers, less because of what he said he would do and more because of who he is: a man of sorrow acquainted with grief.

Biden's tragic self now rises to meet two American tragedies, one very immediate, one long and slow. The immediate one is the malign mishandling of the pandemic. Trump, at his inauguration four years ago, spoke of 'American carnage'. He did not say that he would cause it. The most powerful country in the world, with vast scientific and logistical capacities, has allowed close to 400,000 of its people to die from Covid-19, very many of them because of lies and misgovernment.

Trump did not feel this pain, either personally or electorally. Biden does feel it. His own sorrows have made him deeply attuned to the meaning of death, but also profoundly resilient in the face of its depredations. If the purpose of tragedy in art is to allow us to look death in the eye and not be defeated by it, Biden's life experience has uniquely fitted him to fulfil that purpose in public life. He can allow Americans to grieve, while also restoring their faith in science, reason and good government.

If he does this successfully, he will also have the authority to address the other, historical American tragedy: the irony of great republican ideals built on foundations of cruelty, oppression and structural inequality. He will have a moment in which he can confront the other truths that are self-evident: that gross racial, social and economic inequity has always disfigured the US. If the tumult of the last two years has made anything clear, it is that the denial of this truth cannot persist.

In this, his familiarity with the dark can be Biden's great strength. In his own life, he has been there and come back. He knows that it cannot be denied, but that it can be transcended. He can invite America to encounter its own darknesses – the legacy of slavery, the persistence of official and unofficial white supremacist violence, the failure to provide the access to education and healthcare necessary for the equal dignity of citizens – while reassuring its citizens that after such acknowledgement can come real change for the better.

The great problem of American political discourse has always been – strangely for such a biblical culture – a refusal to accept the idea of original sin. Tragic narratives are driven by some version of this idea: something went wrong at the beginning and, until it is confronted and expiated, it will continue to play itself out in havoc and pain.

The mainstream American narrative has worked in the opposite direction. The foundational acts are sacred. If the present has gone wrong, it is because we have deviated from our origins. We must return to those foundations and we will be great again. Trump repeated exactly this story; Biden must break from it once and for all.

The current conservative image of the American polity is as a solid house unfortunately invaded by a boor, who took possession of it for four years and wrecked the joint. It is time to call in the restorers: Joe Biden & Co.

The truth is closer to that vanished house in Nantucket that so haunted Biden. The Trump years represented the crumbling of a building 'no longer able to hold its ground'. His increasingly deluded and destructive ramblings are 'the sharp crack as its moorings failed'. The ramparts of law and order that were supposed to protect it failed and it has been flooded by a high tide of proto-fascism.

You don't try to rebuild on land that has been washed away. You move elsewhere. In his own mad, intuitive way, Trump has already done this for his followers. He no longer even pretends to occupy the terrain of democracy. He has built his own new piece of real estate in which the US is a demagogic despotism, wholly owned by himself and his family. Even after the deadly debacle of 6 January, a huge part of the American polity is content to up sticks and follow him there.

Biden has to create an equal and opposite space, with an equally bold departure, away from the hollow promises of the American dream and towards a new awakening of real equality. He has, after all, little to lose, not just in the political sense of having no second term to win, but in the personal one of having already endured so much loss. He has the paradoxical freedom of knowing that nothing that lies ahead of him is likely to be as bad as what lies behind him. In that freedom lies the possibility of a courage adequate to the fight he has promised to engage in – a relentless struggle for America's soul.

23 JANUARY

The cat has plenty to say. But why should I listen?

TIM DOWLING

My phone says it's 7.50am, but the sky outside looks more like 4.15. Rain is striking the window in handfuls, like flung gravel. It has been raining all night, and it promises to rain all day, possibly for the rest of the month. I dress by the light of a reading lamp and close the bedroom door behind me.

'Hello?' says the cat from somewhere in the darkness below.

'Quiet,' I hiss. The cat is sitting at the bottom of the stairs, waiting for me.

'Hey, hi,' it says.

'I get it,' I say.

Over the past several months, the cat has acquired a small number of English words in a bid to communicate its needs to me more urgently. I find this immensely patronising – like a rich American learning how to say, 'Please start with the ironing' in Spanish.

For that reason, my morning routine is based around putting the cat's needs last: first I open the curtains in the sitting room. Then I unlock the back door, so I can fling the old grounds from the coffee machine on to the grass. Then I make coffee. The cat follows me from room to room.

'You!' it says, stopping at the cupboard where the cat food is kept.

'Your English is poor,' I say, taking the milk from the fridge. 'Your accent is atrocious.'

'Hello,' the cat says.

'You've tried that,' I say.

'Ma'am,' it says.

'Wrong,' I say, sitting down with my coffee. 'I think I'll check my email.'

The cat crosses the room, jumps on to the worktop, sits down at the edge of the sink and turns in my direction.

'Ray,' it says.

'I'm not Ray,' I say. But I know well enough what the cat wants: for me to run the water at a trickle so it can drink from the tap. I stand up and walk over to the sink.

'What's the magic word?' I say.

The cat looks at the tap, and then at me.

'Now,' it says.

Only after I have made myself a second cup of coffee do I feed the cat. As usual it stares at me as if I have just filled its bowl with sand.

'It is what it is,' I say. 'Cat food.' I take the coffee out to my office shed and settle down to work. From time to time, when my concentration wanes, I sit back and look towards the kitchen. At one point I see the dog perched on the windowsill, eating from the cat's bowl. The rivalry between the cat and the dog is such that they only really enjoy each other's food.

Just before lunch I return to the kitchen, where the oldest one is now working, hunched over his laptop, vaping absent-mindedly. The cat is at the back door waiting for me when I walk in.

'Miaow,' it says.

'It's back to miaow now, is it?' I say.

I spy a tidy heap of cat sick in the middle of the kitchen floor, threaded, as is traditional at this time of year, with a strand of Christmas tinsel.

'Miaow,' the cat says.

'He wants you to feed him,' the oldest one says.

'I have fed him, and he's eaten tinsel and been sick, and in the meantime the dog's had the rest of his food, and that's where we're at,' I say.

'Miaow,' the cat says.

'I'm not feeding you again,' I say, bending down to clean up the cat sick. 'Bother somebody else.'

'He only does this to you,' the oldest one says.

'Believe me,' I say, 'I know.'

'Miaow,' the cat says.

After lunch I return to my office. Every time I look up, I see the cat sitting at the back door staring across the garden at me. It's unnerving, but I think: I can wait this out.

The rain continues, and the sky darkens further. Sometime after sunset, I glance up and notice that the cat has left his post. Finally, I think, turning back to my computer. Suddenly the security light outside my office snaps on. I turn to see the cat standing just the other side of the glass.

'Jesus,' I say. The cat looks up at me.

'Why?' it says.

2 FEBRUARY

The real thing: my battle to beat a 27-year Diet Coke addiction

SIRIN KALE

The greatest love story of my life has been with a carbonated beverage.

I can't remember a time when I wasn't addicted to Diet Coke. Some memories: I am sitting at the kitchen table at my grandmother's house in northern Cyprus, screaming because my mother won't refill my yellow-and-green patterned glass. I am four or five years old. My grandmother looks on, disturbed, as I wail disconsolately. My mother does not give in.

I am a teenage anorexic. After a long day starving myself, I walk to the corner shop and reward myself with a bottle of Diet Coke. (My mum won't buy it for the house any more, because of my addiction.) My low blood sugar makes the artificial sweetness taste euphoric.

It is my 30th birthday. I am at work at my former employment. To much fanfare, my boss brings in an eight-pack of Diet Coke, with a burning candle stuck in it. I am delighted.

I drink Diet Coke from the moment I wake up until I go to sleep. Five cans on a good day, seven cans on a bad day. My boyfriend jokes about my morning routine: wake up, pad to the kitchen. The sound of a can cracking a hiss. Glug, glug, glug. Yes, every morning.

Using some back-of-a-fag-packet maths, I estimate that I have drunk 11,315 litres of Diet Coke in my 31 years on this Earth. (I have been conservative with these numbers – it is almost certainly more.) That is more than 11,000 litres of caramel fizz, fermenting my insides, bathing my liver in foam.

I really want to stop drinking Diet Coke – and not only because I spend at least £500 a year on the stuff. It is embarrassing and bad for me. When I go on holiday, I fill up the supermarket trolley with Diet Coke, to the amusement of my friends. I get anxious if I don't have any Diet Coke in the fridge as bedtime approaches; I run to the shop in the middle of the night to ensure there is a cold can waiting for me in the morning. I recently spent a year on prescription medication for a stomach condition that was almost certainly triggered by my overconsumption of Diet Coke, according to my GP.

I quit smoking in my twenties on my first attempt, but Diet Coke is my aluminium Annapurna: I daren't even attempt the summit. So I pitched this feature – mostly as a way of holding myself accountable – and set myself a target. By the end of January 2021, I would be Coke-free. If I am being honest with you, I didn't think I could do it myself.

My attempt to quit Diet Coke does not start well. I finish my stockpile on New Year's Eve, suckling from a two-litre bottle like a baby drinking from the teat.

On New Year's Day, I wake up hungover and watch TV in bed with my boyfriend. We order pizza. 'Add a can of Diet Coke,' I instruct him. 'I thought you were quitting?' he replies. My head is pounding; only the caramel smack of Diet Coke will do. '*Order it*,' I say, my tone leaving no room for discussion. When it arrives, I down it, making little whimpering noises of pleasure.

The following day is worse. I find myself craving Diet Coke in a way that is alarming and unexpected. I envisage a tiny part of my brain – roughly parallel with my tongue and upper palate – that won't become activated unless I drink Diet Coke. I want to dump a bucket of Diet Coke on this spot and watch it fizz. I know that my headache won't go away otherwise. I feel horrific.

This – according to Dr Sally Marlow of King's College London, a specialist in addiction and mental health – is because I am in physical withdrawal from the caffeine in Diet Coke. The average can of Diet Coke contains 42mg of caffeine, the equivalent of roughly two-thirds of a shot of espresso. Caffeine is a medically recognised addictive substance that, when taken in excess, activates the brain's reward circuitry. 'The caffeine will be stimulating neurotransmitter pathways, including dopamine,' says Marlow. 'Your brain has become used to having a certain amount of caffeine in it and, when you take that away, you go through withdrawal. It's physical. You get crashing headaches.'

Marlow confesses something unexpected: like me, she is a Diet Coke addict. 'I managed to stop drinking it four years ago, but had to go cold turkey,' she says. 'I don't think it's an option for me to have an occasional Diet Coke – it would rapidly escalate to five or six cans a day.' It took her four attempts to kick the habit.

It is validating to hear an expert tell me that my Diet Coke addiction is just that, rather than a bad habit. 'Oh, it's real,' Marlow laughs. She explains that addiction has a biological component and a psychological component. The biological component is your body's physiological craving for an addictive substance, such as caffeine, nicotine or alcohol. 'The minute you get that substance into your body, your brain knows about it and gets a hit from it,' she says. 'Over time, you develop a tolerance for the substance.'

In a statement on its website, Coca-Cola denies that its products are addictive. 'Many people enjoy sweet tastes from time to time, and that's normal ... Regularly consuming food and drink that taste good and that you enjoy is not the same as being addicted to them ... Caffeine is a mild stimulant, and if you have it regularly and then stop abruptly, you may experience some headaches or other minor effects. But most of us can reduce or eliminate caffeine from our diets without serious problems.'

Then there is the psychological pull of a can of Diet Coke, something Marlow knows first-hand. 'I would crack a can open and it was almost like Pavlov's dog,' she says. 'I'd anticipate having the Coke in my mouth. That's the psychological aspect of the addiction.' She tells me that it takes 17 days to begin to kick an addiction. 'The first few days are very intense,' she says. 'Hang in there.'

I don't have the fortitude to do as she did – go cold turkey – so I improvise an extraction plan.

I will taper myself off Diet Coke: two cans a day for the first week, reducing to one can a day for the second week and no cans thereafter. I run to the shop and purchase an eight-pack. My mouth is watering as I carry it home.

How did I get to the point where I found myself umbilically attached to a sugar-free carbonated drink?

Like many women, I was cruel to myself in my teens. I grew up in the 00s, when the body-positivity movement was nonexistent. Rachel Zoe's tribe of identikit US size zero (UK size four) waifs stalked the pages of every fashion magazine. Models spoke about subsisting on cigarettes and Diet Coke. 'Nothing tastes as good as skinny feels,' said Kate Moss in 2009. I internalised that message wholeheartedly.

Every girl at my school aspired to be as thin as possible. The toilets smelled of vomit. At lunch, groups of dieting girls – myself included – would walk arm in arm to the corner shop, skipping food to buy Diet Coke, which filled you up and had zero calories. Diet Coke denoted thinness and social cachet. We all wanted a taste.

Over time, I flirted with other soft drinks – Pepsi Max is a favourite, because it is slightly sweeter than Diet Coke – but I always found myself returning to my original love.

Diet Coke was launched in 1982, seven years before I was born. I grew up watching the 'Diet Coke Break' adverts, featuring a group of businesswomen ogling a topless hunk. The Coca-Cola Company already had a diet drink – Tab – but Diet Coke was marketed more smartly. 'It has been a spectacular success since its launch,' says Prof Robert Crawford, a marketing expert at RMIT University in Melbourne and the co-editor of *Decoding Coca-Cola*. 'It tapped into the zeitgeist, which was professional women making their way in the workplace, looking good and feeling good. It also reflects the fitness craze of the period.'

In the 00s and 10s, Diet Coke leaned heavily into its association with the fashion world, recruiting Jean Paul Gaultier and Karl Lagerfeld as creative directors. More recently, as the body-positivity movement has gained traction, Diet Coke has pivoted away from this association. But as someone who grew up associating Diet Coke with skinny models, the imprint remains. To me, Diet Coke is diet culture in a can.

'I don't want to make you beat yourself up even more,' says Aisling Pigott of the British Dietetic Association, when I ask her to tell me why drinking so much diet soda is bad for me. I can take it, I say. She relents.

'It will cause tooth erosion and lead to fillings,' says Pigott. My stomach will also be taking a battering, as I know from personal experience. 'You're at increased risk of gut ulcers, as well as irritable bowel syndrome,' she says. 'And there are links between carbonated drinks and reduced bone density, meaning you're more at risk of getting fractures as you get older.'

Although I was concerned about the health risks of aspartame, the sweetener in Diet Coke, Pigott tells me not to worry. 'Aspartame is a heavily tested sweetener,' she says. 'There is no strong evidence linking it to any health consequences.' In the grand scheme of things, Pigott says, Diet Coke isn't terrible. 'It's definitely a better option than full-sugar Coke. But it's the amount you're having that is potentially harmful,' she says.

The first week of my regime passes without incident. I join a Facebook support group for Diet Coke addicts who want to quit.

Week two of my tapered extraction programme. The first day is OK, but on day two I snap and drink four cans. I hide the cans in the bottom of the recycling bin, hoping my boyfriend won't notice, but he had counted the cans in the fridge that morning. Rumbled.

Week three: a week without Diet Coke. I anticipate this like I do a cervical smear, only with less enthusiasm. On my first day, I feel like I am going to cry. I miss it. I miss Diet Coke.

The hypnotherapist and addiction specialist Jason Demant has helped people beat far tougher addictions. 'Cocaine, alcohol, that sort of thing,' he says. 'Do you often feel like you have to toe the rules in your life?' Demant asks. 'Are you always a good person? Do you always do the right thing?'

Yes, I respond, slowly. I work hard at my job, I try to be a good friend and partner, to eat well, to exercise. Diet Coke is the one thing where I think: fuck it. I am going to do what I want to do, which is drink gallons of this stuff. Demant explains that Diet Coke is triggering my inbuilt reward system, which is why I can't seem to let it go. 'It's a break from the obligations of life. What you need to do is find something else that gives you that feeling. What about, instead of rewarding yourself with Diet Coke, you could do things for yourself that felt loving?'

I incorporate small gestures of self-care into my day. I spend more time playing with my cat. I watch trashy TV. I read in the bath. In the twilight period between brushing my teeth and going to bed, I listen to the hypnotherapy recording Demant sent me after our session. 'You have no need to drink Diet Coke,' Demant intones over a gentle piano soundtrack. Yes, I nod. I don't want it.

Something miraculous starts to happen. I stop thinking about Diet Coke. There is no longer any Diet Coke in my fridge – and it is OK. I don't miss it. To my astonishment, I lose a kilo. I am indifferent to the weight loss, but it is fascinating. It suggests that the artificial sweetener in the Diet Coke was triggering my appetite for sweet things. (Studies have shown a link between drinking diet drinks and higher sugar consumption.)

More than anything, I feel peaceful. Demant explains that I have to be watchful in the future, so I don't slip into old habits. 'With any pattern that is compulsive or addictive, you have to be on the watch all the time,' says Demant. 'Because you may think: "Oh, I've conquered this," and then five minutes later you can go to the shop to buy Coke. Always be on guard.' Marlow agrees. 'What we know with most addictions is that people relapse when they think they can have just one,' she says. 'For many people, it's simply not possible.' She has not drunk a Diet Coke in five years.

It has been a month now and I no longer drink Diet Coke. When I take out the recycling, it doesn't sound like a steel band at Notting Hill carnival. I drink water in the morning – and I like the taste of it. I have swum out of the foaming caramel tide into an ocean of clear, clean sea: water all around me and not a drop of fizz to drink.

5 FEBRUARY

'Since March, we have spoken every day': how a call to California got me through lockdown

LAURA BARTON

It is morning in Los Angeles, and my friend Tess is making breakfast. I watch her pad about the kitchen in her pyjamas, fixing coffee and oatmeal, and all the while we are talking – about politics, and soup recipes, and Guns N' Roses, about the peculiarities of pandemic life. In England, the day is fading. Beyond my computer screen, my window looks out to a pinkening sky, and the last bright flashes of parakeet and magpie.

We are eight hours and five and a half thousand miles apart, but throughout the strangeness of the past year, Tess has been my steady companion. Since March, we have spoken every day. Sometimes twice. Sometimes for an hour or more. The pandemic has brought a fervency to some of my friendships: I don't think I have spent so many hours taking telephone calls of ambling nothingness since my teens. This is not the same as those early pandemic Zoom gatherings, many faces spread across a screen, but an increasingly concentrated attachment between two people.

For medical reasons, I chose not to form a bubble. I have not seen anyone for months. And while I am quite content alone, I have found these points of contact with friends quite profound. I have noticed, too, that those I speak to most frequently all share a similarly intensified experience of isolation: the solo-dwellers, the single parents, the partnerless, the shielders, the new mothers.

I have no family or emotional connection to the town where I live, and some days, as I walk through the woods, or along the sea road, I think how location is increasingly irrelevant; instead, the people I speak to each day have become my home.

Like me, Tess lives alone. We are both single, both writers, the same age. We met in California seven years ago and have been firm friends ever since. Before Covid, our daily conversations were generally text-based and governed by time difference: I would awake to a stream of messages – thoughts on relationships, work, links to Rebecca Solnit essays and Bruce Springsteen songs. But when the pandemic descended, we began to video-chat.

In the early weeks, we spoke with one eye on the rolling news, our conversations peppered with headlines, infection rates, the new, unwieldy terminology of our modern plague days. In the months that followed, our exchanges softened to encompass professional dilemmas, romantic interludes, male privilege, Etsy purchases. A year on, we have developed a closeness that is intricately bound: I am familiar with her hopes, her annoyances, her half-thoughts; I know what time she went to sleep, what she dreamed, what she ate for breakfast, lunch, dinner.

This year, all of my closest friendships have been marked by such cumulative detail. With one, I swap voice notes. He records long, meandering messages as he takes out the bins, feeds the cat, cooks ramen; I speak to him as I walk across fields, clean the bath, or chop onions, eyes streaming.

Another calls me most days as she cycles across London, taking pictures. When she tells me that the light is making Hyde Park look like a Jack Vettriano painting, or how quiet Euston Road is tonight, I feel I am beside her, lungs full of cold city air.

Such intimate detail is not a matter of mitigating the tedium, or filling the long hours with chatter and irrelevance. Rather, it is a way of reaching out towards the connection we have lost; of

recognising how much life is held in the humdrum, the unfil-
tered, the domestic. 'I don't know exactly what a prayer is,' the
poet Mary Oliver wrote. 'I do know how to pay attention.' And
perhaps this is what this pandemic year has reminded me about
friendship: that in attentive communication we find a new reverence for one another.

Most days, I spend the hours before Tess wakes making
mental notes of things to tell her; the momentous and the
minutiae. I don't much care for the old life – for the scrolling
of social media posts, the perpetual fear of missing out. What I
fear missing now is the small things: the wonder of the human
voice, warm down the line. The sound of a friend chopping
carrots. The delight in seeing a favourite face, unwashed and
lovely, in the California morning.

6 FEBRUARY

'I've been called Satan':
facing abuse in the Covid crisis

RACHEL CLARKE

Please imagine it, for a moment, if you can bear to. Being wheeled
from your home by paramedics in masks who rush you, blue-lit,
to a hospital. Then the clamour and lights, the confusion and
fear, the faceless professionals, gloved and gowned, who eddy and
swirl past your trolley. Your destination is intensive care where
too soon, or perhaps not soon enough, you will arrive at a point
of reckoning. You will blanch when they tell you, because you've
watched the news and know what it signifies: you are going to

be put on a ventilator. You will understand, as clearly as they do, that your doctors cannot promise to save you.

Here, though, is the detail that haunts me. For every patient who dies from Covid-19 in hospital, from the moment they encounter that first masked paramedic, they will never see a human face again. Not one smile, nor pair of cheeks, nor lips, nor chin. Not a single human being without barricades of plastic. Sometimes, my stomach twists at the thought that to the patients whose faces I can never unsee – contorting and buckling with the effort of breathing – I am no more than a pair of eyes, a thin strip of flesh between mask and visor, a muffled voice that strains and cracks behind plastic.

Of all Covid's cruelties, surely the greatest is this? That it cleaves us from each other at precisely those times when we need human contact the most. That it spreads through speech and touch – the very means through which we share our love, tenderness and basic humanity. That it transforms us unwittingly into vectors of fatality. And that those we love most – and with whom we are most intimate – are the ones we endanger above all others.

It's late January. The wards and ICUs are overwhelmed, awash with the virus. The patients seem younger, the new variant more virulent. We are drowning, drowning in Covid. The sight of a doctor or nurse breaking down has become unremarkable. Too close, for too long, to too many patients' pain, we have become – just like them – saturated. Behind hospital doors, tucked out of sight, we seem to suffer as one.

Outside, on the other hand, the virus has once again carved up the country into simmering, resentful, aggrieved little units. It's too old, too cold to be doing this again. One way or another, lockdown hurts us all. But instead of unity, community and a shared sense of purpose – that extraordinary eruption of philanthropy last springtime – we seethe like rats in a sack, fractious, divided.

During the first wave, I knew the public had our backs. This time round, being an NHS doctor makes you a target. For the crime of asserting on social media that Covid is real and deadly, I earn daily abuse from a vitriolic minority. I've been called Hitler, Shipman, Satan and Mengele for insisting on Twitter that our hospitals aren't empty. Last night a charming 'Covid sceptic' sent me this: 'You are paid to lie and a disgrace to your profession. You have clearly sold your soul and are nothing more than a child abuser destroying futures. I do not consent to your satanic ways.' A friend, herself an intensive care doctor, has just been told by another male 'sceptic' that he intends to sexually abuse her until she requires one of her own ventilators. And this morning, another colleague, also female, was told: 'You evil criminal lying piece of government shit. You need to be executed immediately for treason and genocide.'

In short, we have reached the point in the pandemic where what feels like armies of trolls do their snarling, misogynistic utmost to silence NHS staff who try to convey what it's like on the inside. Worse even than the hatred they whip up against NHS staff, the deniers have started turning up in crowds to chant 'Covid is a hoax' outside hospitals full of patients who are sick and dying. Imagine being forced to push your way through that, 13 hours after you began your ICU shift. Some individuals have broken into Covid wards and attempted physically to remove critically ill patients, despite doctors warning that doing so will kill them.

I well understand why they want to gag us. Our testimony makes Covid denial a tall order. We bear witness not to statistics but to human beings. Our language is flesh and blood. This patient, and then this patient, and then another. The pregnant woman in her twenties in the ICU, intubated and lifeless. The three generations of one family on ventilators, each of them dying one after the other. We humanise, empathise, turn the unfathomable dimensions of the 100,000 dead into mothers, fathers, sisters, brothers. Increasingly, speaking out feels like a moral imperative. Because perhaps – if we can only disprove enough untruths, if we can just slow the onslaught of disinformation – we may have fewer dying hands to hold in the future.

Please don't flinch. Please don't look away. The truth of conditions inside our hospitals needs telling. To dispel a few prime ministerial press conference myths, the NHS is not 'close to' or 'on the brink of' being overwhelmed. We are here and now in the midst of calamity. The Covid patients keep on coming, so unnervingly unwell, and we race to find space for them. But all the spare staff have already been snatched from their day jobs. Elective surgery has shut down, everything inessential postponed. ICUs are filled with obstetricians, paediatricians, psychiatrists and surgeons doing their amateur best to support the small pool of staff with proper expertise. On wards across the country, where Covid patients live and die in their thousands, the medics are stretched perilously thinly. And still the new admissions come.

This week, a doctor friend in another trust sent me this, having been newly redeployed to her hospital's ICU: 'The situation at work is just dreadful. Once I've donned PPE and gone into ICU, hours and hours go by. And it's just awful in there. It's not calm like the news videos, it's chaotic with alarms going constantly, patients being intubated and proned. Most of us are NOT trained to do this or deal with this. We are surgeons, anaesthetists, physicians, nurses, HCAs, porters etc. We are NOT ICU staff.'

Newly qualified doctors with scarcely six months' experience sometimes struggle single-handed on the Covid wards at night, their seniors unable to leave crashing patients elsewhere. Whoever deteriorates overnight may live or die according to whether a bed can be found in an ICU. This is rationing, without being named out loud as such. An unacknowledged peacetime form of battlefield triage: lives being lost because there aren't enough staff to go around. No one here is being 'protected', not the patients, not the nurses, not the doctors, not the families, and certainly not the NHS writ large.

Sometimes, colleagues confess that they feel suicidal. Sometimes, in the darkness, a patient pleads to die. They cannot take the claustrophobic roar of their CPAP mask any longer. The struggle to breathe is costing them more than they can bear. A student I used to teach looks close to collapse. 'I feel as if it might be my fault when they die,' he tells me in a monotone. 'If I'd been a doctor for longer, I might know how to do something different. Maybe it's me – maybe I'm not cut out to be a doctor.' I watch him wrestle to keep his tears at bay, unable even to reach out to give him a hug. The wrongness of it all constricts my chest until it hurts. He's too young, too green to be standing here like this, accusing himself of failing the pandemic dead, who themselves have been failed by so many in power above. At what cost do these night shifts worm into his soul?

The truth is, patients of necessity are falling through our cracks. We cannot hold them all, we're too few and too ground down. Rationing does not declare itself in a fanfare of noise. It sidles in, bit by bit, as the Covid cases rise. Intensive care nurses, used to working with a concentration of one nurse per patient, are asked to stretch themselves across four patients or more. Standards start to slip as battered, shell-shocked staff do their brave and hopeless best against the ever-surging human tide. The truth – and don't we know it, if we're honest? – is that doctors and nurses are neither angels nor heroes. We're human. Merely human. We can only do so much.

I can't sleep. I can't sit still. I feel sick. I want to scream. Something monstrous, like cancer, is twisting in my chest. One morning, on the way to work, the politicians and the trolls and the suffering and the death become too much. All of a sudden, I'm unable to drive. In a layby I cringe, doubled up, fighting for breath. My body is in mutiny, it's overruled my head. You clench your teeth, wipe your cheeks, turn the ignition, set off again. You must go on. I can't go on. I'll go on.

A unity of sorts emerges with the stupefying news that in Britain, an island, the cumulative Covid death toll has surpassed 100,000. On the same day, we learn that our death rate per head of population is the highest in the world. As the country reels from these calamitous statistics, the prime minister insists that his government 'truly did everything we could to minimise loss of life'. Yet a quarter of those deaths have occurred in 2021 – during the last four weeks alone – making Boris Johnson's words a patent lie. He didn't lock down promptly, he didn't close our borders, he didn't protect care homes, he allowed tens of thousands of elderly and vulnerable residents to die. And then, instead of future-proofing Britain from a second surge last summer, he offered bribes for social mixing. But our eating out, far from helping out, sent Covid cases ticking hungrily upwards.

This second wave has been turbocharged by Downing Street's procrastination. Putting off lockdown until the 11th hour has – yet again – wreaked havoc. Urgent cancer surgeries should not be postponed. Covid patients should not be calling Ubers to rush them to hospital because the ambulances they need are nowhere to be found. Doctors and nurses should not be suicidal with stress, nor tended by their own as they suffocate and die on ventilators. It did not have to be like this. None of these horrors were inevitable.

How – from where – can we find cause for hope when our political leaders, despite a track record like this, insist they've behaved infallibly? Well, by early spring, the country's most vulnerable citizens should be vaccinated, a prospect that makes me ecstatic.

And lockdown has already sent new cases plummeting downwards. The deaths, we know, will follow. Momentum too is building towards a zero Covid strategy – the complete elimination of the virus – as demonstrated so successfully by countries like New Zealand, Taiwan and Vietnam.

But my main reasons for optimism lie closer to home, flickering and sparking amid the darkness. I turn my gaze from the dizzying statistics and look instead to the human beings around me. Their ingenuity and kindness give me the steel to go on. One day, for example, a peculiar procession outside the hospital turns heads on the high street. It is led by a strangely immaculate tractor, freshly waxed and wreathed with flowers, gleaming beneath the winter sun. The tractor is destined for a nearby village, hauling an agricultural trailer on which a coffin has been laid. Several cars follow, their stern-faced drivers dressed in black. It's the funeral cortege of a larger-than-life farmer, known to all in his village and far beyond. Pre-Covid, hundreds of locals would have packed into the village church, eager to pay tribute to a man much loved. Now, though, a virus dictates our forms of mourning. No large gatherings are allowed.

When the tractor arrives in the village, lumbering slowly towards the empty church, something magical and startling begins to unfold. Word of mouth and social media have told the neighbours when the cortege will pass and now, on their doorsteps and in porches, behind their gates, on garden paths, they assemble at a respectful social distance. As the tractor passes, so begins the applause. First a ripple, then a clatter, then a thunder, then a roar. In physical estrangement, a population finds its voice. This community, unbowed, celebrates a man they loved – and how. My heart lifts. I feel hope flicker. For however bleak the times, however grim our prospects seem, human kindness finds a shape and form: it will not be locked down.

All across the hospital, you see it. In the tiny crocheted crimson hearts, made by locals for patients and delivered in their scores so that no one feels alone. In the piles of donated pizzas, devoured at night by ravenous staff. In the homemade scrubs, whipped up by an unstoppable army of self-isolating grandmothers whose choice of fabrics is fearlessly floral. In the nurses and carers and porters and cleaners who keep on, despite everything, smiling. I may be tired and angry and sometimes mad with grief, but every single day at work, I see more kindness, more sweetness, more compassion, more courage, more resilience, more steel, more diamond-plated love than you could ever, ever imagine. And this means more and lasts more than anything else, and it cannot be stolen by Covid.

7 FEBRUARY

Don't mess with Jackie Weaver, boys. She's got a mute button and knows how to use it

GABY HINSLIFF

Someday, there will surely be a statue to Jackie Weaver.

Women will take their small daughters to see it and deliver homilies about the importance of standing your ground with pompous and aggressive men in meetings, which their daughters won't understand at the time but will remember with startling clarity once they actually start work. And just as MPs entering the Commons chamber used to touch the bronze foot of Winston

Churchill's nearby statue for luck, aspiring politicians will stop and offer silent thanks to Jackie, the patron saint of women who are having absolutely none of your nonsense.

Well, we can dream. But, if nothing else, the heroine of last week's most unexpected viral content has given everyone something other than Covid-19 to think about. Weaver was the host of an extraordinary (in every sense) Zoom meeting of Handforth parish council's planning and environment committee, footage from which ended up on YouTube, after it had descended into a terribly British form of naked power struggle.

First, she removed the obstreperous chairperson from the online meeting despite his protests ('You have no authority here!'). Then the incandescent vice-chair stormed off his sofa in solidarity ('Read the standing orders! Read them and understand them!'), leaving the studiedly calm Weaver to lead more mild-mannered colleagues in getting some actual work done. Nevertheless, as the saying goes, she persisted.

Hopefully, someone has shown the video clip to Yoshiro Mori, the former Japanese prime minister now running the Tokyo Olympics organising committee, who last week complained that meetings with women 'take so much time'. The problem, he suggested, was that when one person says something, women feel they have to say something back, rather than nod mutely in agreement. It's a revealing insight into the kind of meeting he prefers to run, which presumably doesn't involve much listening, or at least not to women. But it's also an illustration of what the Weavers of the world are up against.

For the record, research suggests that if anyone is dragging out meetings intolerably, it isn't women. A now-classic study by Barbara and Gene Eakins recorded seven university faculty meetings and found that, in each one, men spoke more often and for longer than women did. That was in 1976, but it seems times

haven't changed all that much. In 2019, a Montreal city coun-
cillor who had taken up knitting in meetings decided to knit in
red wool when a man was speaking and switch to green when
women did. There are no prizes for guessing which colour made
up most of Cllr Sue Montgomery's scarf.

The issue isn't that women talk more, but that a woman
speaking up is still seen as more surprising (or even annoying)
than men doing so, and thus registers more. Men who can't take
having their authority challenged by women may find it particularly objectionable. No wonder, then, that for some female
politicians the Handforth footage stirred less than fond memories. The Labour frontbencher Dr Rosena Allin-Khan praised
Weaver for sticking to her guns but tweeted that 'people doing
their best in local politics, especially women, shouldn't have to
put up with that'. Rather poignantly, Weaver said later that if
they had all been physically in the room rather than separated by
their computer screens, she might have been 'frankly afraid' to
stand her ground. And that's where it stops being quite so funny.

More than one Labour MP has quietly told me over the past
year that it was a relief when constituency party meetings moved
online during lockdown. It's harder for aggressive members
to physically intimidate other attenders – something that has
happened to both men and women all too often for comfort in
recent years – when they're all in their separate living rooms.

Heckle or threaten now and you can be muted, too. It's a power
that could, of course, be abused in order to silence dissenting
voices, but in the hands of a sensible chair, it could also encourage
people scared off by a toxic political climate to come back and get
involved. It was oddly touching to hear Weaver use a barrage of
post-match interviews to talk about the genuine importance of
taking part in local democracy; how it wasn't all twee *Vicar of
Dibley* stuff, but about volunteering to serve your neighbour.

Nobody who has ever spent a rainy Wednesday evening sitting in a church hall, staring at the minutes of the previous meeting and longing for death, will be surprised that this one turned sour. Westminster's Punch and Judy show has nothing on the barely suppressed rage occasionally engendered by local politics at its most parochial and least political; neighbourhood watch meetings that have long since turned horribly passive-aggressive or any form of neighbourhood gathering that touches on the picking up of dog poo or who hasn't cut their hedge. As a cub reporter on a local paper years ago, I once covered a public meeting on village speed limits that got so fraught the parish council sent me a box of Milk Tray by way of apology for the language.

But there are thousands of blameless men and women across the country patiently giving up their spare time to tenants' meetings or the PTA or the council and you would be amazed by what some of them get done, in between resignedly shouting, 'You're on mute, Roger!' at one of their neighbours for three hours.

Jackie Weaver isn't just a heroine to women shouted down in meetings. She's a model to both sexes of how to get things done, without fuss or fanfare, and preferably (at least once the pubs reopen) in time for last orders. And that's all the authority she needs.

7 FEBRUARY

I learned by touring Europe in the 60s. Young artists need the same chance

ELTON JOHN

In 1966, I went to Hamburg. I was the keyboard player in Blue-sology, and we had a residency at the Top Ten Club, where the Beatles had famously cut their teeth. It was a real baptism of fire. We played on the Reeperbahn, five hours a night in among the brothels and sex shows, to audiences who hadn't come to see us. But it was still great: we played so much we didn't have any choice but to improve as a band. Certainly, it was better than my solo debut on the continent a few years later, when some bright spark booked me as the support act to Sergio Mendes in Paris. One audience member was so aggrieved at having his evening of bossa nova interrupted by the strains of 'Your Song' that he threw his hotdog at me. Clearly, the only way was up. I kept touring Europe and gradually built up an incredibly loyal audience.

This was all a long time ago. If I was the keyboard player in a young band, or a solo artist just starting out now, it's unlikely I'd get the chance to go to Hamburg, or indeed have hotdogs thrown at me in Paris. As a result of Brexit, British artists who want to play in Europe will now need visas, work permits and equipment carnets for each country they visit. It's an administrative night-mare that vastly increases the cost of staging a European tour.

Of course, none of this affects me. I'm lucky enough to play big venues and have a huge organisation supporting me. My tours can absorb these costs, and I have people working for me who can sort out the admin. But in a way it does affect me, because I don't want to live in a world where the only artists who can afford to tour properly are those who have been going for decades and have already sold millions of records.

I've always been passionate about new music. During that tour, I spent all my spare time in record shops, and 50 years later I still spend hours each week going through new-release schedules, buying new albums and listening to songs on streaming services. As a successful artist, one of my raisons d'etre is to promote younger artists and to be on their side. I'm in an incredibly privileged position, and it seems only fair to use this to help people who are starting out. It's not an act of charity: my favourite thing about music is the energy and the raw excitement that a new artist transmits when you see them live. It's hugely inspiring, and it's something you only normally get from a younger artist.

It's absolutely vital for new artists to tour Europe. Getting your music across to crowds from a different culture to your own, who don't necessarily speak the same language as you, just makes you a better musician. As I discovered in the 60s, you can spend months in a rehearsal room painstakingly perfecting your craft and you won't learn as much about live performance as you do in half an hour trying to win over an unfamiliar audience. You have to have that visual contact with other human beings.

Touring Europe allows you to absorb different influences, understand different crowds and meet new musicians. It helps you get inside your art. You not only play better, you write better songs as a result. During the Covid-19 pandemic, we've seen many other ways of promoting music to a global audience: artists have used social media and live streams, and have created pay-per-view online events. Some of these formats have been incredibly creative. But not one of them has come even remotely close to replicating the experience of going to a gig, and not one of them is going to have the kind of impact on an artist that touring does.

The situation we're now in is ridiculous. Music is one of Britain's greatest cultural exports. It contributed £5.8 billion to the British economy in 2019, but was left out of the Brexit trade negotiations when other industries weren't. Workers from some professions are still allowed to travel on business without applying for a visa. But not musicians. Either the Brexit negotiators didn't care about musicians, or didn't think about them, or weren't sufficiently prepared. They screwed up. It's ultimately down to the British government to sort it out: they need to go back and renegotiate.

But renegotiating freedom of movement is complicated and is going to take a lot of time. If you've just made your first album, and you've got that fresh momentum building behind you, it's no use waiting for two or three years before you tour – you have to catch that energy while it's on fire, you have to go out and play, and you have to take yourself to as many different audiences as possible.

What musicians need now is a short-term fix. We should set up a support organisation, funded partly by the music industry itself, where artists who don't have the kind of infrastructure that I benefit from can access lawyers and accountants to help them navigate the touring problems created by Brexit. The pandemic has put a stop to live music in the immediate future, so we should use the window of opportunity we have now to set this support organisation up.

Just to reiterate: this isn't about Elton John. It's about ensuring that emerging artists have the space to nurture their own talent and broaden and build their audiences. We need a new generation of superstars, not least because one generation of superstars – my generation – are getting older, retiring and dying off. This is about more than just pop music: it affects folk singers and jazz players, classical musicians, orchestras and opera companies too. And it's also about cult bands and performers and artists who are making stuff that is too experimental for mass appeal.

In fact, if you hate every note I've recorded, because your tastes are edgier, weirder and more exploratory – if you think that the Parisian hotdog thrower had a good point – you need to support musicians' ability to tour. Because if Brexit prevents many new musicians from touring, the only artists who are going to have any meaningful kind of live career are big, august, mainstream artists like me. And, trust me, I don't want that any more than you do.

19 FEBRUARY

British grief centres mainly around the making of sandwiches

GRACE DENT

In the befuddlement of grief, I have achieved very little in the kitchen other than the occasional sub-par frittata. I lurk by the hob, my safe place, but largely I just wipe and sterilise. Our days of vigilant shielding are over. The Covid monster did not catch my mother but, in the meantime, his ghoulish cousin, cancer, made an incremental land grab, taking lungs and bones, then liver, and then, worse than any of that, it stole her appetite.

This stage felt the most hopeless. I am from a family of sturdy-hipped women who have never willingly eschewed a bowl of wobbly, custard-smothered trifle or a toasted, buttered hot cross bun, all sticky with cinnamon glaze. When Mam began refusing these things, well, we knew that time was tight.

Joe Biden was elected 46th president of the US in November 2020, receiving over 81 million votes – more than any other presidential candidate in history. ANGELA WEISS/AFP/GETTY

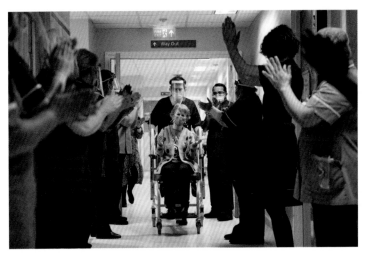

The Covid vaccine rollout was one of the big success stories of 2021. Here, Margaret Keenan, 90, becomes the UK's first recipient in December 2020. JACOB KING/PA WIRE

Onlookers dive for cover as protestors break into the US Capitol on 6 January, after Trump urged his supporters to 'fight like hell' against the election result. ANDREW HARNICK/AP PHOTO

America's youth poet laureate Amanda Gorman wows the crowds at Biden's inauguration on 20 January. She described 'The Hill We Climb' as a call for 'unity and collaboration and togetherness'. ALEX WONG/GETTY IMAGES

Women are arrested at a gathering in London on 13 March to commemorate the life of Sarah Everard after her kidnap and murder. HANNAH MCKAY/REUTERS

The Queen cuts a lonely figure at a Covid-regulated funeral for her husband, Prince Philip, on 17 April. They had been married for 73 years. JONATHAN BRADY/
AFP/GETTY IMAGES

Jennifer Lopez performs onstage during Vax Live, billed as 'a concert to reunite the world', California, 8 May. KEVIN MAZUR/GETTY IMAGES FOR GLOBAL CITIZEN VAX LIVE

Boris and Carrie Johnson's son Wilfred entertains his mother and other leaders' partners during the G7 Summit in Cornwall in June.
SIMON DAWSON/NO 10 DOWNING STREET

The England team celebrate Harry Kane's winning goal against Denmark on their way to the final of the UEFA European Championships in July.

Silver medallist Kye Whyte holds Bethany Shriever aloft after she wins gold in the women's BMX racing competition at the Tokyo Olympics on 30 July.

A member of Extinction Rebellion's Red Rebel Brigade protests against fracking in Dublin, Ireland, on 23 March. CLODAGH KILCOYNE/REUTERS

Desperate Afghans wave their credentials at Kabul airport as they attempt to flee the country after the Taliban swept to power in August. AKHTER GULFAM/EPA

Teams work round the clock to bury victims of Covid-19 in Indonesia, 11 August. To date, Indonesia has recorded over 140,000 Covid deaths as it struggles to cope with the Delta variant. ULET IFANSASTI/GETTY IMAGES

Wildfires hit Greece in August during its worst heatwave in decades. The same month, an IPCC Report confirmed that climate change is 'widespread, rapid and intensifying'. KONSTANTINOS TSAKALIDIS/BLOOMBERG/GETTY IMAGES

Eighteen-year-old Emma Raducanu becomes the first qualifier to win a
Grand Slam final in tennis history at the US Open on 11 September.
KENA BETANCUR/AFP/GETTY IMAGES

A 'full flower supermoon' rises behind the Temple of Poseidon near Athens,
26 May. LOUISA GOULIAMAKI/AFP/GETTY IMAGES

I've deliberated many times about discussing grief in a food column – you're possibly here to read about new ways with couscous yet the two topics are more linked than one might imagine. Victoria Wood once said that British grief centred mainly around the making of sandwiches. 'Seventy-two baps, Connie. You slice, I'll spread,' she quipped, mimicking the stoic capability of a widow stood behind a 2kg catering tub of Stork.

This always rang true to me. As a child, I learned that, although funerals were to be dreaded and the church bit was weird and jarring, the buffet afterwards would taste like delicious, carefully restored semi-sanity. First the crying, wailing and throwing of soil, which was horrible, but then everyone went to a chintzy hotel or the pub's back room for tinned salmon on Mothers Pride, pork pie and jam tarts. For the adults, there were nips of Bell's whisky on a tray. 'A good spread,' all would agree while debating the best route home, the traffic lights on the new bypass and the best part of nothing much.

But somewhere between the cocktail sausages with dipping mustard and the madeira cake, there would be a perceptible thawing of the mood; a general unsaid agreement that, amid the mouthfuls of scotch egg and the nibbling of cubed cheddar skewered on sticks atop small pickled onions, the grief had taken a slightly different shape.

Something shifted again when the mourners, who had started out stiffly in the main room, began gathering wherever smoking was permitted. Black ties would be loosened and women would nurse double gin and tonics – in short glasses, scant ice, never lemon. The first sounds of laughter would ring through the air, feeling decidedly cleansing. 'They had a good send-off,' the grownups would agree. Into sadness, some joy was clawed back.

In the grand scheme of things, my family are relatively fortunate. We are allowed to visit the chapel, in masks, socially distanced but sort of together. Over the past 12 months, millions of grieving people have not been so comparatively lucky. Nevertheless, dealing with death in a time of Covid, with wakes for up to six and no pubs, hotels or restaurants open, is a strange, awry sensation. My grief has been oddly nomadic. Death is here, I can feel it – I even have the paperwork to prove it – but there is no known fixed point to stumble towards, featuring people and hugs and stories and scones on three-tier cake stands.

My mother loved sweet things and, by God, if I could, I'd provide them. I'd fill that trestle table in that imaginary room until it was groaning. I'd fill it with trifle, tipsy cake and bowls of black forest gateau. The nips of Bell's would be more than a finger; they'd be generous, cheek-warming and numbing. No mourner would leave without a take-home treat in their handbag, without fruit loaf, bakewell tart or eccles cake stuffed in a purse. Good-suit pockets would forever be crumb-strewn, from leftover funeral flapjacks wrapped roughly in a napkin and forgotten until the next trip to the dry cleaners, when a hand in the pocket would remind you of a great funeral buffet.

But that cannot happen right now. We bury our dead, sad in spirit and very much empty of stomach. Full of love, but not of egg mayo and cress sandwiches, cut into neat triangles and piled on a stainless-steel platter. It's an odd sort of grieving, is this.

On hope: 'Look for the rainbow'

MATT HAIG

I always think it is interesting that arguably the most hopeful song of the 20th century – 'Over the Rainbow' – arrived in arguably its darkest year. *The Wizard of Oz*, adapted from L Frank Baum's novel, opened in cinemas on 25 August 1939, the day Hitler sent a telegram to Mussolini to tell him he was about to invade Poland. Within a week, the second world war was under way in Europe.

'Over the Rainbow' was the most popular piece of music in 1939, and has become shorthand for that bittersweet sense of being in tough times and walking towards better ones. Yip Harburg's heartfelt lyrics speak of hope, but so does Harold Arlen's music – and when the tune jumps a whole octave within the elongated 'some-*where*' it flies over a metaphorical rainbow of seven notes to land on the eighth. And it is that leap that really feels like the essence of hope: half rooted in reality, half up in the sky. Half present, half future. Part Kansas, part Oz.

Of course, 1939 and 2021 are very different years. And sure, the felt-tip rainbows children drew in support of the NHS had become faded and sun-bleached long before the second wave of the pandemic crashed to shore, but hope is still in demand. The trouble is, hope can be hard. For every buoyant thought about vaccines, it is easy to sink back into a black hole of news and ongoing catastrophe. And it seems impossible sometimes to resist the downward gravitational pull of new strains and scary statistics and the sheer social, economic and psychological magnitude of all this.

It is easy to feel, quite literally, hopeless. We might actively try to resist it and stay inside the low octave of pessimism. As gloomy old Nietzsche saw it, hope is the absolute 'worst of all evils' because it prolongs our torments rather than relieves them. But that is defeatist, and this last year has shown us that, despite our collective flaws as a species, we don't easily give up on a better future. I prefer Anne Lamott's idea of how hope 'begins in the dark – the stubborn hope that if you just show up and try to do the right thing, the dawn will come'. Because that is the thing about hope. Its stubbornness. It is Emily Dickinson's singing bird perched in the soul that *never stops at all.*

This actually gives hope a very real and practical purpose. Far from it being a Nietzschean torment, something that dangles like a carrot eternally in front of a donkey's nose, reasons for hope can be found not just *after* despair but inside it. In the face of this slow-moving tragedy we have been living through, we have seen so many acts of everyday goodness and courage, in hospitals and care homes and on our own streets.

Maybe, then, the hope we could work to cultivate is less the passive cross-fingers-and-wait variety, but more the look-for-the-rainbow kind, or the sleeves-rolled-up-and-make-it-happen kind. In desperate times, beauty shines brighter. I can remember reading about how Steven Callahan, a sailor who was adrift at sea for 76 days, noticed through pain and hunger the sudden majesty of the night sky. He wasn't noticing this beauty *despite* his life being in peril but *because* of it.

In depression I used to cling to such moments, even as the weight of illness pressed into my mind. Beauty shone like a promise of another world within this one. Even amid the collective trauma of this year, it is also still possible to detect a collective hope. 'It is in collectivities that we find reservoirs of hope and optimism,' observed the civil rights activist Angela Davis. So just as a virus highlights our interdependence on each other in an ominous way, hope shows how togetherness is as much solution as problem. Whether developing a vaccine or wearing a mask or shopping for a relative or contacting an elderly neighbour, there is always something we humans can do for each other.

Hope isn't about waiting for a hypothetical future. Hope is finding the goodness in the dark and protecting it like a flame. Maybe – let's hope big – we will emerge from this mass experience with a better idea of how we should live, just as we did after the second world war. And, in the end, we might not need ruby slippers because we have each other to lead us home.

9 MARCH

Meghan and Harry v 'The Institution': another royal fairytale turned Grimm

MARINA HYDE

Well, now: a '21st-century monarchy'. As an oxymoron to run a mile from, it's up there with 'fourth-century brain surgery'. Trying to clean up after the Meghan and Harry interview feels a little like asking a series of decapitated mafia soldiers if they can produce an email trail showing they raised their issues with their line manager.

The institution headed by the Queen, 94, is accused of racism, along with an as yet unnamed member of the royal family on whom the net of fevered suspicion is likely to close. A lot of people will have dealt with racist family members of their own, of course

– but concerns about bloodline mean so much more coming from any royal house founded on intermarriage. Even so, it feels a little late for the royals to be taking an interest in genetics. A child being a quarter African American is somewhat less of a talking point than one side of that child's family having repeatedly bred with its cousins for half the 19th and 20th centuries.

Still, on with the show. It's fair to say the house of Windsor has failed to end its marrying-an-American-divorcee hoodoo. As for the idea that there is some sort of HR process in train to investigate both Meghan's complaints and complaints against Meghan, I'm sure it's a nice idea, but ... do me a favour. The royal family can't even begin to pretend 'the firm' is like 'a firm'. No firm I've ever worked for feels they still have to pay the bezzie of an international paedophile, who himself has had to deny having sex with a trafficked 17-year-old. Actually, hang on – when I started as a secretary on the *Sun*, the paper's chief reporter had been allowed back to work after being convicted of strangling and drowning his wife. So yes: always good to hear from certain sections of Fleet Street on what counts as conduct beyond the pale. 'Meghan's Baby Shower Shame', is it? Righto.

Unsurprisingly, the Duchess of Sussex is not the first person connected with this 'firm' to feel suicidal. When the Queen and Princess Margaret's devoted nanny Crawfie wrote a discreetly adoring and anodyne memoir, *The Little Princesses*, the royal family effectively destroyed her. Some kind of published reminiscences had initially been the Queen Mother's idea, but Crawfie was utterly cast out and demonised for the next 30 years – forever parted from the two children she had effectively raised, at an age where she was now unable to have her own. Desperate for reconciliation, she bought a house on an Aberdeen road down which the family drove on their annual summer decampment to Balmoral. They never stopped. When she attempted to take her own life, as she did twice, Crawfie left a note which read: 'I cannot bear those I love to pass me by on the road.'

The more Harry and Meghan used the words 'the institution' in their Oprah interview, the more it sounded once again like somewhere known locally as 'The Institution'. As in, a nightmarish place, with staff instructed not to speak to townsfolk about what happens there. Just assume the Queen has a wacky sign on her desk: 'You don't have to be mad to work here – but you will be by the time you leave.'

Moneywise, I'm sure it's unfortunate being 'cut off financially' in your mid-thirties, in a way that forces you to leave a taxpayer-funded house to purchase a \$14.5 million (£10.4 million) Californian mansion. But it feels even more so when Buckingham Palace advertises jobs at below the living wage, given a lot of the duties sound like something you might be expected to perform if you were being held without your passport in exchange for 'room and board' in a shed.

Whenever the tasks of royal servants are itemised, I can only imagine them being listened to by a fictional police officer from a specialist unit, probably played by Sarah Lancashire. 'And you say your job involved squeezing toothpaste on your master's toothbrush ...? OK. And what would happen if you put the toothpaste on wrong? ... Right. I see. And you're saying you had to hold the specimen bottle when he gave a urine sample? No, it's all right, love. I know it's hard. Let's take a break, get you a cup of tea.'

But we know all this. Perhaps the last truth some dare not speak about royal dysfunction is their own addiction to it. Speaking my own truth, I note I am writing another column about the drama the second in three weeks. And for all the outrage on Monday, there was a sense of high excitement to many people's engagement with the latest bombshells, as they condemned/ supported the dramatis personae thrice hourly on social media.

I was reminded of the woman I met in Windsor the day before Meghan and Harry's wedding who was one of those camping out to see the happy couple. 'It's terrible what they've done to her,' she fumed to me of the tabloids, three of which she had bought that morning and was working her outraged way through.

There's plenty of precedent here. Contrary to the pompous way in which it is often discussed, people loved the abdication crisis. The whole drama gave them quite the lift in otherwise depressing times. I've quoted a passage from Evelyn Waugh's diaries here before, but let's wheel it out again: 'The Simpson crisis has been a great delight to everyone. At Maidie's nursing home they report a pronounced turn for the better in all the adult patients. There can seldom have been an event that has caused so much general delight and so little pain.'

The shock death of George VI was also luxuriated in, according to the Bloomsbury-group diarist Frances Partridge, who noted 'bulletins of thunderous gravity and richly revelled-in emotional unbuttoning'.

'The whole effect is of ham acting,' she continued, 'and a lot of nonsense is being talked about the relief necessary to our tortured feelings. What the public is feeling is a sense of great drama, not at all unpleasant.'

My own long-held belief is that a sense of great drama is what people truly want from the royal family. It's not what people say they want, of course. People say they want dutiful ribbon-cutters who speak in platitudes, and only biannually. They say they want fist-gnawingly dull copy about how the Queen is wearing a brooch she wore on her honeymoon to this or that engagement, and what that might mean. They say they want 1,500 words of torpid and painfully uneventful bollocks about William and Kate boarding an easyJet flight. But what they really want is high drama, pure mess, grotesque villains and a side to take.

They've certainly got one now. Early polling suggests that sympathy for the palace and the Sussexes is split deeply on generational lines – which is a problem if you're in charge of something that has to get handed down the generations. It is increasingly clear that the Queen has constructed a monarchy that only works with her specific, unreplicable personage at the helm. Or, to put it another way, if you want to tell a coming blockbuster horror story in just two words, try this pitch for size: 'Charles III'.

12 MARCH

'Non-fungible tokens': the etymology behind this new digital swag

STEVEN POOLE

When is an album not an album? Why, when it's a 'non-fungible token', a new form of digital swag, related to cryptocurrency, being sold by artists and musicians such as Kings of Leon and Grimes. They are called NFTs for short, but why?

The Latin verb *fungi* means to discharge some office or perform some task, and so *fungibilis* means 'useful', and English 'fungible' describes useful things that are interchangeable. If I order five spoons of a certain design, it doesn't matter exactly which five of those spoons you send me.

The *OED* says the word was first used in English by the diplomat Anthony Ascham in 1649, though the citation it gives is actually, according to Early English Books Online, from a 1676 treatise on maritime law, *De Jure Maritimo et Navali*, by Charles Molloy and Robert White. Of money, they write: 'Take away this fungible Instrument from the service of our necessities, and how shall we exercise our Charity?' Money is the paradigmatically fungible good, since one £10 note is as good as any other. Writers, though, are definitely not fungible.

12 MARCH

Cast out: the Yazidi women reunited with their children born in Isis slavery

MARTIN CHULOV AND NECHIRVAN MANDO

Bundled up in oversized scarves and coats, and squirming over lounge chairs, the 12 young children seemed startled as nine strange women with outstretched arms hurried towards them. Some of the women sobbed as they embraced the bemused toddlers who stared at them blankly, not recognising their mothers or understanding what the fuss was about. One mother stood motionless with her head in her hands, while another stared intently into her tiny daughter's eyes.

The nine mothers, all members of the Yazidi community, and their children, all born to the terrorists who enslaved the women, had been reunited for the first time since the collapse of Islamic State in early 2019. And after two years of preparing for such a moment, the women were about to make the most momentous decisions of their lives.

The extraordinary scenes at the Iraq–Syria border crossing last Thursday were the culmination of months of lobbying by officials, including from the Biden administration, protracted debates among the Yazidi community and the determination of young mothers cruelly stripped of the children born to them to reclaim what was theirs, no matter the price. Each of the women had used an excuse to slip away from their family. The last time most of them had been at the Samalka crossing, they had been rescued from the giant al-Hol refugee camp in eastern Syria where the remnants of Isis's collapsed so-called caliphate were collected.

The Yazidi were allowed to return to Iraq, but their children were seized from them before the border and taken to an orphanage. Yazidi elders had since refused to allow the children to join their mothers. To the community, the children were outcasts who could never be assimilated into Yazidi society. The unwritten reckoning was that if the mothers chose their children, they would need to forgo their community.

Until last week it appeared unlikely that the women, all aged between 19 and 26, would ever be able to make such a decision. The children had been banned from entering Iraq and only a few mothers had been able to enter Syria on day passes to visit the orphanage. Then came a convergence of people and circumstances that made the seemingly impossible suddenly doable.

Nemam Ghafouri, an organiser of the Yazidi mothers and founder of Joint Help for Kurdistan, an NGO, received a phone call from Peter Galbraith, a former US diplomat and long-term contact of Kurds on both sides of the border. The Syrian Kurds were prepared to do a deal, he told her, and he was flying to Erbil to make it happen.

Galbraith worked on the US Senate foreign relations committee for 14 years and has been a friend of Joe Biden since 1980. Like him, the new US president had taken an interest in Kurdish issues. The calculation on both sides of the border was that doing business on an issue such as this might pave the way for more extensive re-engagement after the turmoil of the Trump years.

'I asked Nechirvan Barzani [president of the Kurdish regional government] to talk to Mazloum Abdi [commander of the Syrian Democratic Forces] and he agreed,' he said.

After fraught discussions throughout Wednesday during which Galbraith called the White House to secure the transfer, Syrian Kurdish officials bundled the 12 children – who could all be definitively linked to the nine mothers waiting for them – into a minibus and headed for the border.

Ghafouri, who had been waiting with the mothers in a hotel, brought them to the border, and waited. In the following hours officials in Kurdish Iraq demanded to know the provenance of the children before clearing the mothers to reclaim them. The women had been enslaved in their early teens from the community of Sinjar, which bore the brunt of the Isis genocide, and had stayed with the group throughout its rise and fall. Some of the mothers did not know who the fathers of their children were.

'People need to realise why some of these women have such bonds with their babies,' said Ghafouri. 'When they got pregnant, it meant the end of selling and raping by new men. This child brought an end to part of their suffering. Once being pregnant and giving birth, it was the end of it. The mother stayed with one man until he was killed.'

By midnight last Thursday the mothers were on their way to a prearranged safe house.

But news of the reunions has been met with anger by leaders of the Yazidi community. 'We don't accept this. This should be a Yazidi nation decision,' said Prince Herman, a representative of the senior Yazidi leader, Prince Hazem. 'The mothers are always welcome to come back home, but the children are not accepted.

They can give their children to whomever they want, but they cannot live with us.

'Those people who brought back those children without asking Yazidis, or Yazidi leaders, will pay the price for what they did. There is no difference between those missionary NGOs and Isis because they are playing with our girls and taking them from us.'

The Yazidi spiritual leader, Sheikh Ali Ilyas, said the women were now exiled. 'Neither I or the Yazidi community will accept those children,' he said. 'They are free to go wherever they want, except our community. They are no longer our issue and are free to make their own decisions.'

In the safe house, sounds of children playing echoed over two floors. Eight mothers moved into the house, with one returning to her family in a refugee camp. Those who stayed are now looking for relocation to Europe or Australia.

'I wasn't sure what I'd do until I saw my daughter again,' said one of the mothers. 'I love my mother a lot and know what this means for me. But I love my daughter too. I want a new start.'

A second mother said she was overwhelmed by the support she had felt over the past week and now realised she needed to cut ties with her society. 'I have family living abroad, and even they won't accept me. This has to change, and we're going to make it happen. When I told my parents, they said: "You are no longer a member of our family."

'I am very happy that I am with her. At first she didn't recognise me, but it's getting better day by day. When I came back after being separated, and I realised the community wasn't accepting us, I decided to make my life my daughter. Children are innocent. They haven't made any mistakes.'

Yazidis have been granted resettlement in Europe and elsewhere, but the issue of children born to Isis fighters remains vexed for governments.

'They have no safe place not only in Iraq but in the entire Middle East,' said Ghafouri. 'The only thing they want is to be resettled as a group in a third country. This has been an infected wound for the Yazidi community. The only healing is reuniting those mothers who want their children and resettling them.

'We need to find solutions now. I don't necessarily blame Yazidi communities or Kurdish communities in either Iraq or Syria, but I do blame the UN and the international community.

'They are victims again being victimised by those people saying they are supporting them, but not doing anything.'

Additional reporting by Barzan Salam.

20 MARCH

We always speak of women's safety. Let's talk about male violence instead

ANNE ENRIGHT

Rapists are not a talkative lot. They don't discuss the deed much, after they have been caught. And you might think this is because they feel remorseful, but often they don't seem to know that they have done something wrong. Or they know that they have done something illegal, but the act itself is fine by them. They admit to nonconsensual sex 'but not rape'. They admit to rape but not to blame: 'I felt I was repaying her for sexually arousing me,' a man in one of the few studies says.

On a Reddit forum where, at the onset of the #MeToo revolution, my soul went to die, men wrote 'from the other side' of sexual assault. Their accounts implied covert participation – 'She just had this unusually sexual way of carrying herself' – or active reciprocation: 'In my mind, at the time, she wanted it.' This man looked at the woman's face and realised he had been mistaken.

A few things are striking about the comments: one is that desire – and I think this is true for women also – turns the sexual object into a fragmented object. When people are having sex, they can get a bit lost in it. We do not always look into our lover's eyes, not all the time, so yes, it is a good idea to check back with the entire person to see if your needs are still aligned. The sense of entitlement is, with the vengeful or narcissistic types, always breathtaking. This is something society does not encourage or allow in women, for which you might almost be grateful. Who wants to be like that? There is also the mechanism of blame, that magical projection machine. These men speak as though arousal comes from somewhere outside the self, and that it, even more strangely, continues to happen outside the self. There is no reality check. She started this. She wants this. It comes from her.

The courts don't laugh at these projections, they magnify them. We have all seen women destroyed by a justice system that puts them on trial for being attacked. The courtroom discussion becomes all about the victim, her clothes, her 'mistakes', while the perpetrator remains a blank.

This gap in the argument is an odd absence that requires a lot of energy to maintain. This is why strange things happen in court: why a woman's thong is waved by the defence, as in a case in Cork last year; or a woman's silence during a gang rape is taken as a sign of her enthusiasm, as happened in a 2019 trial in Pamplona, Spain. A good part of female outrage, the years of #MeToo, has been taken up by raw disbelief. These courtroom arguments are a bit mad. They are also a distraction from the man in the dock. There is a kind of trick happening here.

Men do not just disappear in court, they disappear from the discussion, they disappear from the language we use. Rape is described as 'a women's issue'. We speak of 'women's safety concerns', not 'concerns about men's violence'. We call it 'an abusive relationship' as though the relationship were doing the abusing, or an 'abusive home' as though the walls were insulting the occupants for fun. The notorious line 'she was asking for it' is not so different to 'a woman was raped': both take the rapist out of the sentence.

Male agency is routinely removed from descriptions of male violence, and this helps men get away with it. I still can't figure out the contradiction, though, that the violent assertion of male potency also involves a kind of vanishing act. It seems very self-defeating.

The American theorist and activist Jackson Katz is one of the few men who states the obvious fact that men's sexual violence is first of all an issue for men. He also says male silence about this so-called 'women's issue' is a form of consent. His remarks about the use of the passive voice hit Twitter in a week of renewed social unrest about sexual crime. 'When you look at that term, "violence against women", nobody is doing it to them. It just happens. Men aren't even a part of it!'

In his popular Ted Talk Katz describes men's ability to go unexamined as 'one of the key characteristics of power and privilege'. We do not talk about men, because that is the way they like it. For Katz, a tendency to blame the victim is not about sex or even gender, it is just what humans do. 'Our whole cognitive structure is set up to blame victims,' he says. Katz teaches a bystander programme, in which he urges men to interrupt other men who talk abusively about women. He wants us to know that this is not a call for greater sensitivity, however – he seems to realise how sensitive men can get when you ask them to be 'sensitive' – no, this is a leadership thing, 'because the typical perpetrator is not sick and twisted. He's a normal guy in every other way, right?'

Well, how would I know? I can't say if a perpetrator is a 'normal guy' because I am not a guy, and the men who do know are saying nothing. I do think misogynists are 'twisted' because of the way they twist the truth of their own psychology and I think some men are aware of this and some men are not.

Is that why society maintains a silence about rapists, because we secretly think that they are just 'normal' guys, they are just 'male'? It is possible that men worry this is the case and Katz wants to reassure them that their fantasies, their swagger, do not automatically turn them into monsters. He is, very cannily, working with and not against male bonding, which has a big role in the formation of male sexuality. But he is also accurate to the fact that most rapists do not commit other crimes. In social terms, they can be anybody.

Most rapists do not end up in jail. The rapists who do end up in jail, according to one American study, are also more likely to have committed non-sexual crimes. Work within this cohort shows that convicted rapists tend to start young, have female-hostile peer groups, like rape-pornography (which is more than 80 per cent of pornography), often report feeling rejected in some way and suffer from a lack of empathy.

The vengeful sentence 'I felt I was repaying her for arousing me' feels very familiar to women, who are long tired of the weirdness it contains. But the man who said it also seems to consider arousal to be a kind of punishment. It is not pleasant. It is unfair. The man who says, 'This is her fault, she did this' feels as though he has been acted upon. He is passive, perhaps unbearably so. This man is taking himself out of his own desiring; you might say he is obliterating himself.

If I were a man, I might want to put my self back into the discussion, I might want to do a reality check. But if I were a man, I wouldn't be writing this because writing about rape, talking about rape, protesting against rape and being raped are all women's work. This despite the fact that the weekend of protests in London was also a weekend during which footage was circulated online of an RAF recruit being sexually threatened by a group of his peers brandishing a piece of military hardware. In America the figures show that one in six men has been the victim of sexual violence of some kind, as opposed to one in three women, and that 99 per cent of the perpetrators are male. The difference between the victims, sadly, is that society has long been happy to blame the women.

29 MARCH

What we're getting wrong in the conversation about mental health

LUCY FOULKES

Many years ago, in the fading hours of a house party, I sat outside in the garden with an old friend. From inside came the distant thud of music and pockets of laughter – a thousand miles from the conversation we were having. My friend's relationship had ended a few weeks previously, and that night his heartbreak was palpable and raw. He told me how disconnected he felt from the people inside the house, from his life. 'When I look into the future,' he said, avoiding eye contact, 'I can't see anything ahead of me.' At that moment, I thought, something became clear: he was clinically depressed.

Over the following days and weeks, I told my friend what I knew about the disorder, and the benefits of therapy and anti-depressants, and encouraged him to go to the doctor. Even though he was reluctant, I was sure of how much he would benefit, so I persisted. But then, after about a month of checking in with him, something strange happened: he started to feel better, without any professional help at all. I distinctly remember the moment, a disin-tegration of what I thought I understood about mental health.

Evidently, since my friend's acute distress passed within a few weeks, he didn't sit clearly in the territory of what we might call 'mental illness'. But he certainly wasn't mentally healthy for those weeks either. Instead, I realised, he was somewhere in the vast grey plains between the two.

Everything we might think of as a 'symptom' of mental disorder – worry, low mood, binge eating, delusions – actu-ally exists on a continuum throughout the population. In the terrain of mental health, there is no objective border to cross that delineates the territory of disorder. On top of this, the thoughts, feelings and behaviours that appear temporarily as a natural response to hardship and stress – such as when we're heartbroken – exactly mimic those that, should they persist, are defining features of mental disorders.

But this messy truth is not part of the public conversation about mental health. In the past decade or so, there has been a huge push to destigmatise mental illness and talk more openly about our distress. Broadly, this is a good thing. But when you attempt to smooth down a vast and thorny landscape into punchy hashtags and ad-friendly slogans, nuance gets lost – and there has been some collateral damage.

The current conversation can be summed up as follows: you should notice, scrutinise and seek help for negative psychological experiences. Of course, for some people, this message will be essential. But the message misfires when it implies that all negative states are *problems*, health problems – and things that can and should be fixed.

This is not to say people who fall below the threshold of a 'disorder' should be silenced or ignored. I am vehemently opposed to the accusatory, dismissive language aimed at 'snowflakes'. We do need to encourage people with milder or more transient difficulties to talk: first, because any form of distress is horrible to experience alone; second, because what seems mild may be the beginning of a more serious problem. But we need to figure out a way to talk about these negative emotions without sending the message that there's something dysfunctional about you for feeling that way.

This means resisting the temptation to label all negative feelings with psychiatric terminology. When I was a psychology lecturer, I spoke to an undergraduate who said that everyone in her year group – around 150 students – described themselves as having either depression or an anxiety disorder or both. From what we know from population-based studies, it's nigh-on impossible that they all met criteria for these disorders. What seems more likely is that individuals in more hospitable parts of the mental health terrain have started to co-opt terminology that really needs to be reserved for people trapped farther in its depths.

This is no one's fault. We all want language and labels to interpret our experiences, especially difficult ones, and thanks to the public conversation psychiatric terms such as depression, post-traumatic stress disorder and social anxiety disorder are readily available. Psychological distress, whatever its intensity, is hard, and diagnostic labels allow you to say: I'm suffering, my problem is real, and I need help.

But this framing, used inappropriately, can ironically compound people's distress. Research shows that interpreting your low mood as a sign of depression, for example, can actually cause you to spiral into the very depression you're worried about. It also doesn't help the people who actually *do* have depression: a devastating disorder that hijacks body and mind, leaving people unable to live the life they want or, in some cases, any life at all.

The public conversation as it stands therefore seems to be underserving people across the spectrum: some people unnecessarily label themselves as disordered, which can make them feel worse, while others who are seriously unwell are still not being heard.

We need to recalibrate. First, we need to tell more stories about individuals with severe and debilitating mental disorders, so we clearly understand what these disorders involve and what can help. Second, we need to promote the idea that a great number of distressing psychological experiences can be managed – sometimes with professional help – without needing to reach for the psychiatric dictionary. This is not meant to be critical but to empower, and reassure: don't feel you have to take on a psychiatric diagnosis, or consider there's something medically wrong with you, unless you really do find that framing helpful.

The next time one of my friends is heartbroken – which will happen, of course, as night follows day – I'll take a different approach. I'll still discuss the value of getting professional help; I'll still remember that relationship breakdowns can and do contribute to mental disorders and even suicide in some individuals; I'll still keep checking in, and being a good friend. But I'll also hold another possibility in mind: that with a bit of talking and time, their pain will pass on its own. That we may be in the realm not of psychiatric disorder, but rather in the tangled landscape of our rich and painful lives.

Spring

'The fear is that this will get bigger': six nights of rioting in Northern Ireland

RORY CARROLL

It is not hard finding the next riot spot in Northern Ireland. You can check Facebook or other social media for locations and times. You can follow young people visiting petrol stations to fill up jerry cans. Or you can tag along with older people who gather, phones in hand, to watch and record the show.

One older woman came to Lanark Way off the Shankill Road on Wednesday well wrapped up, bathrobe over her coat, for what promised to be a long, cold, eventful evening. 'Not long now,' said a man to no one in particular.

The soon-to-be rioters were young males, many teenagers, in dark fleeces and tracksuits. They made their preparations openly and with swagger, conscious they had an audience of several hundred.

Some collected rocks from an adjacent waste ground, making little piles on the pavement and in their pockets. Others broke pallets and lit a fire in the road. Tyres sent a black plume into a darkening sky.

The atmosphere was giddy. Boys of about 17, with younger apprentices, appeared with brown bottles, some filled with liquid.

Kevin Scott, a *Belfast Telegraph* photographer, was assaulted and his camera was smashed. White police Land Rovers arrived, lights flashing, and the fusillade began.

Rocks, bottles and petrol bombs crashed off the vehicles. Spectators scattered back, or went home, leaving the stage to the main performers. Two youths entered a Translink double-decker bus emptied of driver and passengers. An older man appeared to guard the entrance while they fiddled with the controls. They exited, the bus rolled and a petrol bomb exploded inside, creating a fireball on wheels.

A vehicle that connects the city – connects people – destroyed by children of the 1998 Good Friday agreement that drew a line under the Troubles: it was a dispiriting spectacle.

By yesterday, the disturbances across Northern Ireland had left 55 police officers injured and aggravated a political crisis that encompasses policing, Brexit and the endless tug-of-war between nationalists and unionists.

'Last night was at a scale we haven't seen in Belfast or further afield in Northern Ireland for a number of years,' said the assistant chief constable, Jonathan Roberts. 'We are very, very lucky no one was seriously injured or killed.'

Translink said the bus driver was shaken but unhurt. Ten people have been arrested over the past week, including a 13-year-old boy.

The British and Irish governments expressed grave concern that scenes supposedly consigned to history had returned. The region's power-sharing executive at Stormont held an emergency meeting with Simon Byrne, the chief constable. Politicians from all parties condemned the violence. Brandon Lewis, the Northern Ireland secretary, planned to meet faith, community and political leaders.

But there were reports that loyalists are planning fresh protests this weekend. And there was no sign of a detente between Sinn Féin and the Democratic Unionist party to chart a way out of the crisis.

In some ways things are not as bad as they look. The protests have been small, usually just a few dozen people. The main loyalist paramilitary groups have not thrown their weight behind them. Stormont is still functioning and giving primacy to peaceful, constitutional politics. No one has died. But the undercurrents driving the unrest are deep and turbulent.

'We're second-class citizens. Protestants are second-class citizens, it's not right,' said Jay, 16, as his friends prepared to skirmish with police. They repeated grievances like a mantra: second-class citizens, picked on by police, abandoned by unionist parties, betrayed by government and, worst of all, bested by nationalists.

According to this perspective, nationalists were able to flout pandemic rules at a huge funeral for Bobby Storey, an IRA commander, last summer because the police are now biased towards Sinn Féin; the DUP let Boris Johnson weaken Northern Ireland's link to the UK to clinch a Brexit deal; loyalism has been ignored, and the only way to get attention – to hit back – is to cause some mayhem.

'Youse weren't here till we started lighting fires,' said one.

Some analysts believe that the DUP has demanded the chief constable's resignation over the policing of the Storey funeral, to deflect anger over the party's role in creating the Irish Sea border.

Middle-aged men have hovered in the middle of some riots, prompting suspicion that elements of loyalist paramilitary groups such as the Ulster Defence Association are orchestrating events. This could be to let youngsters blow off steam, to stiffen the resolve of unionist leaders, to punish the police for a recent spate of arrests and drug busts, or all of the above.

The irony is that in Northern Ireland's centenary year it is unionists and loyalists, not nationalists or republicans, who highlight the region's shortcomings and show that this part of the UK, post-Brexit, doesn't work.

In Belfast on Wednesday night, however, some nationalists were happy to help them make the case. After monitoring loyalist postings about the Lanark Way protest, they gathered on Springfield Road on the other side of the 'peace wall' and launched rocks and bottles.

A barrage of stone, glass and flaming petrol came in response, a sectarian air battle peppered with sectarian insults. One of the gates caught fire and was breached. For a fleeting moment it resembled 1969, the dawn of the Troubles, when mobs burned homes, but the skirmish ended without serious injury. 'It's very disheartening,' said Cailin McCaffery, 25, a postgraduate researcher on the Springhill Road side. 'The PUL [Protestant unionist loyalist] community is destroying its own community.'

Northern Ireland had progressed greatly since the Good Friday agreement, for instance with cross-community support for LGBT rights. Yet here were Catholic teenagers sucked into a tribal battle with Protestant teenagers living over the wall, said McCaffery. 'The fear is that the disturbances will get bigger. We don't want to relive what our parents lived.'

On Thursday morning, calm returned to the Shankill Road, and traffic passed the scorched carcass of the bus. The wheels were still smoking.

9 APRIL

First thing I turn to in a book? The thank yous at the back

HANNAH JANE PARKINSON

I have something to acknowledge: I love acknowledgements. They are the first thing I read in a book. (Often, I won't read an author's introduction until after I have finished, in case it contains spoilers. Yes, I know.)

Gratitude is one of the most important things. If someone doesn't say thank you after I hold a door open for them, they might as well be a serial killer. Acknowledgements are the literary equivalent of thanking all the people who made a book possible; who held the door open. (Or gave the writer a key to their cottage by the sea for a writing retreat. Lots of those.)

I am quite a nosy person, so I enjoy scanning the names to see if there is someone I recognise; as though I am spotting two people I did not know were friends dining together in a restaurant. I enjoy the turns of phrase writers come up with to avoid repeating themselves. The in-jokes.

We even get a glimpse into the circumstances of an author's life and the backdrop against which the book was produced. Those who acknowledge Arts Council grants or thank the NHS, and even food banks and housing charities, as was the case in Anna Burns's Booker-winning novel *Milkman*; a mini-political commentary in itself.

I am currently reading Benjamin Dreyer's brilliant *Dreyer's English*, which has eight pages of acknowledgements; a commendable level of generosity (though if this were an Oscars speech, the orchestra would have played him off by page two). I suppose the longer the list, the more likely someone will be miffed if left out; but also the shorter the list, the danger that more people will be miffed. What a minefield.

Dedications are much more likely to be read, so funny or touching ones are often more memorable than something similar tucked away at the back. What a shame, though, if the acknowledgements page at the back of Brendan Pietsch's *Dispensational Modernism*, which starts: 'I blame all of you', had gone unnoticed.

But it's the love coming off the pages that makes acknowledgements so special. Knowing that the book I am about to read (for others, usually the book just read) could not have come into being without all the support and advice and friendship and hard work of others. The reiteration that, no matter the trope of the toiling writer in a solitary study, life – in all its glory and achievement – is a team sport.

15 APRIL

We can mourn Prince Philip, but not the monarchy

AFUA HIRSCH

Within minutes of Prince Philip's death having been announced, I began receiving messages from friends in Ghana. 'My sincere condolences for your loss,' one said. 'May God bless you and everyone in the UK who is grieving,' said another. On a human level, acknowledging respectfully the loss that comes with death makes sense. But why did these messages describe it as *my* loss?

I am not alone in feeling that the monarchy is an institution that cannot be embraced – although, even now, it is not easy to say so. If I fail to express my deference and loyalty, I will be viciously attacked by those who regard me as unpatriotic. I will be the bad Black person, the ungrateful 'guest' (never mind that this is my country), the disloyal colonial subject who forgot how much Britain did for me.

The public reaction to Prince Philip's death has centred on how much he, personally, has done. By all accounts he was the most active member of the royal family, having conducted, apparently, more than 20,000 engagements, and holding more than 800 presidencies and patronages. Many young people benefited from the Duke of Edinburgh awards scheme.

But these acts of public service come with strings attached. We become complicit in a toxic transaction that, in exchange for their privileges, deprives the royals of their privacy or control over their own destinies and entitles us to endless and poisonous coverage of the minutiae of their lives.

On our side of the bargain, we abandon our supposed commitment to meritocracy and equality by accepting that these human beings are born deserving of special reverence. We receive access to their charity but in return lose our freedom to challenge their authority. The royals' good deeds are not in themselves a justification for the monarchy.

The truth is that there is no escaping the haunting legacy of empire. Its ghosts have long taken possession of our royal family, turning them into emperors without colonies, bounty hoarders without raids, conquerors without wars. Instead, they are heads of a Commonwealth in which the colonised are rebranded 'friends' with 'a shared history'. This is fantasy stuff.

As is the idea, ludicrously popular in tributes to Prince Philip, that he was some kind of frustrated comedian. We have all by now been reminded of his famous remarks: telling the Nigerian president, Olusegun Obasanjo, who was wearing national dress, 'You look like you're ready for bed'; or advising British students in China not to stay too long or they would end up with 'slitty eyes'. A Black British, Cambridge-educated friend of mine received a classic Prince Philip 'compliment' when she met him: 'You speak English beautifully!' he said.

In the past few days we've heard numerous euphemisms deployed to cover these outbursts without calling them what they were. 'His "gaffes" were typical of the clubbish humour of the officer class.' He was 'politically incorrect', and 'blunt'. Nobody likes to speak ill of the dead, but these are not excuses for Philip so much as alibis for British commentators desperate to avoid confronting the real legacy of British imperial expansion: racism. A dirty word that inconveniently undermines the glorious narrative the royals still help project. The colonisation of 'lesser peoples' was by definition a project of white supremacy, and one personified by the royal family at the head of the empire: of course he made racist jokes.

If calling Prince Philip 'a man of his time' is an admission that the royals exist in something of a time capsule, then I have to agree. The institution is, as the experience of the Duke and Duchess of Sussex has made clear, outdated. Both Meghan's presence and the racist press treatment to which she was subjected offered the monarchy a unique opportunity to embrace a woman of African heritage, acknowledge its complicated relationship with this heritage in the past, and at least appear committed to a new era of equality. It could not have failed the test more dramatically.

Meanwhile, Britain's honours system continues to glorify the pain felt by survivors of colonialism and their descendants. This system – which is still being actively promoted – rewards British people for their achievements on remarkable terms. It asks us to aspire to see ourselves as 'Members', 'Officers' or even 'Commanders' of the British Empire – a painful act of betrayal to our histories.

For those who object to projecting this painful history on to a single, recently deceased old man, this is the very problem with the concept of monarchy. Of course, there is an individual analysis in which Prince Philip was a fascinating historical actor whose passing points towards the end of an era. His childhood was shaped by the Ottoman empire's collapse. His body carried the genetic memory of the Bolshevik revolution and its fatal consequences for the Romanovs: in 1993, his DNA was used to identify their remains.

Philip's marriage is a legacy of Queen Victoria's project to unite Europe through dynastic marriages, based on a deep appreciation of the need for peace on the continent. It's a virtuous ideal with much to offer the same people most noisily prostrating themselves before the royals, if they actually cared to learn.

But our personal relationships with the monarchy cannot exist in a vacuum. Before expressing any fondness for the royals, I have to ask myself: am I subconsciously seeking the approval of the predominantly white society that rewards particular Black people for showing their allegiance? Am I threatened by the penalties for not engaging in this period of forced mourning? Many TV journalists like me are, after all, at the mercy of a governing party that has made clear its willingness to upbraid broadcasters who do not appear sufficiently patriotic.

Above all, the unspoken requirement for us to publicly celebrate the monarchy's gains – or mourn any of its losses – demands that I internalise a history of violence and racism against my own ancestors. The instinct I still feel to apologise for not doing so is evidence of how strongly those forces still exist. So, if there is a fitting tribute to the passing of Prince Philip, I believe it would be to learn, with honesty, the lessons from both his life and the reaction to his death.

26 APRIL

Breakaway leagues are nothing new and nor are the negative reactions

SIMON BURNTON

In mid-April 12 clubs who fancied themselves to be the biggest around made a controversial announcement. They had decided to set up a league together. Cue outrage. 'A dozen clubs, who style themselves the pick of the talent, have joined hands for their own mutual benefit, apparently without a care for those unhappily shut out in the cold,' raged one newspaper. Another fumed: 'The league is not formed for the purpose of encouraging football, it is formed so the allied clubs can make more money than they already do,' describing the clubs involved as 'nothing better than circus shows' and the idea as 'a huge strategy to dip into the pockets of the public'.

It was 1888, and the first season of the Football League was being planned. Precisely 133 years and one day later, the launch of a new international super league was announced. Within 48 hours it had died under a deluge of outrage, and other than the sheer quantity of it leaking from social media platforms there was little to differentiate most of it from what has come before. Football is not a game that tends to react well to innovation, or to be able to differentiate between the positive kind – setting up a league rather than playing constant friendlies and assorted cup competitions, for example – and the genuinely harmful.

The idea of a European super league has not always been unpopular. In 1960, after Bristol Rovers proposed a reorganisation of English football (one 18-team top flight fed by two regional second divisions, four regional third divisions and so on), *The Times* wrote about the 'crying need to create an upper cadre, forming a super-league of no more than 16 clubs who can perform and grow wiser in some newly established European League'. At the same time the *Observer* proposed 'a Premier League of 16 clubs chosen for their playing record, ground facilities, financial strength and spectator population' from which 'the best teams [would] enter a European league'. In 1972 the Conservative minister for sport Eldon Griffiths hosted a meeting at his London apartment where he tried to persuade the Football League to launch a European equivalent. In February 1957 the *Guardian* reported 'some voices within the Football Association would favour a supernational European league bringing into opposition the finest talent in all the countries'.

Mostly, however, the idea has met, as this year, with hostility. 'A European league would skim the cream off English football, and to support such a scheme would be for the Football League tantamount to suicide,' the *Guardian* wrote in 1957. 'Its effect at least initially must be to increase the prosperity of the leading clubs and to decrease that of the poorer.' That was the first season in which an English club played in Europe, Manchester United ignoring the Football League's 'strong request' not to take part and reaching the semi-finals of the European Cup. In 1958 there was speculation that United could be expelled from the league for accepting an invitation to play – offered in response to the Munich air disaster – despite not having won their domestic title, which was considered a terrible precedent. But speculation about breakaway leagues really ramped up in the 1980s.

In 1985 talks took place between Liverpool, Everton, Manchester United, Tottenham and Arsenal – plus Manchester City, Newcastle and Southampton – to discuss a breakaway league and the *Guardian* raged about the prospect of 'the few richest and most successful clubs' setting up on their own, declaring the idea 'tawdry and greedy'. In 1988 the story simmered once more, with Silvio Berlusconi plotting a European version, and the *Guardian* wrote about a project that 'is all about money and television', adding: 'The top clubs, believing, correctly, that the armchair fan only wants to watch them, see no reason why any of the money should go anywhere else. [But] the English game is about 92 clubs, not 10 or 13.'

The following year David Lacey, the *Guardian*'s football correspondent, noted: 'Always you get the feeling that one day the threats are going to be more than a series of back-page headlines designed to keep the hoi polloi in order.' And in 1991 the domestic breakaway happened, with the 22 First Division clubs resigning from the Football League to set up alone. The *Observer* wrote: 'It remains to be seen how the new arrangements will quench the thirst for money and power of the big clubs ... The push towards a further breakaway may come from Europe, whose more influential figures have pressed for a Continentwide super league.' In 1990 there was talk of an agreement between 16 clubs across Europe, with Liverpool and Rangers representing Britain. In 1992 the European Cup became the Champions League – but the plotters barely paused.

The owners of the six English clubs involved in the latest attempted breakaway were all born and are based abroad, a fact that many have blamed for their readiness to cast tradition and history aside – but in 1998, when representatives of a dozen European clubs were reported to have met in London, Manchester United had a chairman from Cheshire, Liverpool had an owner from Merseyside, Everton's was from Birkenhead, Arsenal and Tottenham's were from London and Manchester City's from Lancashire. It didn't seem to make much difference.

'The projected European super league is pure, naked, unadulterated greed,' wrote Jeff Powell in the *Daily Mail*. 'Not content with having loadsamoney and bags of influence, the giant clubs of this continent appear to want all the money and absolute power.' And not much, it seems, has changed since.

28 APRIL

'We are witnessing a crime against humanity': India's Covid catastrophe

ARUNDHATI ROY

During a particularly polarising election campaign in the state of Uttar Pradesh in 2017, India's prime minister, Narendra Modi, waded into the fray to stir things up even further. From a public podium, he accused the state government – which was led by an opposition party – of pandering to the Muslim community by spending more on Muslim graveyards (*kabristans*) than on Hindu cremation grounds (*shamshans*). With his customary sneer, he stirred up the crowd. 'If a *kabristan* is built in a village, a *shamshan* should also be constructed there,' he said.

'*Shamshan! Shamshan!*' the mesmerised, adoring crowd echoed back.

Perhaps he is happy now that the haunting image of the flames rising from the mass funerals in India's cremation grounds is making the front page of international newspapers. And that all the *kabristans* and *shamshans* in his country are working properly, in direct proportion to the populations they cater for, and far beyond their capacities.

'Can India, population 1.3 billion, be isolated?' the *Washington Post* asked rhetorically in a recent editorial about India's unfolding catastrophe and the difficulty of containing new, fast-spreading Covid variants within national borders. 'Not easily,' it replied. It's unlikely this question was posed in quite the same way when the coronavirus was raging through the UK and Europe just a few months ago. But we in India have little right to take offence, given our prime minister's words at the World Economic Forum in January this year.

Modi spoke at a time when people in Europe and the US were suffering through the peak of the second wave of the pandemic. He had not one word of sympathy to offer, only a long, gloating boast about India's infrastructure and Covid-preparedness. I downloaded the speech because I fear that when history is rewritten by the Modi regime, as it soon will be, it might disappear, or become hard to find. Here are some priceless snippets:

'Friends, I have brought the message of confidence, positivity and hope from 1.3 billion Indians amid these times of apprehension ... It was predicted that India would be the most affected country from corona all over the world. It was said that there would be a tsunami of corona infections in India, somebody said 700–800 million Indians would get infected while others said 2 million Indians would die.

'Friends, it would not be advisable to judge India's success with that of another country. In a country which is home to 18 per cent of the world population, that country has saved humanity from a big disaster by containing corona effectively.'

Modi the magician takes a bow for saving humanity by containing the coronavirus effectively. Now that it turns out that he has not contained it, can we complain about being viewed as though we are radioactive? That other countries' borders are being closed to us and flights are being cancelled? That we're being sealed in with our virus and our prime minister, along with all the sickness, the anti-science, the hatred and the idiocy that he, his party and its brand of politics represent?

When the first wave of Covid came to India and then subsided last year, the government and its supportive commentariat were triumphant. 'India isn't having a picnic,' tweeted Shekhar Gupta, the editor-in-chief of the online news site ThePrint. 'But our drains aren't choked with bodies, hospitals aren't out of beds, nor crematoriums & graveyards out of wood or space. Too good to be true? Bring data if you disagree. Unless you think you're god.' Leave aside the callous, disrespectful imagery – did we need a god to tell us that most pandemics have a second wave?

This one was predicted, although its virulence has taken even scientists and virologists by surprise. So where is the Covid-specific infrastructure and the 'people's movement' against the virus that Modi boasted about in his speech? Hospital beds are unavailable. Doctors and medical staff are at breaking point. Friends call with stories about wards with no staff and more dead patients than live ones. People are dying in hospital corridors, on roads and in their homes. Crematoriums in Delhi have run out of firewood. The forest department has had to give special permission for the felling of city trees. Parks and car parks are being turned into cremation grounds. It's as if there's an invisible UFO parked in our skies, sucking the air out of our lungs. An air raid of a kind we've never known.

Oxygen is the new currency on India's morbid new stock exchange. Senior politicians, journalists, lawyers – India's elite – are on Twitter pleading for hospital beds and oxygen cylinders. The hidden market for cylinders is booming. Oxygen saturation machines and drugs are hard to come by.

There are markets for other things, too. At the bottom end of the free market, a bribe to sneak a last look at your loved one. A surcharge for a priest who agrees to say the final prayers. Online medical consultancies in which desperate families are fleeced by ruthless doctors. At the top end, you might need to sell your land and home and use up every last rupee for treatment at a private hospital.

None of this conveys the full depth and range of the trauma, the chaos and, above all, the indignity that people are being subjected to. What happened to my young friend T is just one of hundreds, perhaps thousands of similar stories in Delhi alone. T, who is in his twenties, lives in his parents' tiny flat in Ghaziabad on the outskirts of Delhi. All three of them tested positive for Covid. His mother was critically ill. Since it was in the early days, he was lucky enough to find a hospital bed for her. His father, diagnosed with severe bipolar depression, turned violent and began to harm himself. He stopped sleeping. He soiled himself. His psychiatrist was online trying to help, although she also broke down from time to time because her husband had just died from Covid. She said T's father needed hospitalisation, but since he was Covid positive there was no chance of that. So T stayed awake, night after night, holding his father down, sponging him, cleaning him up. Finally, the message came: 'Father's dead.' He did not die of Covid, but of a massive spike in blood pressure induced by a psychiatric meltdown induced by utter helplessness.

Things will settle down eventually. Of course, they will. But we don't know who among us will survive to see that day. The rich will breathe easier. The poor will not. For now, among the sick and dying, there is a vestige of democracy. The rich have been felled, too. Hospitals are begging for oxygen. The oxygen crisis has led to intense, unseemly battles between states, with political parties trying to deflect blame from themselves.

On the night of 22 April, 25 critically ill coronavirus patients on high-flow oxygen died in one of Delhi's biggest private hospitals, Sir Ganga Ram. The hospital issued several desperate SOS messages for the replenishment of its oxygen supply. A day later, the chair of the hospital board rushed to clarify matters: 'We cannot say that they have died due to lack of oxygen support.' On 24 April, 20 more patients died when oxygen supplies were depleted in another big Delhi hospital, Jaipur Golden. That same day, in the Delhi high court, Tushar Mehta, India's solicitor general, speaking for the government of India, said: 'Let's try and not be a cry baby ... so far we have ensured that no one in the country was left without oxygen.'

Ajay Mohan Bisht, the saffron-robed chief minister of Uttar Pradesh, who goes by the name Yogi Adityanath, has declared that there is no shortage of oxygen in any hospital in his state and that rumourmongers will be arrested without bail under the National Security Act and have their property seized.

Where shall we look for solace? For science? Shall we cling to numbers? How many dead? How many recovered? How many infected? When will the peak come? The number of Covid-protocol funerals from graveyards and crematoriums in small towns and cities suggests a death toll up to 30 times higher than the official count.

If Delhi is breaking down, what should we imagine is happening in villages in Bihar, in Uttar Pradesh, in Madhya Pradesh? Where tens of millions of workers from the cities, carrying the virus with them, are fleeing home to their families, traumatised by their memory of Modi's national lockdown in 2020. It was the strictest lockdown in the world, announced with only four hours' notice. It left migrant workers stranded in cities with no work, no money to pay their rent, no food and no transport. Many had to walk hundreds of miles to their homes in far-flung villages. Hundreds died on the way.

This time around, although there is no national lockdown, the workers have left while transport is still available, while trains and buses are still running. They've left because they know that even though they make up the engine of the economy in this huge country, when a crisis comes, in the eyes of this administration, they simply don't exist. This year's exodus has resulted in a different kind of chaos: there are no quarantine centres for them to stay in before they enter their village homes.

These are villages where people die of easily treatable diseases like diarrhoea and tuberculosis. How are they to cope with Covid? Are Covid tests available to them? Are there hospitals? Is there oxygen? More than that, is there love? Forget love, is there even concern? There isn't. Because there is only a heart-shaped hole filled with cold indifference where India's public heart should be.

The precise numbers that make up India's Covid graph are like the wall that was built in Ahmedabad to hide the slums Donald Trump would drive past on his way to the 'Namaste Trump' event that Modi hosted for him in February 2020. Grim as those numbers are, they give you a picture of the India-that-matters, but certainly not the India that is. In the India that is, people are expected to vote as Hindus, but die as disposables.

'Let's try and not be a cry baby.'

Try not to pay attention to the fact that the possibility of a dire shortage of oxygen had been flagged as far back as April 2020. Try not to wonder why even Delhi's biggest hospitals don't have their own oxygen-generating plants. Try not to wonder why the PM Cares Fund – the opaque organisation that has recently replaced the more public Prime Minister's National Relief Fund, and which uses public money and government infrastructure but functions like a private trust with zero public accountability – has suddenly moved in to address the oxygen crisis. Will Modi own shares in our air-supply now?

'Let's try and not be a cry baby.'

Understand that there were and are so many far more pressing issues for the Modi government to attend to. Destroying the last vestiges of democracy, persecuting non-Hindu minorities and consolidating the foundations of the Hindu Nation makes for a relentless schedule. There are massive prison complexes, for example, that must be urgently constructed in Assam for the 2 million people who have lived there for generations and have suddenly been stripped of their citizenship.

There are hundreds of students and activists and young Muslim citizens to be tried and imprisoned as the primary accused in the anti-Muslim pogrom that took place against their own community in north-east Delhi last March. If you are Muslim in India, it's a crime to be murdered. Your folks will pay for it. There was the inauguration of the new Ram Temple in Ayodhya, which is being built in place of the mosque that was hammered to dust by Hindu vandals watched over by senior BJP politicians. There were the controversial new Farm Bills to be passed, corporatising agriculture. There were hundreds of thousands of farmers to be beaten and teargassed when they came out on to the streets to protest.

Then there's the multi-multi-multimillion-dollar plan for a grand new replacement for the fading grandeur of New Delhi's imperial centre to be urgently attended to. After all, how can the government of the new Hindu India be housed in old buildings? While Delhi is locked down, ravaged by the pandemic, construction work on the 'Central Vista' project, declared as an essential service, has begun. Workers are being transported in. Maybe they can alter the plans to add a crematorium.

There was also the Kumbh Mela to be organised, so that millions of Hindu pilgrims could crowd together in a small town to bathe in the Ganges and spread the virus even-handedly as they returned to their homes across the country, blessed and purified. This Kumbh rocks on, although Modi has gently suggested that it might be an idea for the holy dip to become 'symbolic' – whatever that means. There were also those few thousand Rohingya refugees who had to be urgently deported back to the genocidal regime in Myanmar from where they had fled – in the middle of a coup.

So, as you can tell, it's been busy, busy, busy.

'Let's try and not be a cry baby.'

Anyway, what about the vaccines? Surely they'll save us? Isn't India a vaccine powerhouse? In fact, the Indian government is entirely dependent on two manufacturers, the Serum Institute of India (SII) and Bharat Biotech. Both are being allowed to roll out two of the most expensive vaccines in the world, to the poorest people in the world. This week they announced that they will sell to private hospitals at a slightly elevated price, and to state governments at a somewhat lower price. Back-of-the-envelope calculations show the vaccine companies are likely to make obscene profits.

Under Modi, India's economy has been hollowed out, and hundreds of millions of people who were already living precarious lives have been pushed into abject poverty. A huge number now depend for survival on paltry earnings from the National Rural Employment Guarantee Act (NREGA), which was instituted in 2005 when the Congress party was in power. It is impossible to expect that families on the verge of starvation will pay most of a month's income to have themselves vaccinated. In the UK, vaccines are free and a fundamental right. Those trying to get vaccinated out of turn can be prosecuted. In India, the main underlying impetus of the vaccination campaign seems to be corporate profit.

As this epic catastrophe plays out on our Modi-aligned Indian television channels, you'll notice how they all speak in one tutored voice. The 'system' has collapsed, they say, again and again. The virus has overwhelmed India's healthcare 'system'.

The system has not collapsed. The 'system' barely existed. The government – this one, as well as the Congress government that preceded it – deliberately dismantled what little medical infrastructure there was. This is what happens when a pandemic hits a country with an almost nonexistent public healthcare system. India spends about 1.25 per cent of its gross domestic product on health, far lower than most countries in the world, even the poorest ones. Even that figure is thought to be inflated, because things that are important but do not strictly qualify as healthcare have been slipped into it. So the real figure is estimated to be more like 0.34 per cent. The tragedy is that in this devastatingly poor country, as a 2016 *Lancet* study shows, 78 per cent of the healthcare in urban areas and 71 per cent in rural areas is now handled by the private sector. The resources that remain in the public sector are systematically siphoned into the private sector by a nexus of corrupt administrators and medical practitioners, corrupt referrals and insurance rackets.

Healthcare is a fundamental right. The private sector will not cater to starving, sick, dying people who don't have money. This massive privatisation of India's healthcare is a crime.

The system hasn't collapsed. The government has failed. Perhaps 'failed' is an inaccurate word, because what we are witnessing is not criminal negligence, but an outright crime against humanity. Virologists predict that the number of cases in India will grow exponentially to more than 500,000 a day. They predict the death of many hundreds of thousands in the coming months, perhaps more. My friends and I have agreed to call each other every day just to mark ourselves present, like roll call in our school classrooms. We speak to those we love in tears, and with trepidation, not knowing if we will ever see each other again. We write, we work, not knowing if we will live to finish what we started. Not knowing what horror and humiliation awaits us. The indignity of it all. That is what breaks us.

The hashtag #ModiMustResign is trending on social media. Some of the memes and illustrations show Modi with a heap of skulls peeping out from behind the curtain of his beard. Modi the Messiah speaking at a public rally of corpses. Modi and home minister Amit Shah as vultures, scanning the horizon for corpses to harvest votes from. But that is only one part of the story. The other part is that the man with no feelings, the man with empty eyes and a mirthless smile, can, like so many tyrants in the past, arouse passionate feelings in others. His pathology is infectious. And that is what sets him apart.

The crisis-generating machine that we call our government is incapable of leading us out of this disaster. Not least because one man makes all the decisions in this government, and that man is dangerous – and not very bright. This virus is an international problem. To deal with it, decision-making, at least on the control and administration of the pandemic, will need to pass into the hands of some sort of non-partisan body consisting of members of the ruling party, members of the opposition, and health and public policy experts.

As for Modi, is resigning from your crimes a feasible proposition? Perhaps he could just take a break from them – a break from all his hard work. There's that $564 million Boeing 777, Air India One, customised for VVIP travel – for him, actually – that's been sitting idle on the runway for a while now. He and his men could just leave. The rest of us will do all we can to clean up their mess.

No, India cannot be isolated. We need help.

'I seek a kind person': the *Guardian* ad that saved my Jewish father from the Nazis

JULIAN BORGER

On Wednesday 3 August 1938, a short advertisement appeared on the second page of the *Manchester Guardian*, under the title 'Tuition'.

'I seek a kind person who will educate my intelligent Boy, aged 11, Viennese of good family,' the advert said, under the name Borger, giving the address of an apartment on Hintzerstrasse, in Vienna's third district. The small ad, costing a shilling a line, was placed by my grandparents, Leo and Erna. The 11-year-old boy was my father, Robert. It turned out to be the key to their survival and the reason I am here, nearly 83 years later, working at the newspaper that ran the ad.

In 1938, Jewish families under Nazi rule were scrambling to get their children out of the Reich. Newspaper advertisements were one avenue of escape. Scores of children were 'advertised' in the pages of the *Manchester Guardian*, their virtues and skills extolled in brief, to fit the space.

The columns read as a clamour of urgent, competing voices, all pleading: 'Take my child!' And people did. The classified ads – dense, often mundane notices that filled the front pages, and coffers, of the *Guardian* for more than 100 years – also helped save lives.

Richard Nelsson, the *Guardian*'s information manager and archivist, emailed me a picture of the ad in January. Its existence had been the subject of family myth, but I had never seen it before.

Its emotive impact took me by surprise – three lines of anguish, from parents willing to give up their only child in the hope he would be safe. The Nazi annexation of Austria, the *Anschluss*, had taken place five months before my father's ad was placed, while the Nuremberg race laws had been imposed in May, stripping Jews of basic rights. Groups of Nazi *Sturmabteilung*, the brownshirted SA, had free rein in Vienna to beat and humiliate Jews.

My father was identified as a Jew by his classmates and at one point was grabbed by an SA gang, who locked him inside the local synagogue. My grandfather Leo, who owned a radio and musical instrument shop, was summoned to Gestapo headquarters to register. He was ordered, like other Viennese Jews, to get down on his hands and knees and wash the pavement, in front of jeering crowds.

'The SA still captures Jews in the streets and makes them scrub floors and lavatories,' the *Manchester Guardian* reported on 1 April 1938. 'Many prominent Jews commandeered for such work have appeared in top-hats and morning coats with all their decorations on.'

The next time my grandfather was called, he was held overnight. He may have been held for longer periods after *Kristallnacht* on 9 November 1938, when Jewish businesses were ransacked and most of Vienna's synagogues were destroyed. Many – perhaps most – Viennese Jewish men were taken to Dachau, the camp in Bavaria, and had to be ransomed out.

The Nazis were keen to drive Jews out of the Reich, but did not make it easy. Emigrants had to fill in the right forms and were fleeced of almost everything they owned.

By late summer in 1938, many Viennese Jews were advertising in the *Manchester Guardian*'s 'Situations Wanted' column as butlers, chauffeurs and maids. There was a shortage of domestic workers in the UK, with the expansion of prosperous suburbs and the opening up of other work opportunities for British women creating vacancies for outsiders.

Scrolling through the classified ad pages of the newspaper, you can see the wave of panic gather pace. Prior to May 1938, the only references to Vienna concerned tourism and opera. On 10 May, Erna Ball offers herself as a housekeeper, then, a fortnight later, Julie Klein describes herself as a 'distinguished Viennese lady, Jewish, good appearance, blond, 35'.

On 7 June, the first of the children appeared: Gertrude Mandl, a 'young Viennese Girl ... not Aryan' who 'seeks position as Cook Housekeeper'.

She was the first of 60 Viennese Jewish children advertised in the newspaper over the following nine months, rising to a peak in August, September and October and then falling off after November 1938, when the UK launched the *Kindertransport* scheme for groups of unaccompanied minors. This brought 10,000 Jewish children to Britain in the months leading up to the outbreak of war.

The *Guardian* ads in early 1939 reflect the plight of those left behind. On 14 January, under the new section 'Refugee Advertisements', there is a three-line plea: 'Father in concentration camp, three boys, 8–12 and three girls, 13–16, have to leave Germany. Is anybody willing to help?'

On 11 March, another ad issued an 'urgent appeal. Who will help to get out of concentration camp two Viennese boys, age 21 and 23, by offering trainee posts.'

Similar appeals were placed in *The Times* and the *Telegraph*, but the *Manchester Guardian* was seen as more sympathetic by those seeking to flee. The city was home to the biggest UK Jewish community outside London; it had ties to Vienna through the textile trade, as well as an energetic Quaker community that set up a refugee committee after *Kristallnacht*, which helped resettle large numbers of central European Jews.

The *Guardian* also focused more than the rest of the British press on the plight of Jews under Nazi rule and the hardships of those in the UK. It ran an anonymous column by a Jewish maid in a British home, identified only as 'J', giving the view from below stairs.

'The *Manchester Guardian* had a justified reputation for being supportive of the Jewish plight and especially being pro-refugee, so it would be a natural place to advertise in, especially if there were commercial agencies and also refugee organisations at either end,' says Tony Kushner, a University of Southampton professor and the author of *Journeys from the Abyss*, a book about the Holocaust and forced migration.

'Certainly, the way the *Manchester Guardian* reported Nazi antisemitism and supported the entry of refugees – and then their protection in Britain – during the Nazi era can be regarded as one of the proudest moments in the newspaper's history,' adds Kushner.

A couple of Welsh teachers, Nancy and Reg Bingley, responded to the ad for my father and fostered and educated him through his teen years in Caernarfon. My grandmother Erna (Omi to us) got a job as a maid for a family in Paddington, so was able to get a visa and make the train and ferry journey to the UK with her son, but not to live with him once they arrived.

In March 1939, a visa was secured for my grandfather Leo, as well as a job as a cutter at Silhouette, an underwear factory run by a German Jewish family that employed refugees, first in London, then in Shrewsbury, after the war started.

Leo stayed in the same job the rest of his working life; there were always bales of offcut knicker elastic in our cellar. My father would speak German with his parents, but if they reminisced much about the old days in Vienna, they rarely told us.

Having read the ads, I was determined to find out what had become of the other children who had appealed for help alongside my father. He had been relatively lucky, it turned out. Many of the children did not settle happily and spent their first years in Britain, at the age of 12, 13 or 14, searching, with little help in a foreign language in a strange land, for ways to save their parents.

Liese Feiks, an 18-year-old girl advertised on 28 June 1938 as a multilingual 'shorthand writer and typist', was saved by a British family, but struggled with the domestic work she was given. Her son, Martin Tompa, a computer science professor emeritus at the University of Washington in Seattle, says: 'She told me many times they were the most miserable years of her life.'

Liese's parents waited too long to leave Vienna. By spring 1940, escape westwards was no longer an option. Instead, they headed for Shanghai, which would take Jews without visas, on the Trans-Siberian railway. From Shanghai, they tried to get to the US, but were captured by the Japanese and spent the rest of the war in an internment camp near Manila in the Philippines.

In his advertisement on 29 July 1938, Adolf Batscha, a Viennese dry goods merchant, appealed for a family to take in his only daughter, 14-year-old Gertrude, who was 'well mannered, able to help in any household work, speaks German, French, and a little English' and played the piano.

A Somerset family called the Partingtons responded and agreed to take her in. In February 1939, Adolf and his wife, Walburga – 'Vally' – saw Gertrude off at Vienna's main railway terminus. 'I hope never to know such desperation as prompted them to decide to part with me and send me away alone,' Gertrude would later write in a memoir for her children, decades after she had emigrated to Israel and become Yehudit Segal.

She would never see them again. Gertrude's daughter, Ruthie Elkana, told me her grandparents did not act in time. 'It was just too late for them,' Elkana says. 'They prepared themselves. He prepared himself to be a butler and she prepared to be a housekeeper, to sew and all that, so they could earn money in the UK. But it didn't help them.'

In October 1942, Adolf and Walburga were deported to the Maly Trostenets death camp, outside Minsk in the Nazi-occupied Soviet republic of Belarus. Gertrude didn't give up hope for them until she received a letter from the Red Cross after the war, confirming their deaths. In her memoir, she said the dread of losing them was compounded by 'the fear of forgetting what they all looked like'.

Elkana says she was overcome by emotion when she saw the small ad for the first time, in 2014. 'Our mother told us about this advert,' she says. 'It was really so exciting to find it. It's heartbreaking.'

Ernst Schanzer was 16 in November 1938, when his parents described him as 'well-bred', an 'excellent stenotypist' and a 'good sportsman'. He was given a place at a commercial college in Newcastle before being interned on the Isle of Man (like my grandfather and most other male Jewish refugees) as an 'enemy alien' in 1940, when public opinion turned against the strangers in their midst. He was then evacuated to Canada.

As Ernest Schanzer, he became a renowned Shakespearean scholar and a professor in Munich. Unable to obtain a visa to the west, his parents and his elder brother, Peter, got as far as Latvia, but were captured there by the invading Soviet troops and deported to Siberia in 1941. Ernest's parents died there, but Peter somehow survived six years of near starvation and bitter cold. He made his way back to Vienna after the war, but it would be many years before the brothers were reunited. Canada denied Peter entry, seemingly because of forgiving comments he made about some of his Soviet jailers. He emigrated to Australia instead and raised a family there.

Ernest never married, but he enjoyed life as a single man in Munich. 'He had a rich social life, staging himself as a playboy, as it were, being invited by many and inviting his friends to celebrations of his clematis in flower on his balcony overlooking the fairly posh Englschalking suburb of Munich,' says his closest friend, the English professor Manfred Pfister. Pfister says he and his wife visited Vienna often, but Ernest, 'without spelling out his reasons, understandably never joined us on these trips'.

Speaking to other descendants of refugees, fellow children of the *Manchester Guardian* small ads, some common themes emerged. Most of us had been taken, at some point in our lives, on melancholic visits to Vienna. We went in the mid-70s, when I remember staring up at the apartment block where the family had lived; the nearby park, with its huge concrete gun emplacements, too big and solid to destroy; and the site of the old shop, Radio Borger, which became a stationer's shop and now sells discount women's clothing.

Another common strand was the lifelong burden our parents had carried, from the experience of separation from their parents in a foreign land to the weight of surviving while countless relatives, left behind in Vienna, perished.

When my father took his life, it was my task to call his foster mother, Nancy. After a sharp intake and a pause, Nancy said he had been the Nazis' last victim. There were certainly other factors: his career did not work out as he had hoped, and he had made a mess of his family life. But she always saw the 11-year-old boy who had arrived in Caernarfon, so scared they had to take the whistle off the kettle as it reminded him of the SA doing their roundups.

The longest-surviving child of the classified ads died in February. Karl Trommer, and his sister Hella, appeared in an ad on 11 November 1938, their parents calling for 'any kind-hearted family' to take them in. They survived and moved to Palestine after the war. Karl, as Akiva Trommer, fought in the Palmach, the Jewish special forces before the creation of Israel.

Hella died in 1980, but online records showed Akiva was still alive, with a home telephone number. When I called in late March, his son answered. I was a few weeks too late. I offered my condolences and sent a copy of the *Manchester Guardian* ad.

For most of the descendants to whom I spoke, the ad was a poignant footnote in family history, a reminder of the delicate chain of events that made the difference between survival and obliteration. It held particular sway for me, as the reverence for the *Guardian* in our childhood home no doubt shaped my ambition to work here. At the time my dad's ad appeared, my mother, his future wife, was growing up in the Rusholme district of Manchester. Her father would bring the *Manchester Guardian* home from his job as a railway shipping clerk and tell her the newspaper offered a reward for readers who could find any spelling mistakes.

In August 1938, she would have been a bit young for spell-checking, but I like to think of her running her finger over those lines on the second page: 'I seek a kind person who will educate my intelligent Boy.'

7 MAY

The day of 'female rage' has dawned – and Kate Winslet is its fed-up face

EMMA BROCKES

There's a scene in *Mare of Easttown*, the new crime drama on HBO/Sky Atlantic starring Kate Winslet, that with minimal fuss captures a mood rarely seen on TV. Winslet plays a detective in small-town Pennsylvania, where – when she's sitting on her sofa one night eating an enormous sandwich – a neighbour throws a gallon of milk through her window.

She stops eating, briefly, to survey the wreckage, before returning with exquisite deliberation to the sandwich. Through Winslet's character, Mare, *Easttown* nails that rarely excavated, beautifully enacted vibe of the fed-up middle-aged woman. It is hard to overstate how much excitement this and similar scenes have caused among women in the US since the show started airing, two weeks ago.

It's not merely that Mare reflects back at us the bombed-out, personal-grooming-gone-to-seed reality of life at the tail end of the pandemic. Nor is it a case of the overused trope of a movie star eschewing makeup as a shorthand for integrity. (I loved the movie *Nomadland*, recently bombarded with Oscars, but Frances McDormand has in recent years perhaps over-ploughed this furrow to the extent that it can have the opposite effect, making the act of appearing 'ordinary' seem a little stagey and performative.)

By contrast, the heroine of *Easttown*, while operating on her last nerve and declaring her life to be a mess, displays a range of behaviours that never quite adds up to defeat. She wears a lot of flannel, eats a lot of junk, and snaps constantly at her mother (played brilliantly by Jean Smart) and teenage daughter.

What remains curious is what precisely as viewers we're responding to in Mare. *Easttown* was created by Brad Ingelsby, who grew up in the working-class Pennsylvanian town where the show is set; and the show's attention to detail – a character in a vintage Dave Matthews Band sweatshirt, dinners of Tater Tots and microwave mac and cheese – give it an unfakeable air of reality. In the heroine, however, there is something that transcends the show's context. Mare has been compared, favourably, to Sarah

Lancashire's cop in *Happy Valley* and Olivia Colman's in *Broadchurch*, and there's some matter-of-fact quality in all three actors that one connects, intangibly, to their Britishness.

Her success with viewers is also a question of timing. The aftershocks of #MeToo won't wear off for many years, and still the stories keep coming. In the past month alone we heard of alleged abuses by Hollywood producer Scott Rudin, and the almost unbelievably novelistic horror of Blake Bailey, lauded biographer of Philip Roth, being the subject of multiple accusations of rape and sexual assault, resulting in the book being hastily withdrawn.

We've had it. We're done with it. Those years of Trump compulsively commenting on women's looks, the intensity of demands made of women handling families and jobs throughout the pandemic, and the fact that women over 40 – particularly those in flannel and Timberlands – are still expected to remain largely invisible, have created a condition for this show to hit home. The absolute I'm-over-it energy of the heroine channels some broader snap in a willingness to go along with all this and a yearning for some reflection of how many are feeling.

It's not even anger; much has been made of 'female rage' in the past few years, but to my mind it's more muted and long-suffering than that. It's irritability, crossness, the oh-for-God's-sake complete lack of surprise when the latest outrage comes along, with the occasional florid meltdown. In one scene, a middle-class character sensitively counsels Mare to open her heart to the daughter-in-law with whom she's about to get locked in a custody battle. Instead, she storms over to her house, mocks her addiction, threatens to see her in court, then frames her for a crime she didn't commit. I mean, it's not ideal. But one appreciates a certain emotional truth.

There is, perhaps, one amusingly and I guess unavoidably false note in all this. Early on in the show, Mare meets a suave, middle-class character played by Guy Pearce, and reluctantly agrees to go out on a date with him. She throws on some makeup, finds a dress and a hairbrush, and – stepping out of her house – hey-ho, it's Kate Winslet. Even that, I sense, we'll give her. It goes badly; the guy's a douche. She shrugs and goes home.

8 MAY

Window on the world:
a pandemic poem

SIMON ARMITAGE

'THE SKY STRETCHED THIN'

The sky stretched thin
     over the frame
          of day.
Downdraft and throttle –
     the air ambulance carving
          its high yellow arc,
the millpond ronkled, jittery,
     wood pigeons rousted
          out of the wood,
an embarrassed fox
     in its winter coat,
          flushed from the copse.
Night hunched
     in the east, ready
          to fill in the gaps.

I'm watching all this
through
bullet-proof glass.

I was just about the busiest I'd ever been when lockdown arrived, so it was a huge change, and some of that's been quite good for me. I've slowed down, I've caught up with a lot of deadlines. But from a creative point of view, everything has just become a little bit overfamiliar. I've written three poems about my Velux window. And there's probably more to come.

'The Sky Stretched Thin' is typical of the kind of poem that I've been writing. It starts with a look out of the window in the morning and a bit of a sigh. 'Here we go again.' On that day, there was an air ambulance, which ruffled the feathers of the environment around it and ruffled my feathers a bit, too. I saw it as a token of the emergency that's going on, but also the fact that it's slightly anonymised for a lot of people. There's both a sense of something urgent happening and being somewhat detached from it.

What I've really missed are the chance encounters and accidental collisions and ear-wigging. The unexpected. I miss my friends, going out for a meal, a drink, getting on trains, seeing the world go past through the window. I miss giving readings and travelling: picking up different feelings and ideas and getting that chance to express yourself outwardly. Not being able to do that has become a kind of artistic claustrophobia.

Marcus Rashford: 'Whenever I hear "no", I ask myself: why not?'

SIMON HATTENSTONE

Imagine being Marcus Rashford. You're just going about your business, playing football for Manchester United and England, being an everyday sporting superstar. Then you put out a Twitter thread suggesting that the country's poorest children need to be supported better in the pandemic, and it's the government's responsibility to help them. And the tweets go viral. And the public agrees with you. And suddenly you're no longer just a footballing hero, you're a leader, a sage, Mahatma Rashford, Marcus Mandela, a footballing messiah. Just imagine being Marcus Rashford, a supremely successful footballer, a shy young man who has never really shared an opinion publicly before, and you're now dictating government policy. How profoundly must it change you?

Ordinarily footballers are interviewed about football. And yet today we're meeting to talk about child literacy, Rashford's latest passion. He tells me he didn't start reading properly till he was 17 (which, let's remember, is only six years ago). Once he started, he couldn't stop. He mentions his favourite book, *Relentless* by Tim Grover, the personal trainer who took some of the world's greatest athletes, including Kobe Bryant and Michael Jordan, and made them even better. *Relentless* is a self-help book about how to maximise your potential. Its subtitle is 'From Good to Great to Unstoppable'. And unstoppable is what Rashford aims to be – in all walks of life.

Rashford has not read *Relentless* once or twice, but again and again. 'Every time I read it, I analyse it and highlight things in a certain colour. Then the next time I read it, I'll highlight things in a different colour, and I'll compare what I learned that time with the previous time,' he says. Grover has helped him deal with what he calls the 'hero one week, zero the next' nature of his job: 'Balancing my mood and emotion. Never getting too high, so that the low feels even lower. Just keeping that consistency and that stability.' It's not the fact that he has read this book, but the *way* he has that tells you something about Rashford; about his ambition, his dedication, and his relentless pursuit of the possible.

In January, Rashford was named the most valuable footballer in Europe, with a transfer value of £150 million, according to the research group CIES Football Observatory. Even Manchester United fans might disagree with the ranking, but not with the sense that he is on a relentless upward trajectory. Since making his debut with the club in 2016, he has played more than 260 games for them, 40 games for England and has scored 98 goals in the process. And that, of course, is not the half of it.

It's 14 months since the Twitter thread that resulted in Rashford becoming even more notable for his work off the pitch than on it. He has gone from the back pages of newspapers to the front pages, twice forcing the government to reverse policy on free school meals for the country's most disadvantaged children. He applied himself to campaigning against food poverty with the same discipline he does to football. In October 2020, he was awarded an MBE in recognition of his services to vulnerable children in the UK during the pandemic.

Now he is turning his attention to the estimated 383,000 children in the UK who have never owned a book. Rashford knows exactly how they feel: he was one of them. How times change; not only is he a reader these days, he is also a published author.

You Are a Champion, written with football journalist Carl Anka, is a self-help book for children. Like *Relentless*, it is about overcoming demons and unlocking potential. The message is simple: if someone from my background can become one of the best footballers in the world, you can also follow, and hopefully fulfil, your dream.

The book combines sound commonsense advice (work hard, listen, keep out of trouble, be kind, stretch yourself, believe) with stories from Rashford's life by way of illustration. 'That bit of self-belief can lead to us becoming much, much stronger people,' he says. 'Sometimes you only need a little nudge to become something you could have never imagined. Hopefully this book will provide that push for a lot of young people.'

Rashford is Zooming from his home in Manchester. When we talk, he is just back from training, and lying on the sofa. He looks done in. 'You OK? Sorry for being late,' he says in a sleepy Mancunian monotone. There's something sweet and old-fashioned about him – not least his politeness. As soon as he starts talking about books, he springs to life. 'Reading triggered something in me. I read a lot of books about mentality, because I wanted to play in Manchester United's first team and I knew that to get there and to stay there I'd have to be mentally as tough as I can be. I learned about myself from books.'

There is a lovely dedication at the beginning of *You Are a Champion*: 'To every young person who is trying to find their way. To my mum, for helping me believe that dreams can come true.' Rashford's mother, Mel, is at the heart of the book and his life. He is the youngest of five siblings, and, by the time he came on the scene, Melanie Rashford was a single mother. She worked every hour she could, holding down three jobs: as a cashier at Ladbrokes, returning there after her shift ended to start another as a cleaner, and washing pots at the weekends. And still it wasn't enough. Mel was loving, self-sacrificing and often absent because she was working day and night.

Did she tell Rashford she was struggling? 'No, you would have never known the situation we were in from her. At home every-thing was happy, but sometimes she wouldn't eat. She'd cook dinner and there would only be enough for me and my brothers and sisters. She wouldn't eat that night, but you wouldn't be able to tell.' Because she was always out working, she could say she had eaten earlier. His mother was heroic throughout, he says. 'My values come from my household, the rules and the respect we had for each other. For my whole upbringing, she was the leader in that. Seeing someone living through difficult situations every single day, but waking up the next morning and giving it her best go again – nothing can really top that.'

While so many adults told him to dream small, or not dream at all, Rashford's mother told him anything was possible. 'When you're a kid, a lot of the time you're being told you can't do something, and I always used to ask myself: why not?' What kind of things did people say it would be impossible to do? 'Play for United,' he says. But it must have been obvious to everybody how talented you were? That was irrelevant, he says: 'In my area, there were so many unbelievably talented street footballers but we were always told, "Yeah, you're good but you can't make it in the Premier League or you can't play for Manchester United, you can't play for your country, it's just not reachable."' Why not? 'The size of the club means that if they want a talented footballer, they can just buy one, so in my area it doesn't really happen for kids like me.'

Over the years, Rashford's two-word mantra simply got stronger. Whenever he heard 'no', he asked himself: why not? 'I'd never turn it into an argument or anything, but I'd think, why not? In the back of my mind, it would be bugging me for days.'

Rashford joined the United academy at seven. At 11, he went to live in digs provided by the club, when Mel reluctantly concluded that the club could meet his needs better than she could. He says it was only after he left home, and won sponsorship from Nike, that he began to understand how much the family struggled. 'I didn't need the money, so I just used to give it to Mum.'

Few players have had Rashford's instant impact. In February 2016, at the age of 18, he scored two goals on his debut against Danish club Midtjylland in the Uefa Europa League, becoming the youngest Manchester United player to score in European competition. Three days later, he made his Premier League debut against Arsenal, scoring two and making the other goal in a 3–2 victory. On it went. In May 2016, he made his first appearance for the senior England team against Australia, becoming the youngest player to score for England on his debut, after just three minutes.

When Rashford started to campaign against child poverty, he returned to his old mantra: 'Why not?' This clarity of vision stands out against the waffle of politicians. 'There is a kindness and good-naturedness to him that can make complex situations seem simple,' says his co-author Anka. 'He looks at things like a 10-year-old would – and I mean that in the nicest way. He simplifies stuff. He will look at the obstacles and see if he can tick them off so he can do the thing he wishes to do.'

It has made him an extraordinarily effective campaigner. On 19 March 2020, a day after it was announced that schools would be closing across the UK because of the pandemic, Rashford tweeted that many children relied on free school meals, and that he was working with the charity FareShare to help fill the gap. 'To anyone reading who can spare a few pounds, you could make a big difference ... And to the food industry, we know it's a challenging time, but we ask you to please send any product you can ...'

The tone of the tweet was mature and considered. Rashford had obviously done his research, taken advice, and collaborated with the leading charity on the issue of food poverty.

In April, he announced that his partnership with FareShare had raised £20 million. Two months later, he wrote to MPs asking them to reconsider their decision to cancel the food voucher scheme over the summer holidays. A day later, the government announced the implementation of the Covid summer food fund, ensuring around 1.3 million children in England would receive meal vouchers over the holidays. Rashford was elated, and tweeted: 'I don't even know what to say. Just look at what we can do when we come together, THIS is England in 2020.'

In early October, it was announced that Rashford was to be awarded the MBE. Critics said he had been bought off by the government. Five days later he launched a petition to end child food poverty and extend out-of-term free school meals to all children from a household on universal credit or the equivalent until Easter 2021. Within two weeks, more than a million people had signed it. The government refused to budge. When Rashford pointed out it was now half-term and that many children would be going hungry, the response was astonishing. From the smallest cafes to the biggest supermarkets there were offers of food to people in need. As Rashford retweeted the pledges, he gave a voice to the generosity of people all over the country, in stark contrast to the government.

By now Rashford was both the most celebrated and trolled footballer on social media. Almost a third of comments about him were negative. Rashford said he expected personal attacks, that the rewards outweighed the risks, and continued the fight.

Eventually, and inevitably, there was another government U-turn. Rashford had just returned home from a match when he received the news. In the documentary *Feeding Britain's Children*, he is filmed taking the call from Boris Johnson. He talks to the prime minister as he would to anybody: 'Yeah man, yeah, yeah, yeah, go on can you just say that again please ... yeah, that will be the perfect situation for me ... Thank you on behalf of the families. They'll really appreciate it. Speak to you soon.' Far from being in awe of Johnson, Rashford sees him as somebody who can help him do what needs to be done.

I ask Rashford if he regards himself as political. 'No, not at all. I'm just a young person who was in a difficult situation and managed to find a way out, and now I'm in a position where I can help others.' Rashford is comfortable using social media to speak up about what he believes in. After the murder of George Floyd, he said: 'At a time I've been asking people to come together, work together and be united, we appear to me more divided than ever. People are hurting and people need answers. Black lives matter. Black culture matters. Black communities matter. We matter.'

Last year, Rashford's mother came across a note he had written at school about his ambitions, which he later tweeted. I read it out to him. 'I hope my future is very bright in and out of school, especially in my career as a footballer. I want to have a different lifestyle and make my family and others proud of me.' What was the different lifestyle he wanted? 'I didn't often watch TV, but when I did, those people looked comfortable – they didn't have any stress. They looked happy, and that's what I deemed a different lifestyle. I wrote that when I was 10 or 11.'

He smiles. He has got a lovely smile – gentle, generous, bashful. 'To be honest with you, I didn't understand that football can change your life in that sense. Thankfully, it has managed to do that for me, and I've managed to give the younger people in my family – my nieces and nephews – different opportunities from the ones that I and my older brothers and sisters had. Hopefully it changes things for generations for my family. It's important to do the right thing; to bring others with you along the way.'

Even now, Rashford's detractors say he should focus on his football and improve his goal-scoring record. But there is also plenty of support from within the game. United team-mate Juan Mata recently said: 'Some people say Marcus should stick to playing football but I disagree, because he can do both, as he is showing.' Last June, United manager Ole Gunnar Solskjær said: 'He has changed the lives of so many kids ... which is more important than any game of football he will probably play.'

26 MAY

Dominic Cummings stars in his own jaw-dropping, grubby, delusional miniseries

JOHN CRACE

Not so much a parliamentary hearing, more an eight-hour Netflix miniseries. The one where a lone delusional narcissist drives into town to take revenge on a bunch of other delusional narcissists. With a bit of *Independence Day* and *Spider-Man* thrown in.

Dominic Cummings' appearance before the joint science and technology and health select committee always promised to be good box office and it didn't disappoint. By the end of the session the body count included Boris Johnson, Matt Hancock, half the senior civil servants in Downing Street, Cobra, Carrie Symonds and Dilyn the dog. Not forgetting Cummings himself. It's not in Dom's makeup to resist a self-inflicted wound.

The proceedings kicked off with Cummings blindsiding everyone with an apology. One he was to repeat several times during the course of the day. Senior advisers, such as himself, had failed disastrously and he wanted to say sorry for all his mistakes. He even sounded vaguely plausible.

His was a tale of hubris. The Dominic Cummings who was shocked to find there was a man called Dominic Cummings who had been the chief adviser to the prime minister. The man who could write endless esoteric blogs about why he was right about everything yet was unable to fulfil his basic job description. The chief adviser who was unable to advise.

Which isn't to say the apologies weren't self-serving. Cummings knows that if you want to go on the attack, make sure you've covered your back. First in the crosshairs was the health secretary. Hancock was basically a serial liar who should have been fired in April last year. Saying patients would be tested before being released into care homes was only the greatest in an extensive catalogue of crimes, Cummings claimed. Dom had begged the prime minister to sack him on a daily basis, only for Johnson to refuse because he wanted a sacrificial lamb for the inevitable public inquiry.

Accusing a minister of lying was a serious matter, said joint committee chair, Greg Clark, right at the end. Was there any chance Cummings could provide some evidence? Dom said he would see what he could drag up. Though he wasn't sure it would be ethical to hand over all his private WhatsApp messages with the cabinet secretary – thereby disclosing at least one of his sources. The former cabinet secretary Mark Sedwill's heart must have sunk when he heard this. The grenade-tossing tosser had just tossed his last imaginary grenade.

But it was the revelations about Johnson that were the most startling. Not so much the stuff about herd immunity, 'kung flu', wanting to be injected with coronavirus live on TV, rejecting a

September circuit breaker and letting the bodies pile high rather than have a third lockdown – all these had been heavily trailed. It was the level of sheer incompetence that was gobsmacking. The deputy cabinet secretary who had barged in to conclude: 'We're absolutely fucked'; a cabinet that had ceased to function and a leader unfit for office whose actions had cost the lives of tens of thousands.

Johnson was basically an out-of-control shopping trolley careering from side to side down the aisles. 'The country deserved better than a choice between Boris Johnson and Jeremy Corbyn at the last election,' said Cummings, apparently forgetting he had done more than almost anyone to get Johnson into No 10.

It was by turns jaw-dropping and grubby. But, on balance, it felt as if some light had crept through the cracks. The families of the bereaved deserved better than truths carved out of a desire to settle personal scores. But for now it would have to do.

12 JUNE

My cross to bear: what it means to support England in these divided times

JONATHAN LIEW

It's the morning after my wedding. I'm sitting down to brunch with some friends of the family. While we're waiting for the food to arrive, I pull out my phone and browse the latest sport headlines. 'Oh look,' I announce to nobody in particular. 'We won the Under-20 World Cup last night.' At this, my sister-in-law's boyfriend narrows his eyes accusingly. 'Who's *we*?' 'England,' I respond. He looks at me like I've just sprinkled salt on my cornflakes. 'Huh,' he says. '"We". That's interesting.'

I support England. England is by many objective measures a terrible country ruled by terrible people with a terrible past and a terrifying future, and I support England. None of my forebears were born in England, and I support England. When I watch the news or follow England games abroad or read about politics I often feel utterly disconnected from this country, and I support England.

It was an Englishman who snarled at me on the street last month while I was taking my daughter to nursery: 'Fuck off, Chinaman, and take your Covid patient with you.' Nevertheless, I support England.

I'd like to tell you that I support England as an act of progressive defiance, as a means of reclaiming the cursed red-and-white flag from the reactionaries and the hooligans and the white supremacists. But this would be twisting facts to suit a narrative. The truth is I support England because I've known nothing else. I support England because I loved Gazza and Teddy Sheringham, because Ronald Koeman should have been sent off for fouling David Platt in 1993, because of Jonathan Pearce's commentary on the France 98 version of 'Three Lions'. I support England because it's what you did, because supporting England has given me some of the greatest happiness I've ever known.

For a long time it was possible to do all this while largely ignoring, you know, the other stuff. Everyone knew it was there. But when England fans rioted, or when they smashed up some charming foreign cafe, or when we were shown grainy news footage of shirtless men getting blasted with giant water cannon, it was possible to point to them and say: *those* people do not represent us. *Those* people are a tiny fraction of the whole, the lunatic fringe. Everyone seemed to know the difference between patri-otism and nationalism, and only one of them involved throwing chairs and singing about the IRA.

Meanwhile, in line with the nation as a whole, the traditional England fanbase was slowly changing. It was becoming more gender diverse and ethnically diverse than many club fanbases. During the 2000s it even began to provide an appealing point of contrast with the aloof, entitled squad of players representing them. As recently as 2014 it was possible for the historian David Goldblatt to describe the England fanbase as a 'boisterous, globe-trotting love-fest', a 'more attractive reimagining of the stateless nation than its commercial football or the national team'.

Brexit did not create English nationalism, nor did it invent the divisions in English society that were so effortlessly exposed by the referendum and its fallout. But it certainly demolished the myth of the lunatic fringe. When England fans at Euro 2016 started singing: 'Fuck off Europe, we all voted out', it was harder to write them off as a tiny unrepresentative sample when 53 per cent of the country (slightly higher than the UK as a whole) had essentially just agreed with them.

And so, on the eve of another international tournament, the first to be held in England for a quarter of a century, the question of what it means to support England has never been more fiercely contested. When England players knelt to protest against racial injustice before the friendlies against Austria and Romania, they were booed by their own supporters. Thousands more probably disapproved of the gesture but stayed silent.

When the prime minister – a man of such flawless footballing intuition that he once claimed to support 'all the London teams' – was invited to condemn them, he refused. Instead, he essen-tially derided taking the knee, claiming he was 'more focused on action rather than gestures'. After mounting pressure, Boris

Johnson did finally come out in support of England players taking the knee, at the G7 summit yesterday, with a spokesman saying he 'respects' all peaceful protest in regard to social injustices.

It was easy enough to ignore the far-right's influence on English football when it was a few beery troublemakers in ill-fitting shorts. It was easy to ignore their puerile xenophobic politics when it felt so utterly divorced from the lived reality of England at large. But what happens now *those* people are in the ascendant? What happens now *those* people constitute main-stream opinion in this country? What happens now *those* people are in government? Whose team is this, really? And when we refer to the England football team as 'we', who do we think we're talking about?

One of the myths that has been exploded by British politics over the past decade is the notion that any one person, any one idea, any one cause, can speak for us all. In a much-lauded Players' Tribune article earlier this week, Gareth Southgate proudly discussed his England team's commitment to advocating on matters of equality, inclusivity and racial justice: values that he claimed embodied the nation as a whole. But at the heart of Southgate's unifying message – one nation, under Gareth – is an essentially flawed logic. You can try to represent 'more than 50 million people', as Southgate put it. Or you can recast the England team as a vessel of social justice. But you can't do both.

Personally, I find it immensely cheering that Southgate and his team have doubled down on their anti-racism stance despite the best efforts of politicians and the rightwing media to turn it into a distraction. I am encouraged that they refuse to remotely engage with the disingenuous argument that the multimillion-aire Harry Kane is some sort of Marxist sleeper cell. These values and priorities align closely with my own. But you can't possibly be ignorant of the fact that in doing so they are essentially spurning a significant chunk of the country they purport to represent. (Half? A third? More? Who knows? Who cares?)

Of course, just as Brexit had nothing to do with free trade, the resistance to taking the knee is wrapped up in a complex matrix of often entirely understandable (which is not to say rational or acceptable) fears about the increasing pace of social change in this country. The supermarket is selling something called 'meatless burgers'. You can't say 'trannies' any more. There are women on *Match of the Day*. You hear vague noises about 'defunding the police'. You suspect, on some sinister level, that something you love is being taken away from you, little by little by little. And so, amid this landscape of shifting plates and cultural norms, you have a choice: you can get with the programme and make the necessary adjustments. Or, alternatively, you can stand your ground and fight.

Call these people what you like: 'knuckle-draggers', 'gammon', 'cave dwellers', 'Oliver Dowden'. But it doesn't stop them existing, and it doesn't make them any less a constituent of society than you. This is our England team, but it's also theirs. Perhaps this is why supporting England – and deciding how and why you support England – is a more loaded and political choice than at any point in history.

Insofar as English football is a reflection of English society, you cannot possibly endorse the England football team without tacitly endorsing the society that created it. But perhaps the obverse is also true. Perhaps in aspiring to a better England team, we're articulating something else, too: the hope that England itself can be better, the belief that just as football teams and individuals are capable of change, so too are nations.

If England go deep into this tournament, you will doubtless see and read plenty of sentiment along the lines of how Southgate's team have 'healed a divided country'. And the idea that a football team can unite a nation, particularly in the divine glow of victory, remains a powerful sporting trope. France's twin World Cup triumphs in 1998 and 2018 – the 'Black, Blanc, Beur' sides – were held up by much of the political and media class as triumphs of French diversity. Tangibly, they achieved little more than to make everyone feel very pleased with themselves for a bit.

Perhaps, ultimately, this is all football is good for in the end. It presses the buttons that politicians can't reach. It brings us together like few other spectacles: fleetingly perhaps, illusorily perhaps, but in ways that feel real and profound and cathartic at the time. Perhaps, on reflection, this is all life is good for in the end: the accumulation of pleasant feelings, of experiences that mean something to us.

It's not true that what unites us is stronger than what divides us. That's just the sort of horseshit politicians like to say. I am not one of you and you are not one of us. But for this month, for these 90 minutes, for these sunlit days in June and July, let's pretend we are. Let's build a house together and watch it fall. Let's pick apart Southgate's 3-4-3 and debate the merits of Jack Grealish. Let's elate and commiserate together. The past is the past and the future is the future. In the meantime, I'll see you at the game.

13 June

Enough autism 'awareness': The necessity now is action

JOHN HARRIS

A film comes out this month that is among the most profound, thought-provoking and moving feats of documentary-making that I have ever seen. It is about autism, and a state of being that far too many people either misunderstand or ignore.

The Reason I Jump draws on the revelatory book of the same name, written by the Japanese author Naoki Higashida when he was only 13 and first published in 2007. Diagnosed with 'autistic tendencies' when he was six, Higashida had always displayed the deep difficulties with spoken communication common to many autistic people. But when he learned to use a computer connected to an alphabet grid, he began to map out his world in rich, aphoristic prose that rarely wasted a word.

My eldest child, James, who is now 14, is autistic. And when I first read the translation of Higashida's book by the novelist David Mitchell and his wife, Keiko Yoshida, who also have an autistic son, it confirmed things that my partner and I had long known about James and his rich interior life, as well as highlighting aspects of his mind – and experiences – that we had barely started to think about.

So many plain truths were laid out, from the way in which many autistic people feel and express emotion as a profoundly physical set of events (hence the title), through an instinctive affinity with nature, to the clarity of recollections even from early infancy. Higashida said that while 'a normal person's memory is arranged continuously, like a line', his was 'more like a pool of dots', in which something he experienced years ago might feel just as vivid as an event that has just happened.

The film uses the magic of the camera to evoke and explore these experiences and states. It also focuses on a handful of young autistic people – and their parents and carers – spread across the world, highlighting aspects of their lives that contradict common perceptions of autism (not least a huge capacity for empathy and a need for company), and also what they are up against. Even if the language of 'psychosis' and 'retardation' has dwindled, western societies are still smattered with the attitudes it expressed. Elsewhere, for example in Sierra Leone, there are awful stories of autistic children judged to be demonic and unwanted, and simply abandoned in the bush. Here, clearly, is another frontier of the modern struggle for human rights. Indeed, towards the end of the film comes another of Higashida's elegant sentences, which is as close to a rallying cry as his writing style will allow: 'The hardest ordeal for me is the idea that I am causing grief for other people. Please: keep battling alongside me.'

Such words might suggest anger and desperation, but there is a rising understanding of autism's amazing complexity and a grasp of the condition that would have been unthinkable only a relatively short time ago. The basis of this is science and academic inquiry, and such advances as the British psychiatrist Lorna Wing's revelation that autism is a 'spectrum condition' manifested in a huge variety of ways, which was developed in the 1970s and 80s and is still rippling through society.

But two other factors also stick out. One is the prominence of autism in the world of literature and the arts: before *The Reason I Jump*, a trail was blazed by Mark Haddon's 2003 novel *The Curious Incident of the Dog in the Night-time*, and the American author Steve Silberman's *Neurotribes*, a history of autism and a plea for its acceptance, which, against plenty of expectations, became a bestseller. The other, which marks a huge shift, is the new(ish) world of autistic self-advocacy and the way that the internet has given voice to those who the pre-digital age often condemned to silence, now united by the brilliantly potent concept of neurodiversity.

One truth in particular blares from *The Reason I Jump*: the help autistic people get should be about matching what society and the state are able to do with what voices such as Higashida's tell us. For want of one-to-one support and the right technology, a non-verbal child might remain locked into their own world; if employers don't embrace both the benefits autistic people can bring and how to make their lives easier, oceans of potential will continue to be wasted. The same will happen if we do not redesign parts of the private and public realm in line with autistic people's needs. The world is now brimming with annual rituals all about 'autism awareness'. The necessity is action.

There are increasingly frequent signs of small but significant moves in the right direction. Last week the National Theatre made an announcement about the lead role in its touring production of *The Curious Incident of the Dog in the Night-time*. It said it wanted to give every 'male-identifying actor with a playing age of 14 to 18 who identifies as neurodivergent the opportunity to be seen for an audition', and would 'work closely with the actors who are eventually cast in the role to individualise support on tour – an example of this might be enabling them to tour with a support worker'.

This is what progress looks like. So far it has been measured in small steps: what autistic people await is a quantum leap.

19 JUNE

Young, hot and bothered: 'I was a 31-year-old newlywed – and then the menopause hit'

HARRIET GIBSONE

I'm not crazy about birthdays, but crying in a church is a touch more melodramatic than I anticipated for my 31st. It's January 2017, and my friends and I are watching standup comedy. As laughter ricochets around the gothic architecture, I look down to conceal what's about to happen: flared nostrils, downturned mouth, wincing eyes. Utter devastation.

Sneaky weeping has become my dirty little secret. It started at Christmas, when the sweetness of family and food was kiboshed by the same sudden thwack of melancholy. It was also happening during my work hours, as a music writer and editor: one minute I would be proofing a three-star review of P!nk, then boom, off to a toilet cubicle for a silent scream.

Two thousand and sixteen was a rough year for the world. But, selfishly, I'd got married to an outstanding man, and my fringe was looking good for the first time ever. A brief, golden chapter of my life had arrived: a segue between the scrappiness of my twenties and what I figured would be the seriousness of my forties. The last blast of fun before real life kicked in. I had a steady job, lived in a house in London, one with actual windows and a bath. I was zipping around the city seeing friends at shows or gigs most nights. Until the aforementioned episodes, I felt indestructible.

I visit the doctor and tell him about the sudden short-lived sadness now seeping into hours and days, as if someone has murdered my soul, or something to that effect. 'Would you consider antidepressants?' he asks.

'I'm not sure. This doesn't feel like depression,' I say.

'How are you sleeping at the moment?'

'Terribly,' I reply. I refuse the drugs, leave the appointment promising to meditate and exercise, and decide to take matters into my own hands.

There are other symptoms I've been accruing and, after the usual incurable cancer diagnoses, Google offers what will turn out to be a shockingly accurate suggestion. I really *am* on the cusp of a new chapter of my life – only I've skipped a couple and raced to the part that normally starts at 50. I am a 31-year-old newlywed going through the menopause.

It all started with the sweats, as so many awful things do. Around five times a day, and as many throughout the night. They began when I was 29, but got worse every year. A prickly heat in my face that courses around the rest of my body, taking 10 to 15 minutes to subside. They often arrive before I am about to do something moderately stressful (such as ask for holiday leave, or say a single thing in any meeting) so I presume they are a manifestation of standard workplace worries. It makes life arduous; I accrue a thick film of sweat above my top lip that sometimes drips into my mouth. 'You going through the menopause already, Harriet?' jokes one colleague.

Then there is the rage. At a school reunion in a flat-roofed football club in a field in Essex, I confront a series of people from my youth who I feel had wronged me in some way. A rogue energy ripples through my veins. Furious, and uncharacteristically confident, I ambush otherwise pleasant conversations with boys I used to know by asking, 'Do you realise how [minor incident] made me feel?' They don't, they'd forgotten, and hastily move on to another conversation with someone else about sports day or loft conversions. Another time, I go to a gig and enter my first moshpit for the purpose of trying to push people as hard as I can. Again, not the time or place. It is an Ash reunion concert at the Roundhouse, a grand listed building in Camden, not Megadeth at Bloodstock festival.

By September 2017, I am rocking a full house of menopausal symptoms: a strange feeling of anxiousness that manifests in breathlessness, numbness of my left arm and pain in my chest. Cracking headaches, so piercing that I spend a day waiting in A&E to get one particularly violent attack checked out. The vision in my left eye starts to go. I am unable to sleep: along with the flushes that wake me up with a pinch, I am feeling wired at night, my legs twitching and tense. I sleep on the sofa sometimes, and have night terrors in which a large, dark creature storms towards me and envelops me until I wake, gasping for breath. Then there is brain fog, the most psychedelic of them all: it leaves me confused, exhausted, and unable to form a coherent thought, let alone a sentence. I haven't had a period for a year, but they'd always been erratic. I want also to list vaginal dryness as a symptom, but there is no way of proving it: my sex drive is nonexistent. I google 'Malcolm Tucker shouting'. Still nothing.

I stop showering and exercising, preserving my energy for basic tasks such as 'putting on the same massive grey jumper as yesterday' and for wallowing in my own disgustingness. In spite of my greasy hair and unusual temper, my husband Mark still cares about my wellbeing, and encourages me to be persistent with the GP so we can get an official diagnosis. After a year of puzzled doctors and lots of blood tests, I am summoned to an endocrinologist in a hospital in central London.

As I sit in the waiting room, I imagine how awful it would be if I was actually fine. All the moaning and sketchy behaviour for nothing. Or could there be something fatally wrong with me? A classy funeral, maybe in Edinburgh. Intimate, but a few famous faces come along to pay their respects. Will Mark ever find love again? A doctor calls my name.

'Your FSH [follicle-stimulating hormone] levels are very high: 109,' says the sixtysomething male doctor, giving off a strong 'last appointment of the day' energy. 'For a woman your age, it's normally under 10. So this means you have a condition called premature ovarian insufficiency, or the early menopause. It's not uncommon, but it means you have a less than 5 per cent chance of conceiving.' He unloads the news in such a formal, monotone voice, it's almost as if he's hoping I'll leave without acknowledging I've just been told the worst news of my life.

'But I'll be able to do IVF,' I say.

'You won't be able to do IVF – you have a low egg supply, and your ovarian supply will not respond to IVF drugs.' This is a twist. I had skipped over the fertility details on Google, assuming there would be a simple scientific solution to my eggs being low. This is one of those pivotal moments: the ones where women stand up for themselves at the doctor's. Demanding answers. Not leaving until they have their way. I've heard about them, and only in my wildest dreams have I imagined being obstinate in the face of a health professional.

'I can't do IVF?' I ask, haughtily. The tone doesn't really suit me. I immediately regret it.

'No, but your womb can carry a pregnancy, so a donor egg would be your most viable option.'

My brain spirals into panic. 'Can you write this down for me, please?'

I leave the hospital holding a prescription for hormone replacement therapy drugs, which replace the oestrogen and progesterone that are at a lower level in menopause, and a piece of paper with some diagrams scribbled on it that I shove in a bag and never look at again. The plan is that I'll be on HRT until I'm in my 50s, to prevent the day-to-day symptoms, as well as cardiovascular disease and osteoporosis. For now he's given me a patch called Evra that I stick on my arm, and which pumps oestrogen into my body. If the symptoms continue, I can take the contraceptive pill Yasmin. Blocking that 5 per cent chance of conceiving does feel *slightly* counterproductive, but I used up all my energy with the IVF question, so I accept my fate and move on.

I call my sister Libby. Seven years older than me, often in a car with her two boys, she's the person I normally turn to when things get real. She's driving and I'm on speakerphone.

'It's not great news. I've got premature ovarian insufficiency and I've got less than 5 per cent chance of getting pregnant on my own,' I shout while walking through the rush-hour crowds.

'So what does that mean?'

'I'd need to get someone else's eggs,' I reply.

'You can have my eggs,' she responds, as if at a breakfast buffet. And so begins a dual journey: my quest to get pregnant, and my battle against the demon hormones.

Mark, an optimist, is relieved we have a plan for the former. We'll use Libby's eggs and have a little baby, and we come to the decision as naturally as the offer was presented to us. Obviously, I was hoping I'd get through life without having to understand what happens during fertility treatment, but this will not be the case. The latter question, of hormones, however, is more complex. The patches are awful. The hot flushes are knocked on the head, and for a week I can see colour in the world, but I am furiously hungry, my nice clothes stop fitting, and I begin to change deeply; spiritually almost. My sense of fun slowly fades.

We get to work on the egg-borrowing situation immediately, and are referred to a nearby hospital. My sister, my husband and I meet for the first of many visits. It is the greatest privilege to embark on this with two of my favourite people, and often I am so overwhelmed by the weight of what we are about to do that I turn up on the brink of tears. They are cheerful and encouraging.

In the waiting room is a poster for an infertility support group called Empty Arms, with a grainy black and white image of a woman with a shaggy bob cradling thin air. Like something out of a Julia Davis comedy, only a touch too tragic.

Debbie, our nurse, talks us through the process: blastocysts, fertility investigations, egg transfers. I take notes, but none of the information goes in. Mark gesticulates wildly in time with the doctor's insights, a sure sign that he has no idea, either.

Over the next few months, there's a lot of admin, and even more transvaginal ultrasound scans. We also need 'implications counselling', to ensure we will all be able to cope with the emotional voyage we're about to embark on. During Libby's session, the therapist gently quizzes her about how she might feel once the baby is born. She tells them all she wants is for me to experience the same joy she's had from being a mum. And I am honest, too: I can't see a downside. Any child would benefit from her genetics: her elegant charm and ease with the world. There's no rivalry or baggage. While this is life-altering and enormous, it feels like the most effortless exchange of true love.

All of the above takes about a year. The NHS is busy. I go on a cocktail of new hormones to prepare my body for the eventual egg transfer, but the new HRT they've given me doesn't go down well.

Beyond feeling exhausted, I am shocked by the early menopause diagnosis. My memory loss is getting embarrassing. If I go to a meeting, I write down exactly what I need to say, down to the small talk, but the moment a curveball question is asked, my brain has an enema.

My extracurricular hobby is now trawling message boards. Thankfully, I find the Daisy Network, an organisation set up to support women with POI (premature ovarian insufficiency). I learn a lot about the condition: spontaneous POI affects 1 per cent of women before the age of 40. Approximately 5–10 per cent of women with POI may still conceive. Technically, I could still conceive. For women with POI who still have ovaries, their fertility can be fickle and unpredictable. But is it possible to even consider sex when you can barely look at yourself most mornings?

Social media is a hellscape: I mute or delete friends who have got pregnant by accident, or who post pictures of their weekend family utopias. I avoid seeing people who have children. My gorgeous niece and nephews' birthday parties are painful; we can't stay too long.

I suddenly need a lot of attention and sympathy. Almost every day I consider posting a meme on social media of a cartoon of a woman on the phone saying: 'I'm just in the middle of the menopause, can I call you back in about five years?' but wimp out.

Back to the baby. It's November 2017. A year since I first googled 'have I got the menopause?' and nine months after our first fertility appointment. It's time for the egg collection. Libby heads into theatre for her general anaesthetic and the quick procedure during which they remove her eggs. Once the collection is over, we check on her. Libby lies on a hospital bed completely conked out, her grey pallid skin and still frame giving her the presence of a corpse. It's one of the most chilling moments of my life. As she's not allowed to travel alone, we are joined by Paddy, designated driver, mood-elevator and husband to Libby. The four of us head off to an Italian restaurant to celebrate. I bump into Debbie the nurse on the way out.

'We got three eggs,' she says. 'We'll give you a call tomorrow to let you know how the fertilisation goes.' At 7am the next day I get a call from an unknown number. A nurse from the hospital. She has bad news. None of the eggs has fertilised.

A year of medical tests, desperate anticipation, thousands of pounds of IVF drugs and a sister pumped full of insane hormones. We are all broken. Mark and I spend the day walking around our local park, avoiding buggies.

The next morning I get another mysterious call. It's a nurse and she's in a good mood. As a precaution they kept our eggs in the lab overnight, and one has fertilised – it's a miracle!

We rush into the hospital so they can implant it into my womb immediately. Two weeks pass. On the 14th day we do a pregnancy test. I'm not pregnant. I call my sister to tell her the bad news.

'I'm so sorry, Hat,' Libby says, her words strained with sorrow. It's not an empty platitude; she means it. I reassure her it's not her fault; she says she wants to try again. Barely capable of speech, I quickly thank her, tell her I love her and say goodbye.

In the weeks after the test, my husband can see I am struggling. He is, too. I can't face putting Libby through it again; it's a lot of time and physical and emotional labour. At this stage we are introduced to Dr Luca Sabatini by Debbie. A clean, strong, pragmatic Italian man, who is a consultant obstetrician and gynaecologist. My hero.

'How about an anonymous donor?' the doctor says. 'It's not a big deal. The baby's still yours.' Mark agrees. I nod, but it does feel like a big deal. My body has been a scientific experiment for over a year now, and I need some space. I am horrified by the thought of putting someone else's body into my body.

It helps that Mark has remarkable clarity. We either want a baby, or we don't. And we do, so we decide to put our absolute faith in the professionals and do whatever Sabatini tells us. Because of my condition, I don't qualify for any free rounds of IVF, so we decide we'll see him privately in London, and get the donor from a clinic in Madrid. We make contact and have a series of video chats with clinicians in Spain. They find an anonymous donor with similar colouring to mine, and two months later, we go to Madrid.

It's a tense trip. This time I've been healthy: no alcohol, meditation, lots of exercise, good food – so my body and brain are prepared if it goes wrong. The anticipation is agonising. It's made all the more surreal by the fact that Mark has booked us into a hotel in the gay district that is 50 per cent purple leather, 20 per cent pink fur, 10 per cent black silk and the rest in bowls of condoms. Still, the egg collection goes well – we get nine eggs, and after the fertilisation process have two blastocysts (the strong stage of an embryo, five or six days after fertilisation), which is very positive.

This time we do things differently: I go straight to bed and don't move for four hours. We fly home the next day. Mark carries the luggage. For the next two weeks, I do little physical movement. On day 14, I have a blood test to see if I am pregnant.

At 12:11 I get the email: 'Please find attached a copy of your results which confirms a positive pregnancy test.' We can't believe it.

Pregnancy is a breeze compared with the past few years. It's a profound shift to go from infertile to pregnant, and I am careful not to get carried away with the glee. It's high-risk, but things go to plan. Bit of sickness, a bit of bleeding, lots of apples. But the birth is less straightforward. Plummeting heart rate, baby's stuck, episiotomy, forceps.

'My baby,' I cry, as he is raised from between my legs and immediately moved on to a table. The doctors huddle around his body. Mark is devastated. The baby is unresponsive, blue and limp. 'It's OK, it's OK,' I tell Mark. I am as high as a kite from the epidural, but I am certain, from the depths of my soul, that he will survive.

A few minutes later we hear his cry. A lovely croaky cry.

As I haemorrhage everywhere, I am handed my son for what feels like 20 minutes. I have a bad internal tear. The first set of stitches goes wrong, and the doctors wheel me into theatre, leaving Mark in a room filled with my blood and the overwhelming presence of our tiny naked son.

And what a son he turns out to be. Fun-loving, impressively rhythmic. A club comic and jazz maestro in an elf's body. Beyond being a huge dollop of the most delicious pudding, he is mine. Any kind of spooky emotions about identity that might arise post-natally are nonexistent. I can only compare it to baking a cake.

They are a vital gluing agent, but nobody eats a slice of lemon drizzle and compliments the baker on the egg.

There is a foreboding cloud above me, however. When the pregnancy hormones end, the menopause will return. A few days after giving up feeding, my hot flushes are back and I'm unable to think straight. I'm dizzy, have terrifying heart palpitations, and am not able to get to sleep, which is terrifying when you have a baby who wakes throughout the night.

HRT does its job pretty quickly. I'd like to say this is the end of my hormonal adventure, but my hormones will continue to shift throughout my life. I am constantly weighing up if I am tired-tired or brink-of-mania, HRT-not-working tired. Nothing in excess. Careful with food and alcohol. No caffeine. Tons of supplements. Exercise.

My thirties haven't been the liberating time of calm inner confidence I was promised, and I am far from indestructible. While there's definitely rewiring to do, I've gained a certain fearlessness. I feel as if I am waking from a period of hibernation, not exactly refreshed, but certainly renewed. I am thankful for those who kept me warm. Thankful for my baby, who will know his life was so wanted. And ready to grip the hand of the next hot, teary, angry woman I see hiding her breakdown in a busy room. Or not. Whatever makes her happy.

23 JUNE

Mining's new frontier: Pacific nations caught in the rush for deep-sea riches

KATE LYONS

Travel thousands of metres below the surface of the ocean, and you reach the seabed. Pitch-black and quiet, it is largely unexplored, untouched, unknown.

What is known is extraordinary. The landscape at the bottom of the sea is as varied as it is above water: 4,000m down, abyssal plains stretch for miles like deserts; there are trenches large enough to swallow the Earth's largest mountains; venting chimneys rise in towers like underwater cities; seamounts climb thousands of metres. Hot thermal vents – believed by some to be the places where all life on Earth started – gush highly acidic water at temperatures of up to 400ºC, drawing in an array of creatures.

So little is known about what happens this far under the sea that in the 25 years following the discovery of the hydrothermal vents, an average of two new vent species are discovered every month. They include the yeti crab, a ghostly white crustacean with silky-blond bristles on its claws that give it a resemblance to the Abominable snowman. Others discovered in the last 20 years include the beaked whale and the Greenland shark, which dives to around 1,200m and has a lifespan of close to 400 years, making it one of the world's longest-living organisms.

'Every time you go down into the deep, you see something incredible and often new,' says Diva Amon, a deep-sea biologist and fellow at the Natural History Museum in London who has undertaken 15 deep-sea expeditions.

'There's a bone-eating worm called *Osedax*, which lives on the bones of dead whales in the deep ... Another special one was ... an anemone whose tentacles were eight feet long.'

Anna Metaxas, professor of oceanography at Dalhousie University in Nova Scotia, Canada, recalls the first time she travelled to the deep sea, in waters near the Bahamas. 'The most spectacular part of that dive was the bioluminescence. Because it gets dark at 1,000 metres they all light up, they all flash. I was in a submersible that had a plexiglass sphere, it was like flying through space.'

Ninety per cent of the ocean – and 50 per cent of the Earth's surface – is considered the deep sea (areas deeper than 200m). Only 0.0001 per cent of the deep seafloor has been investigated. Doing so is perilous, technically challenging and expensive. But despite these obstacles, companies have set their sights on the seabed as the new frontier for mining.

Since 1982, the International Seabed Authority (ISA), which is charged with regulating human activities on the deep seafloor, has issued 30 contracts for mineral exploration, taking in an area of more than 1.4 million square kilometres. Most of these sites are in the Pacific Ocean, in the Clarion-Clipperton fracture zone (CCZ).

In particular, companies have their eyes on polymetallic nodules – bundles of ore that resemble potatoes, which litter the surface of the deep sea and are rich in manganese, nickel, cobalt and rare earth metals. The nodules are up to 10cm in diameter and are thought to form at the staggeringly slow rate of just a few centimetres every one million years.

'A battery in a rock,' is how DeepGreen, one of the big players in the nascent industry, describes the polymetallic nodules. The Canadian firm touts deep-sea mining as a less environmentally and socially damaging alternative to terrestrial mining, and says it is crucial for effecting a transition to a greener economy, with the nodules containing the minerals needed for the batteries used in electric vehicles.

Its proposal is to dispatch ships to the CCZ and suck up the nodules through long pipes that stretch to the seabed. The nodules would be processed on the ship, with excess sediment pumped back into the sea.

So far, licences in international waters have only been issued for exploration and not mining, but the ISA is working on a regulatory framework for mining of the deep sea, with DeepGreen saying it will be ready to begin the work by 2024.

There are concerns about the environmental impact deep-sea mining could have on marine ecosystems, particularly given how little is known about them and the very slow pace of reproduction and growth at those depths.

An experiment in 1978, which involved the extraction of nodules from the seabed in the CCZ, pointed to how long-lasting the damage can be. The area was revisited in 2004, and researchers found the tracks made by mining vehicles 26 years earlier were still clearly visible on the seabed. There was also a reduced diversity of organisms in the disturbed area.

'You are talking about the destruction of the habitat on the seafloor. Any area you are mining will be destroyed,' says Duncan Currie, an international lawyer who has worked in oceans law for 30 years. He represents the Deep Sea Conservation Coalition which is calling for a moratorium on deep-sea mining.

Amon was part of a project that conducted baseline surveys in the area of the CCZ that the UK has a licence to explore for potential mining. 'As part of the work we were doing out there, we found that, of the megafauna, the larger animals, more than half of them were completely new to science, and more than half of them relied on the nodules as a surface to attach to. Things like corals, sponges, anemones – they actually need the nodules. So potentially mining in that area could have quite a drastic impact.

'It's also our largest ecosystem so it provides about 96 per cent of all habitable space on Earth,' says Amon. 'I think most people still assume that that space is just sort of empty or there's not a lot happening. But actually, it couldn't be further from the truth; the deep ocean is a vast reservoir of biodiversity.'

Other environmental concerns range from worries that noise pollution will interfere with deep-sea species' ability to communicate and detect food falls, increased temperature from drilling and vehicle operation, materials being discarded and heavy vehicles crushing seabed organisms and compacting the seabed.

Most concerning, Currie says, is the potential impact of sediment plumes. After the minerals are processed on ships, the proposal is to return the non-useful sediment into the ocean via long pipes, or risers, depositing them at a depth of 1,500m.

'The return sediment plume will be almost 24/7 – a continuous plume pumped into the ocean. No one has any idea what it will do: will it go up, go down? Will it interfere with the breeding of squid? We know fish migrate up and down, will it affect that? It's incredibly important and we know almost nothing about it,' he says.

DeepGreen disputes this, saying its modelling and experiments show that the spread of the plumes is far smaller and the amount of sediment injected into the mid-water column is far less than is often cited by campaigners. 'Our goal is to make sure that our activity does not cause any large-scale disruptions to ecosystem services and that we minimise the risk of biodiversity loss,' said a spokesperson for DeepGreen.

Caught up at the centre of this huge push for a new extractive industry are Pacific Island nations. Nations must sponsor companies that want to explore for minerals and among the countries that have issued licences are the tiny Pacific Island countries of Tonga, Cook Islands, Nauru and Kiribati.

DeepGreen holds rights to the exploration contracts sponsored by the Pacific countries of Nauru, Tonga and Kiribati. The relationship between DeepGreen and Nauru is of particular concern to observers of deep-sea mining, who have warned about an imbalance of power between the company and the tiny nation, which has a population of around 12,000.

'The Pacific nations I think are particularly vulnerable,' says Metaxas. 'They have vulnerable economies, this is an opportunity for an economic boom in a country if it's done right, if it's successful. I'm sure it's quite tempting, but I sure hope that there's also some advice about how much to risk and how to manage it all.'

There are still questions to be resolved about whether the company or sponsoring state would be liable in the event of environmental damage or other harm.

Before mining can commence, the ISA needs to release a code for the exploitation of the deep sea. This was due to be released and adopted in July 2020, but was delayed due to Covid. 'It is not implausible to expect that the ISA will be in a position to finalise the code by 2023,' said the DeepGreen spokesperson, who added the company expects to submit their environmental impact statement in 2023 for review in the hope of beginning commercial mining in 2024.

This month the EU parliament advised the European Union to promote a moratorium on deep seabed mining until its environmental impacts could be better understood and managed. But DeepGreen's boss, Gerard Barron, has suggested that, if the ISA moves slowly, the company might invoke the so-called two-year rule, which allows a country sponsoring a mining contractor to notify the ISA that the company intends to begin mining. The ISA then has two years to finalise the regulations for deep-sea mining. If it is unable to do so, the ISA is required to allow the contractor to begin work under whatever regulations are in place at the time.

DeepGreen said the two-year rule is 'only available to sponsoring states to use, not contractors like DG, which cannot invoke it' but that it was 'a valid option available to all member states of the International Seabed Authority'.

25 JUNE

Matt Hancock, the one-time sex cop now busted for a dodgy clinch

MARINA HYDE

Sorry, but the only thing I want to see Matt Hancock doing against the back of his office door is sliding down it with his head in his hands. But he can probably bank on not being sacked by Boris Johnson for having an affair. It would be like being sacked by Stalin for being slightly arsey to work with.

Even so, Hancock will be glad that the British Antarctic Territory has been added to the green list, just as he's been added to the shit list. The South Pole suddenly looks well worth packing his bags for. Temperatures are currently minus 87 but feel like minus 108, making it considerably less frosty than any of Matt's current climes.

That said, if Hancock does end up being resigned for this, it would fit with the general twilight mood in the UK's national story. Nothing says 'country that's going to make a massive success of itself' like a guy getting away with contributing to tens of thousands of unnecessary deaths but having to quit for a knee-trembler. It's like getting Al Capone for snogging.

So, then, to the health secretary's 'steamy clinch' with Gina Coladangelo, the lobbyist and long-term friend he took on as an aide last year (though initially did not declare it), and who was subsequently given a paid non-executive directorship at the Department of Health. Footage of this has somehow found its way from Hancock's office security cameras to the front page of the *Sun*, in a 'WORLD EXCLUSIVE' that feels like a major bollock-drop for the newsdesk of the Matt Hancock app. Guys ... what happened?

Quite how the paper obtained the source material one can only speculate, though I'm suddenly reminded of a quote last April from a Downing Street official, who remarked to the *Sunday Times*: 'There is not much love for Matt Handjob here.' Nor in the Department of Health, perhaps.

In some ways, the only thing you have to remember about Hancock – apart from the app and the parkour and the crying on telly – is that when Prof Neil Ferguson was discovered to have broken lockdown rules in the conduct of a relationship, Hancock went on TV to fume: 'You can imagine what my views are. It's a matter for the police.' So, yes – a shame to see sex cop Matt Hancock busted for sex crimes. But a reminder that cancel culture always devours its children.

Anyway. To the many, many, many sentences your 2019 self would not have understood, do please add: 'BUT THIS WAS TWO WEEKS BEFORE THE BAN ON HUGGING WAS LIFTED!' Absolutely devastating to think that a full 10 days *after* The Clinch occurred, Hancock went on telly specifically to warn people thinking of hugging a loved one that they 'should do it carefully'. Turns out we could have hugged people really hard, with tongues. Unless they were our relatives, I think?

'I'm really looking forward to hugging you as well, Dad,' Hancock smiled into the camera in that same interview. 'But we'll probably do it outside and keep the ventilation going. Hands, face and space.' Honestly, did you ever? How can I possibly trust a politician to lecture me on how to cuddle after this?

Back to the present day, though, and an early statement from another of the health secretary's aides – disguised as an unnamed 'friend' of Matt Hancock – would only say of the sensational revelation that 'no rules have been broken'. Hancock himself has since said he accepts 'that I breached the social distancing guidance', which is one way of putting it; while this morning, he had his honour defended by Grant Shapps. Which doesn't exactly feel like the Kitemark. Arguably the only way this story could now be more dignified is if a 'friend' suggested that the health secretary had – out of an abundance of caution – used a tongue condom.

As for the media maelstrom, I know a lot of your tears might struggle to liquefy, but we can at least remark mildly on quite what a category-five shocker Hancock is currently having. He's being serially stalked by blog-to-kill sniper Dominic Cummings, who released WhatsApp messages from last year in which the prime minister is shown calling Hancock both 'hopeless' and 'fucking useless'. There followed a somewhat excruciating mention in dispatches from the Queen herself on Wednesday. 'I've just been talking to your secretary of state for health,' Her Majesty was filmed saying to Boris Johnson. 'Poor man.'

According to his Downing Street spokesman, Boris Johnson considers the matter of his secretary of state for health breaking his own health advice closed, and has nothing more to add. Something for separated families to fume over as they read about Hancock pushing hard to delay double-jabbed people being able to treat amber countries as green. Meanwhile, I would say that however much the pictures may be amusing some, they probably ought to investigate the CCTV leak as a matter of urgency. It's obviously not great that footage from inside government ministries is being given or sold to third parties.

As for Hancock, I read that his job is now 'hanging by a thread'. Luckily for him, that thread will probably turn out to be made of Spider-Man's super-strength web fluid. After all, it's difficult to escape the suspicion that at some absolutely elemental level, this is what Johnson wants from his cabinet.

It's not just that the prime minister has had a lifelong hard-on for Ancient Times, where the Greek and Roman gods were grotesquely fallible and morally compromised, and where he could quite imagine a creature of his various infirmities and appetites sitting atop Mount Olympus. No, we can only conclude that Johnson wants Matt Hancock and Gavin Williamson and so on to be bad at their jobs, because it provides cover for his own professional inadequacies.

Why else would you keep someone you clearly kept describing as 'fucking useless' as your actual health secretary at the time of an era-shattering pandemic? Why else would you keep someone who constantly and demonstrably fails children and young people as your education secretary at a time when they so desperately deserve better?

The answer, alas, is that by remaining in place, guys like them serve as useful human shields. And I don't see why it shouldn't be the same with these sorts of scandals. Johnson must be only too happy to be surrounded by the erring and the compromised, because now he has shag cover too.

26 JUNE

The Oxford vaccine: the trials and tribulations of a world-saving jab

SARAH BOSELEY

In January 2020, when most of the world was in ignorance of the pandemic coming its way, a group of idealistic scientists at Oxford University got to work on a vaccine to save the planet. They wanted it to be highly effective, cheap and easy to use in even the poorest countries.

Sarah Gilbert, Andrew Pollard and others pulled it off. With speed crucial, they designed it and launched into trials before bringing in a business partner. The Anglo-Swedish pharmaceutical company AstraZeneca would manufacture it, license it around the world – and not make a profit until the pandemic was over.

It was an inspired, idealistic and philanthropic crusade. And yet they have spent the last year being attacked from all sides. As politicians, regulators, the public and the press have all weighed in, the vaccine has gone from hero to zero. So much has gone wrong, the well-intentioned folk at Oxford and AstraZeneca have taken so many blows, that it would be hardly surprising if they wondered whether they have been the victims of a deliberate disinformation campaign.

They have. There is clear evidence that the Oxford vaccine, and others, have been targeted by Russians peddling disinformation in order to promote their own version, Sputnik V. At the university and the company, whose partnership still holds firm, there is bemusement at the disasters and criticism. 'Everyone is ascribing this dark motive to everything we do,' said one company insider.

Sir John Bell, regius professor of medicine at Oxford and the government's life sciences adviser, who has been involved with the vaccine from the beginning, said they had been singled out. 'Of course, the vaccine is not perfect ... we were very clear that we understand that there are complications from the vaccine, as there are with all the vaccines. But ours has had the bloody spotlight, and people just won't let go.

'I think it would be fair to say maybe we haven't handled the negative news as well as we might have handled it. But we're kind of new at this game [and] there was nothing deceitful about what we did. We just perhaps didn't get in front of the dialogue.'

Speaking to experts and insiders, the *Guardian* has pieced together the inside story of the vaccine's fall from grace.

There has been no single enemy with Oxford/AstraZeneca in its sights. Instead, it is a story of cultural and political differences. Of misunderstandings and mistakes. It is a very human story, at heart, featuring people behaving badly or with naked self-interest. The coupling of Oxford University's scientific idealists with Big Pharma was an important contributory factor. This merger of minds and money, idealism and pragmatism, set the Oxford/AstraZeneca vaccine off on the rockiest of roads. 'AstraZeneca isn't really known as a vaccine specialist company,' said Dr Penny Ward, visiting professor in pharmaceutical medicine at King's College London.

A deal had been expected with the US pharmaceutical giant Merck & Co, which is known as MSD outside the US and Canada and has a huge vaccine division. But the health secretary, Matt Hancock, was said to have torpedoed it, because there was no guarantee Britain would get priority once doses were available. By the time AstraZeneca got involved, Oxford's scientists had already set up the early trials. That meant, said Ward, the studies were not tailored to the needs of regulators in a way that big drug companies would have done it. 'There are things that you can do as an academic and it all seems perfectly rational, but don't actually make a great deal of sense in drug development terms,' she said. 'There is a difference between academic science and development of a product.'

Two things happened that would cause serious problems with regulators later on. Oxford had a super-careful approach to older people, and chose to recruit mostly the under-60s for the earliest trials in Britain. Oxford wanted to be sure they would not suffer harm.

Secondly, there was a glitch in the production of vaccine for the studies. A contractor accidentally supplied half-doses, according to AstraZeneca's Sir Mene Pangalos, who headed the research once the company was on board. When the academic researchers found out, they told the Medicines and Healthcare products Regulatory Authority (MHRA) in the UK, and got the go-ahead to continue with two dosing strengths. When the trials reported, it turned out that volunteers given a half-dose followed by a full dose got more protection – up to 90 per cent compared with 62 per cent. Pangalos described it as serendipity. Regulatory bodies such as the Food and Drug Administration (FDA), in the US, don't like serendipity. They like predictability. The oddity of the results sowed doubt at the FDA.

And the Oxford/AstraZeneca explanation of the 90 per cent efficacy turned out to be wrong. Those who got the lower doses also had a bigger gap between shots – that was what improved the outcome. The FDA looked askance. It had already been perturbed by the side-effects in the trials.

Last September, two people were reported to have suffered transverse myelitis – damage to the myelin sheath which protects the spinal cord. Nobody now thinks these were vaccine-related injuries. But the FDA did not consider it had been alerted soon enough. While other regulators suspended the trials for a few days, in the US they did not restart for two months.

News of the setback had been leaked from within the US, where commentators attacked AstraZeneca. Ed Silverman at the influential Stat News wrote an open letter to the firm's chief executive, Pascal Soriot, on 9 September. 'I have concerns about your commitment to transparency,' he said, accusing AstraZeneca of failing to come clean. The following day, the *New York Times* commented in its coverage that 'many details about the trial's suspension and the event that triggered it remain murky'.

At AstraZeneca, they were nonplussed. In all the cancer drug studies they had submitted to the FDA, they had never been called on to account to the public for what they were doing. This wasn't how the industry normally operated.

When the US trials eventually reported in March, AstraZeneca's top executives thought they were home and dry. They reported great results – 79 per cent efficacy against symptomatic illness and 100 per cent against deaths.

Then the world turned upside down again: they had been accused by expert advisers to the US federal government of massaging the data to give a more favourable result. The Data Safety Monitoring Board (DSMB) accused AstraZeneca of putting out 'potentially misleading' figures. It was unprecedented. Data safety monitoring boards don't normally go public. But they had, with no warning.

Next, the national institutes of health (NIAID) headed by Anthony Fauci weighed in behind them. 'We urge the company to work with the DSMB to review the efficacy data and ensure the most accurate, up-to-date efficacy data be made public as quickly as possible,' the NIAID said in a statement. Fauci went on *Good*

Morning America, describing the data issue as 'an unforced error ... this kind of thing does nothing but really cast some doubt'.

Oxford and AstraZeneca's scientists are still astounded by the onslaught. They worked day and night to update the figures. Adding the very latest data pushed the overall efficacy down from 79 per cent to 76 per cent which was barely a drop, and actually pushed up efficacy in the older age group from 80 per cent to 85 per cent. AstraZeneca's vaccine is still not licensed in the US.

Those close to the fray say nationalism may have played a part in the undermining of the Oxford vaccine. But there's also a culture gap. The FDA expects the data to be cut and dried. The UK regulator was willing to think out of the box.

While the US trials were stalled, the new year did not bring AstraZeneca better luck in Europe. In January, the firm revealed it was having production problems at a factory in Belgium. The EU had ordered 400 million doses, with the first 90 million expected by March. AstraZeneca said it could only manage 40 million – and then 30 million – in the first quarter.

As European leaders watched the UK's steady introduction of vaccines, a full-blown row quickly resulted. Soriot insisted Astra-Zeneca had promised only 'best efforts' to deliver the doses to schedule. But the EU commissioner, Ursula von der Leyen, went to war, insisting Europe had a right to doses made in Britain under its contract with AstraZeneca.

Some at Oxford and AstraZeneca believe the row was heightened by Brexit tensions and British bragging about its vaccination programme. With anger rising, the commission threatened to block Pfizer/BioNTech vaccines made in Europe being exported to Britain.

Another huge issue had already rocked public confidence. On 25 January, a German-language business newspaper, *Handelsblatt*, ran a front-page story. 'AstraZeneca vaccine apparently hardly effective in seniors,' said the headline. Efficacy in the over-65s, the age group most at risk of dying from Covid, was only 8 per cent, it said. *Handelsblatt*'s sources were not in the German government. Its journalists had been speaking to regulators and vaccine advisers.

The figure turned out to be inaccurate – and taken out of context. There were too few elderly people in the early Oxford trials, and if you have too few people in a trial, the results are not reliable. The 8 per cent figure was essentially meaningless because there was simply not enough evidence to prove how well the vaccine worked in the over-65s. *Handelsblatt* acknowledged there was too little data, but that was lost in the ensuing row.

Within days, SIKO, Germany's vaccination advisory panel, said it would not recommend the vaccine for the over-65s because of the lack of evidence that it worked in them. In France, President Macron said the jab was 'quasi-ineffective' in the over-65s. Within weeks, he was forced to say publicly he would have the vaccine himself – and by early March it had been approved by France for the over-65s. But the damage had been done.

Bell says you can get only limited data from vaccine trials – you have to see what happens 'in the real world'. 'And yet, throughout Europe we had lots of these little so-called expert committees saying: "Oh God, you can't use it in the over-50s, oh God, you can't use it in the under-50s. You can't use it at all. Well, maybe you could use it if you're upside down, drinking a milkshake." It was unbelievable,' he said.

Real-world data eventually proved the vaccine worked very well in older people. But it also revealed a serious problem in a tiny minority of younger people. On 7 March, Austria suspended the use of a batch of the AstraZeneca vaccine after a woman of 49 died and another aged 35 became seriously ill with blood disorders, shortly after inoculation.

As Covid cases continued to surge, the European Medicines Agency (EMA) said the benefits outweighed the risks, but launched an investigation. The EMA and MHRA eventually ruled the AstraZeneca dose did cause the condition, albeit in only four in a million cases. But it was enough for many European countries to restrict the AstraZeneca vaccine.

These real-world problems were being compounded by misinformation in the virtual world – seeded by pro-Russian state interests who had a vaccine of their own to promote. Sputnik V was designed by the Gamaleya Research Institute, part of Russia's ministry of health and funded by the Russian Direct Investment Fund, a sovereign wealth fund that is headed by Kirill Dmitriev.

Dmitriev christened the AstraZeneca product 'the monkey vaccine', because it uses a chimpanzee virus as its delivery mechanism. Last October, memes, videos and pictures of King Kong injecting a screaming woman and Boris Johnson as part of the cast of *Planet of the Apes* were posted anonymously and went viral.

A report by the EU watchdog, the external action service, found that between December and April, the disinformation intensified. It accused Russia and China of pursuing a campaign to undermine trust in 'western-made vaccines, EU institutions and western/European vaccination strategies'.

AstraZeneca was not the only target, but there are suggestions Kremlin interests hoped to sow dissension across Europe, destabilising Germany and France in particular. Certainly, those behind Sputnik and RT, the Russian state television channel, have amplified the anti-vaccine and anti-mask voices gaining particular traction in France.

For the scientists at Oxford and AstraZeneca it feels personal. Most critics and defenders of the vaccine agree on one thing. The developers, manufacturers and the British government should have come out fighting. Thinking they were saving the world, it didn't occur to Oxford or AstraZeneca that they needed to be proactive. They also agree that the world needs this vaccine – particularly in the developing world.

Dr Peter Hotez, co-director of the Texas Children's Center for Vaccine Development, cited three issues that had gone badly wrong. 'AstraZeneca is not a vaccine company. That's probably one. Two, they're trying to accelerate this in a public health emergency. Three, there is this rare complication, the cerebral thrombosis, happening in an environment of intense anti-vaccine aggression. And you've got now reports from the Russian government trying to discredit their competitors' Covid vaccines.

'It's been a perfect storm ... they've got to figure out a way to communicate this, to walk it back so we can get this fixed.'

27 JUNE

'I could hardly hold back the tears': a diary of *Apple Daily*'s last week

ANONYMOUS

A Hong Kong police national security operation has forced the closure of the city's most vocal and pro-democratic newspaper, *Apple Daily*. Its senior executives arrested, companies charged, and accounts frozen, the paper survived for less than a week after hundreds of officers raided the newsroom, accusing it of foreign collusion. Here a reporter from the 26-year-old paper describes the final days.

Thursday 17 June

I was woken up by a call from my colleague at 7am. I knew these early morning calls are never good, and I was right. He said five of our senior management had been arrested by the national security department, and, as we spoke, hundreds of police officers were at the gates of our office. 'Not again,' I thought to myself. This routine – arrests followed by a raid – had already happened once, last August.

Our livestream was the first thing I turned to. Armed officers in uniform flooded our lobby, and soon our colleagues were ordered to wait outside the gates or in the canteen on the top floor. Even more troubling, the police claimed their warrant granted them power to search and seize journalistic materials. A direct attack at a news institution.

After the police left about five hours later, we rushed back to count our losses: at least 44 journalists' computers had been seized. Hardware can be replaced, but they also froze bank accounts, threatening operations and payment of wages. For the first time, the prospect of shutting down felt very real.

Saturday 19 June

By 8am I was queuing outside the West Kowloon magistrates' court. *Apple Daily*'s chief executive Cheung Kim-hung and editor-in-chief Ryan Law were charged with 'collusion with foreign forces', a crime under the national security law. The others had been released on bail. Dozens of colleagues and ex-colleagues had waited, some since 5am, for a seat inside to show support.

We thought the judge would grant bail, but he didn't, and gave no explanation. We waved at our colleagues. I could only say, 'Hang in there.' Barring a successful appeal, they'll be behind bars until at least mid-August.

MONDAY 21 JUNE

With accounts frozen, we headed to the office, expecting it would be our last day. The shuttle bus to the newsroom was silent, everyone swiping their phones for news.

The board of Next Digital was meeting in the afternoon to decide our fate. At 3pm the news came but it wasn't what we expected. They postponed their decision to Friday, hoping the government would unfreeze our accounts. People were angry and confused. The main issue was the risk of more arrests, not frozen accounts. To drag this on did not make sense.

Some determined to stay on and work till the last minute. Others believed danger was imminent, and one more day at *Apple Daily* meant one more day at risk. There was an exodus. The finance news team stopped updating the website, and all the video editors resigned.

My news team was given two hours to decide. It was one of the most complicated decisions ever. We knew our editor wouldn't leave even if only one reporter stayed, and many of us couldn't live with leaving him behind. Most of us stayed. We focused on a special feature to give our paper a proper send-off.

WEDNESDAY 23 JUNE

Another police raid had been rumoured, and we were told to work from home. I was woken up by another call: the chief opinion writer for the China section had been arrested.

It can't be proved, but most of us saw it as punishment for delaying the closure. The board called a meeting and announced *Apple Daily* would stop publication no later than Saturday. Editorial management pushed it even earlier: today would be our last. And, just like that, our newspaper was ended by a thuggish act of government.

We rushed back. The end of *Apple Daily* was obviously the main focus, and every team worked to publish their special features two days earlier than planned. It was a hectic and emotional day in the newsroom, but professional.

At 10.30pm the photographers told everyone to go to the roof for a final drone shot. A crowd of about 100 passed through the rain to the edge of the roof. Down by our gates hundreds of people waved their phone lights, chanting supportive slogans. My colleagues shouted, 'Thank you!' back at them. I could hardly hold back my tears.

In the final hour before midnight, those who had finished their work backed up as much content as possible before the website shut down and all content was erased, 26 years' worth.

We worked until the literal last minute. The final news update was published at 11.55pm, and it was the resignation of our deputy publisher Chan Pui-man, arrested a week ago. As the front page was signed off by our executive editor, rounds of applause broke out for the senior editors who led us through this incredibly hard time.

Sadness was replaced by a sense of achievement. For once, there was no more news for us to work on; we embraced each other and took farewell photos in an almost graduation day-like mood. On the other side of the office, a record-breaking 1 million copies were being printed and would be sold the next day.

It would be painful for our bosses in jail to see their beloved newspaper cease publication, but from the support we got from the people of Hong Kong, I'd like to think we've done something right these last 26 years, and we handled its last days with dignity. Until we meet again.

28 June

My English will never be 'perfect' – and that's what keeps a language alive

NESRINE MALIK

My first day in an English-speaking school was miserable. It was full of little humiliations: the kind that with the hindsight of adulthood seem trivial, but in childhood plant the seed of a feeling of inadequacy that one can never expel. My family had just moved to Kenya, where English was the official language. I was seven and could not speak a word of it, having grown up in an Arabic-speaking country, and been educated at an Arabic school.

I sat silently in class in a daze, hoping no one would notice my inability. But I drew attention to myself because I had put my schoolbag in the wrong place. And the teacher, who finally had to resort to gestures to get through to me, demanded to know where it was. Out of some childish impulse to hide my awkward self and belongings, I had stashed my inappropriately large bag, overstuffed with provisions by an anxious mum, in a cupboard at the back of the class. I sat in silence as the teacher's interrogation grew more irate. In the end I blurted out where I had put the bag, but in Arabic. The teacher blinked. The whole class laughed. My eyes stung. The bullying started that day and didn't stop until I had learned enough English to lose the stain of difference.

The funny thing is, impossible though it seemed at that moment, I don't actually remember learning English, which I suppose is down to the speed with which children pick up a language. All I recall is one day sitting in humiliated isolation and the next being able to read a whole grade-one book from cover to cover.

Despite the quick uptake, my language challenges weren't over. My English was lopsided – all bloated vocabulary from too much reading to overcompensate for a late start, but no confidence to use the words in conversation. It jostled with, but failed to replace, my first language: Arabic.

Today, even after almost four decades of education and work in the English language, I still falter by the standards my teachers set. My accent is all over the place. I still often have to pause in speech and translate thoughts in my head from Arabic first, which affects my articulacy; and I still mispronounce words.

I am also often corrected, which reflexively takes me back to the classroom. It's usually not an unkind correction, more an amused question. When I say 'meLAN-kolly' did I really mean 'MELON-kolly'? 'Interwined', it was gently pointed out, perhaps had a T in the middle (it shouldn't: much more evocative without it). And the most British correction of all comes in the form of a polite, 'How are you pronouncing that? I think it might be X, but I could be wrong.' It's not as uncommon an impulse as one would think. A recent survey revealed that many people are more than happy to correct friends, family and strangers when they make mistakes.

I don't have time for that kind of preciousness about language any more. Having spent years trying to 'improve' my English, I realised that the more I tried to follow norms, be they related to accent, pronunciation or even inflection and tone, the more hesitant and overly formal my English became. The English I've ended up speaking is dynamic and porous to other influences, and all the more expressive for it.

In my childhood home, the English we learned in school merged with Arabic in ways so organic I couldn't tell you when it began or who started it. Where Arabic constructions seemed hard, simpler English ones replaced them, and vice versa. We added 'ing' to Arabic words to turn them into verbs. Or we transposed simpler Arabic sentence structures on to more cumbersome English ones, dropping words such as 'am' and 'is', which don't exist in Arabic. To this day, we still say 'I tired' or 'I hungry'.

This isn't a quirk of upbringing: it's the experience of most English-speaking people. Far more people speak English in the rest of the world than in native-English-speaking countries. I am even reluctant to use the word 'native', as it implies ownership – some source of correct, unevolving English that exists only in a small number of nations, and is corrupted by others. English is listed as a national language in more than 50 countries across the world. It is used by the Indian government as a supplement to Hindi, and is the language of the Indian judiciary. In some African countries, a version of English is the main language of officialdom, education and the media. Here, a process called 'nativisation' can occur, with local accents, grammar and even cultural concepts (for example, the position of 'senior wife' in polygamous west African countries) influencing the English and subtly changing it.

Even standard English has undergone nativisation of its own through history, absorbing huge amounts of French vocabulary for example, with even a sprinkling of Arabic in there too. No version of English we speak now is 'pure', so policing pronunciation, or indeed any other arbitrary code of language, is futile – the equivalent of patrolling an ever-shifting border.

The purpose of language is to facilitate communication. The magic of language is its capacity to spontaneously evolve to facilitate that communication, incorporating and accommodating the influences, and thus the needs, of those who use it. Caring about the integrity of the English language and allowing it to breathe and change go hand in hand. One could even say they were interwined.

28 JUNE

My dear old dog won't be around for ever – so I will cherish every last walk

EMMA BEDDINGTON

Morning walks are not what they used to be. For years, my whippet, Oscar, and I would take a brisk hour's trot at eight, taking care of business, physical (him) and mental (me). His bladder and bowels got a workout; the rhythm of our steps and the changing-unchanging view provided a gulp of oxygen and thinking time for my groggy brain.

Now, Oscar arrives outside my bedroom door at about 5.45am, making a polite but insistent noise like a slowly deflating balloon. When I get up, he shadows me, still making this noise, his eyes pools of anxiety, until I give up and grab his lead. Despite every appearance of tearing impatience to get out, the minute we leave the house he grinds to a halt by the front step and licks it insistently. If I don't move him on, he will spend five minutes doing this, before peeing slowly on the spot, eyes fixed on me in a way that would be deeply creepy if I didn't know him so well.

This is how our walks go now: he truffles away at lamp-posts, hedges and bins at great length; whenever I start to get into a walking rhythm, he jerks me back, arrested by some particularly compelling pool of urine. Each day, we cover less and less ground and move a little slower. I haven't had an uninterrupted morning train of thought for months.

I would like to be the kind of person who accepts this with Zen patience, but most days I hiss: 'You're driving me mad, Oscar,' or: 'I don't have time for this,' at least once. I often stand in front of his favourite patches of verge to stop him getting stuck for 10 minutes.

My dog is old. I have known and loved him since he was a scrap of a puppy; now, somehow, he is 12. He used to have the muscular gallop of a miniature racehorse and leap into five-foot hedges to retrieve his ball; he still loves a ball, but his legs give up after two throws. His once-black muzzle is silvery white, his breath has the foul stench of a Grimsby trawler in the sun and his body is thinner than ever, battered and balding. Lying on the bed in my office – as he does for hours a day, motionless, more pancake than pet – he has the bruised, almost corpse-like, palette of a Lucian Freud: muddy pinks, greys and putty; still beautiful, but plainly mortal. His flank is bisected by a huge, jagged scar from when a German shepherd attacked him; it still hurts my heart to remember my peaceful gentleman cowering in a ball, not daring to defend himself.

I was terrified we had lost him then – the vet wasn't sure his delicate skin would hold the web of sutures – but now every day is a fractional, inexorable step towards losing him. I forget for a while, then I catch sight of him limping after an unwise ball chase and it brings me up short. He is no emotional support dog – he likes his own company, wants to be stroked only at four each afternoon for no more than five minutes and greets most affection with a martyred sigh – but he has been there, solidly himself, for 12 years: a funny, consoling, reliable presence. It is outrageous that he will not be here for ever.

I had to break off and stroke his silky ears after typing that (he hated it: 9am is not stroking time).

So, I am trying a new approach. On today's walk, I let Oscar stop as often as he wanted and lick as much disgusting street filth as he fancied. Instead of chivvying him on, I watched the bounce of his neatly folded ears as he meandered slowly and enjoyed his happy, pottering absorption. I didn't have a single coherent thought and it took an age: I am horribly behind on everything. But it is abundantly clear that there are a finite number of these morning walks ahead of us; let's squeeze every lingering second of lamp-post-inspecting, pee-licking, bin-sniffing canine joy out of them.

Summer

Our climate change turning point is right here, right now

REBECCA SOLNIT

Human beings crave clarity, immediacy, landmark events. We seek turning points, because our minds are good at recognising the specific – this time, this place, this sudden event, this tangible change. This is why we were never very good, most of us, at comprehending climate change in the first place. The climate was an overarching, underlying condition of our lives and planet, and the change was incremental and intricate and hard to recognise if you weren't keeping track of this species or that temperature record. Climate catastrophe is a slow shattering of the stable patterns that governed the weather, the seasons, the species and migrations, all the beautifully orchestrated systems of the Holocene era we exited when we manufactured the Anthropocene through a couple of centuries of increasingly wanton greenhouse gas emissions and forest destruction.

This spring, when I saw the shockingly low water of Lake Powell, I thought that maybe this summer would be a turning point. At least for the engineering that turned the south-west's Colorado River into a sort of plumbing system for human use, with two huge dams that turned stretches of a mighty river into vast pools of stagnant water dubbed Lake Powell, on the eastern Utah/Arizona border, and Lake Mead, in southernmost Nevada. It's been clear for years that the overconfident planners of the 1950s failed to anticipate that, while they tinkered with the river, industrial civilisation was also tinkering with the systems that fed it.

The water they counted on is not there. Lake Powell is at about a third of its capacity this year, and thanks to a brutal drought there was no great spring runoff to replenish it. That's if 'drought' is even the right word for something that might be the new normal, not an exception. The US Bureau of Reclamation is overdue to make a declaration that there is not enough water for two huge desert reservoirs and likely give up on Powell to save Lake Mead.

I got to see the drought up close when I spent a week in June floating down the Green River, the Colorado River's largest tributary. The skies of southern Utah were full of smoke from the Pack Creek wildfire that had been burning since 9 June near Moab, scorching thousands of acres of desert and forest and incinerating the ranch buildings and archives of the legendary river guide and environmentalist Ken Sleight (fictionalised as Seldom Seen Slim in Edward Abbey's novel *The Monkey Wrench Gang*), now 91. Climate chaos destroys the past as well as the future. The fire is still burning.

It wasn't just the huge plume of smoke that filled us with dread about the adventure to come; the weather forecast of daily temperatures reaching 106F made living out of doors for a week seem daunting. Water level in the river was far lower than normal and due to drop a lot more; the temperature on our rafts and kayaks just above the water was tolerable – but as soon as you walked any distance from the river's edge, the heat came at you as though you'd opened an oven door.

We saw an unusual amount of wildlife on the trip too – mustangs, bighorn sheep, a lean black bear and her two cubs pacing the river's edge – but any sense of wonder was tempered by the likelihood that thirst had driven them down from the drought-scorched stretches beyond the river. We need a new word for that feeling for nature that is love and wonder mingled with dread and sorrow, for when we see those things that are still beautiful, still powerful, but struggling under the burden of our mistakes.

Then came the heat dome over the north-west, a story that didn't appear to make the top headlines of many media outlets as it was happening. Much of the early coverage showed people in fountains and sprinklers as though this was just another hot day, rather than something sending people to hospitals in droves, killing hundreds (and likely well over a thousand) in Oregon, Washington and British Columbia, devastating wildlife, crops and domestic animals, setting up the conditions for wildfires and breaking infrastructure designed for the Holocene, not the Anthropocene. It signified something much larger even than a crisis impacting a vast expanse of the continent: increasingly wild variations from the norm with increasing devastation that can and will happen anywhere. It seemed to get less coverage than the collapse of part of a single building in Florida.

A building collapsing is an ideal specimen of news, sudden and specific in time and place, and in the case of this one on the Florida coast, easy for the media to cover as a spectacle with straightforward causes and consequences. A crisis spread across three states and two Canadian provinces, with many kinds of impact, including untallied deaths, was in many ways its antithesis. There was a case to be made that climate change – in the form of rising saltwater intrusion – was a factor in the Florida building's collapse, but climate change was far more dramatically present in the Pacific Northwest's heat records being broken day after day and the consequences of that heat. In Canada the previous highest temperature was broken by eight degrees Fahrenheit, a big lurch into the dangerous new conditions human beings have made, and then most of the town in which that record was set burned down.

Later news stories focused on one aspect or another of the heat dome. A marine biologist at the University of British Columbia reported that the heatwave may have killed more than a billion seashore animals living on the coast of the Pacific Northwest. Lightning strikes in BC, generated by the heat, soared to unprecedented levels – inciting, by one account, 136 forest fires. The heatwave cooked fruit on the trees. It was a catastrophe with many aspects and impacts, as diffuse as it was intense. The sheer scale and impact were underplayed, along with the implications.

Political turning points are as man-made as climate catastrophe: we could have chosen to make turning points out of the western wildfires of the past four years – notably the incineration of the town of Paradise and more than 130 of its residents in 2018, but also last year's California wildfires that included five of the six largest fires in state history. It could include the deluge that soaked Detroit with more than six inches of rain in a few hours last month or the ice storm in Texas earlier this year or catastrophic flooding in Houston (with 40 inches of rain in three days) and Nebraska in 2019 or the point at which the once-mythical Northwest Passage became real because of summer ice melt in the Arctic or the 118-degree weather in Siberia this summer or the meltwater pouring off the Greenland ice sheet.

A turning point is often something you individually or collectively choose, when you find the status quo unacceptable, when you turn yourself and your goals around. George Floyd's murder was a turning point for racial justice in the US. Those who have been paying attention, those with expertise or imagination, found their turning points for the climate crisis years and decades back. For some it was Hurricane Sandy or their own home burning down or the permafrost of the far north turning to mush or the IPCC report in 2018 saying we had a decade to do what the planet needs of us. Greta Thunberg had her turning point, and so did the indigenous women leading the Line 3 pipeline protests.

Summarising the leaked contents of a forthcoming IPCC report, the Agence France-Presse reports: 'Climate change will fundamentally reshape life on Earth in the coming decades, even if humans can tame planet-warming greenhouse gas emissions [...] Species extinction, more widespread disease, unliveable heat, ecosystem collapse, cities menaced by rising seas – these and other devastating climate impacts are accelerating and bound to become painfully obvious before a child born today turns 30. The choices societies make now will determine whether our species thrives or simply survives as the 21st century unfolds ...'

The phrase 'the choices societies make' is a clear demand for a turning point, a turning away from fossil fuel and towards protection of the ecosystems that protect us.

Every week I temper the terrible news from catastrophes such as wildfires and from scientists measuring the chaos by trying to put them in the context of positive technological milestones and legislative shifts and their consequences. You could call each of them a turning point: the point last week at which Oregon passed the bill setting the most aggressive clean electricity standards in the US, 100 per cent clean by 2040. The point at which Scotland began getting more electricity from renewables than it could use. The point at which New York state banned fracking. The Paris Climate Treaty in 2015. Of course, as with the climate itself, many of the changes were incremental: the stunning drop in cost and rise in efficiency of solar panels over the past four decades, the myriad solar and wind farms that have been installed worldwide.

The rise in public engagement with the climate crisis is harder to measure. It's definitely growing, both as an increasingly powerful movement and as a matter of individual consciousness. Yet something about the scale and danger of the crisis still seems to challenge human psychology. Along with the fossil fuel industry, our own habits of mind are something we must overcome.

12 JULY

England suffer cruel defeat but Southgate and his players lit up the summer

BARNEY RONAY

It was nearly complete, it was nearly so sweet. But it was, lest we forget, still sweet all the same. Italy and not England are the champions of Europe after a gruelling, draining, occasionally wild Euro 2020 final was decided by the final kick of a penalty shootout.

For Gareth Southgate and his young team, defeat came in the cruellest, most operatic fashion at Wembley as England's shot at a first tournament victory in 55 years was decided by another of those brutal little flick-books of joy and despair.

This is an England manager whose public identity has been defined for much of the past quarter of a century by failure at the same ground in a European Championships penalty shootout. As the final stretched into extra time Southgate watched from his touchline, shuffling his substitutes, trying to put a brake on this train.

There were scares, bruising collisions, weary attempts to break the game open. But, of course, it was heading this way, a twist pulled from football's schlockiest of scripts. There were tears in the crowd for the three England players to miss in the shootout: Bukayo Saka, Jadon Sancho and Marcus Rashford, aged 19, 21 and 23.

As Italy's players collapsed on to the turf in spasms of joy following Gianluigi Donnarumma's decisive save from Saka, as the white shirts slumped into a frieze of sadness, there was a feeling of vertigo around Wembley, but beneath it the sound of something else too. Italy are deserved champions, a fine team who played some thrilling football. England produced moments of clarity too, and were bold and unafraid in their first men's tournament final since 1966.

There will be pain in defeat. But that sound at the end was a gentle hiss of applause. Down the years moments such as these have been met with a reflex splurge of blame, hurt, recrimination, tears, hurled plastic chairs. But this was something else. For the past four weeks, Southgate's fine, likable young team has been a tonic, his clarity, decency and willingness to speak across football an uplifting thing at a time of dissonance and weak leadership elsewhere.

At times Southgate has seemed like the last sensible person left. This England iteration may or not go on to further glories from here. But when something is good it's never gone, and this fine young group of footballers made a mark here that will not be lost. After a year and a half of fear and isolation football has, for the last few weeks, provided a reminder that other things also exist, that there is also hope and warmth to be found, other stories to be written.

Wembley was a beautiful spectacle, the grass a deep green, the huge open tiers throbbing with bodies, flags, banners, people blinking in the lights, as though struggling to believe this waking dream. There was a pause before kick-off as the players of both sides took the knee in the final of the world's third largest televised sporting event, quite a moment for that ritual. Taking the knee is a nudge. It's a note of sympathy. It costs nothing. It has no hard political outline, unless tolerance and anti-racism seem like startling new concepts. But billions of people watched this final. The warm ripples of that gesture will be felt in unexpected places.

The anthems had already passed at a pitch of hysteria, the cameras lingering on the gorgeously soft, brutish brows of Giorgio Chiellini as Italy's poster boy belted out '*Il Canto degli Italiani*'. We are prepared to die, the final refrain insists. But what Italy weren't prepared for was Luke Shaw.

There was something glorious in the fact England's opening goal after two minutes was scored by one full-back and made by two others. When Southgate picked his squad there was an idea he would be hoist by his own full-back fetish, that this was excessive, crankish caution. Well, three of those full-backs made a goal in the final. Kyle Walker's run created space and time for Kieran Trippier to measure a perfect pass to the back post, dipping in a perfect parabola into Shaw's stride. The volley into the corner was perfectly executed.

As the ball spun around in the back of the net Shaw leapt and waved an arm a little vaguely. As of that moment the last two England players to score in a final were Geoff Hurst and Luke Shaw, two minutes of game-time and 55 years apart on this same pitch. England got to half-time still ahead, but paddling for the end. And, as the second half dragged past its midpoint, they began to fade. Or, rather, Italy began to play. And they are a wonderful team, strong in every area, coached in fine-point detail.

Southgate frowned on his touchline, occasionally muttering but still collected, still with the air of a junior cavalry officer on his way to a country wedding. At 1–1 England were hanging on a little right to the end. Full-time came and went, with England looking like a young team now, stretched thin by Italy's pressing in midfield, their ability to control the tempo. Harry Maguire showed defensive leadership when it was needed, patrolling that stricken backline like a police horse shepherding a testy crowd. Then came that grand final twist, and a defeat that felt as bad as defeat ever feels, but not quite like the end.

21 July

Data leak raises new questions over capture of Princess Latifa

DAN SABBAGH

For a few days Princess Latifa had dared to think she could relax. An extraordinary plan to escape from a father she said had once ordered her 'constant torture' was looking as if it might work, as she sat on a 30-metre yacht on the Indian Ocean, her home city of Dubai further and further away.

Yet the daughter of Sheikh Mohammed bin Rashid al-Maktoum, the ruler of the glittering Emirati city, still wanted to connect with home – to tell family and friends something of her freedom, send emails, WhatsApp messages and post on Instagram from what she thought were two secure, brand-new 'burner' pay-as-you-go mobile phones.

It was a decision that may have had fateful consequences, according to analysis by the Pegasus project, a special investigation into the NSO Group, which sells hacking spyware to governments. At the height of the escape drama, it can now be revealed, the mobile numbers for Latifa and some of her friends back home appeared on a database at the heart of Pegasus. It raises the possibility that a government client of the group was drawing up possible candidates for some sort of surveillance.

It was late February 2018, and Princess Latifa, then 32, had been desperate to flee her father's emirate for many years. She had made a 'very, very naive' first attempt in 2002, arranging to be driven across the border to Oman, but was easily recaptured. This time she hoped it was different, but had prepared for the worst.

When planning her second escape, Latifa had prepared a video to be released online if the latest effort was foiled. In it, she described how she had been beaten and tortured between 2002 and 2005, forcibly injected with sedatives, and once told by her captors: 'Your father told us to beat you until we kill you.'

They were extraordinary claims of abuse that were accepted as truthful in a fact-finding judgment from an English judge – part of a custody battle between Sheikh Mohammed and his sixth and former wife, Princess Haya, over their two young children. Part of that continuing case turns on how Dubai's ruler treated some of his other children, although after the fact-finding ruling, Sheikh Mohammed insisted it had only told 'one side of the story'.

Alongside Latifa onboard the yacht – the *Nostromo* – was her best friend and confidante, a Finn with a taste for adventure, Tiina Jauhiainen. She had first met the princess at the end of 2010, when she was asked to become her fitness instructor, and had become so close that the princess asked for her help to get out of the country, in an elaborate scheme worthy of a film.

Also onboard was Hervé Jaubert, a former French spy, who was captaining the vessel. It was Jaubert who had devised the yacht end of the escape plan after Latifa recruited him – Jauhiainen later told a London court he was paid €350,000 – having come across a book he had written about escaping from Dubai when a business deal he was involved in ran into trouble nearly a decade before.

Latifa and Jauhiainen believed their communications, via the yacht's satellite uplink, were secure. They had taken some precautions: Jaubert had turned the ship's tracking device off and their phones were new, as were the sim cards.

Latifa and Jauhiainen began their escape at 7am on 24 February from downtown Dubai. The princess's driver had dropped her off to meet her friend, then Latifa changed clothes in the cafe's bathroom, where she ditched her normal mobile phone.

Likening themselves to the ill-fated Thelma and Louise, the duo drove six hours to Muscat in Oman. There, with the help of Christian Elombo, a friend and former French soldier, they made a difficult journey by dinghy and jetski 13 miles out into the ocean to international waters, where Jaubert's boat the *Nostromo* was waiting.

Meanwhile, back in Dubai the hunt for the missing princess had started. A day later, on 25 February, Latifa's phone appeared in the leaked data list – by Dubai's doing, it is thought, although not much may have been gleaned, given that it had been left behind in the cafe.

Elombo and his girlfriend, who were supposed to leave Oman, were picked up a day later and questioned by the authorities on behalf of the neighbouring state. Realising contact with Elombo had been lost, and becoming a little more nervous, Latifa and Jauhiainen revised their plan. Jauhiainen said they had intended to go to Sri Lanka, from where Latifa would fly to the US to claim asylum, but instead they opted to land in India.

Yet it did not appear to matter much, because for the first four days at sea, until 28 February, there was nobody on their tail. Latifa and Jauhiainen were thrilled to have made it, although conditions were not luxurious: there was an ever-expanding number of cockroaches onboard and, apart from watching a few bad movies, there was not much to do. Inevitably they ended up spending time on their phones.

On the same day, 28 February, the numbers of some of her friends began appearing on the list that is determined to have come from Dubai.

At home, one of Latifa's few freedoms had been skydiving; she had jumped frequently with Jauhiainen among others. But it was other members of the daredevil club whose numbers were being added to the list in the days that followed, including Juan Mayer, a photographer who regularly took pictures of the princess in mid-air, which had formed the basis of a short magazine feature.

The data indicates other numbers began to appear too: those of Lynda Bouchiki, an events manager, and, more significantly, Sioned Taylor, a Briton who lived in Dubai, working as a maths teacher in a girls' school. Taylor had also been a member of the skydiving club. Bouchiki and Taylor had acted as Latifa's chaperones. After she had been released from prison, the princess was never allowed out unsupervised. Friends say that Taylor, in particular, had also become a close friend.

On the *Nostromo*, Jauhiainen, who spoke to the *Guardian* in April, remembers Latifa messaging Taylor and Bouchiki. The latter did not reply, but she clearly remembers that the princess was chatting with Taylor while they were onboard. At one point, Latifa even became suspicious, saying: 'I'm not sure this is Sioned,' but the communications continued.

What that signified precisely is unclear, but what the database shows is that Taylor's phone was listed repeatedly – on 1 and 2 March and on the day Latifa was to be captured, 4 March. Bouchiki's number appeared again on 2 March.

Without forensic examination of the phones, it is not possible to say whether any attempt was made to infect the devices, or whether any infection attempt was successful.

But at sea the situation had changed, ominously. Jaubert says it was on 1 March, a day after Latifa's friends and family were first targeted, that he noticed the first ship following the *Nostromo*, taking the same route and following at the same speed. Spotter planes followed soon after. It was clear they had been picked up by the Indian coastguard. Jaubert became increasingly nervous, also emailing a campaign group, Detained in Dubai, for help, worrying that he might run out of fuel as he headed towards the Indian port of Goa. But they were never to arrive.

After 10pm on 4 March, about 30 miles offshore, in an operation authorised by the Indian prime minister, Narendra Modi, at the request of Dubai, about 15 commandos in 'full military gear' stormed the yacht, firing stun grenades to incapacitate those onboard. Latifa and Jauhiainen panicked, running below deck and locking themselves in the bathroom. Latifa frantically rang Radha Stirling from Detained in Dubai, who said the princess was 'frightened, hiding, [saying] that there were men outside and that she heard gunfire' on the emergency call.

But the two women had to give themselves up, as smoke poured in through the vents. They were captured and dragged to the deck, and, according to Jauhiainen, Latifa was screaming, in English: 'Shoot me here, don't take me back' as she was handed over to Emirati forces, tranquillised and returned to Dubai.

Dubai did not respond to a request for comment. Sheikh Mohammed did not respond, although it is understood he denies having attempted to hack the phones of Latifa or her friends or associates, or ordering others to do so. He has also previously said he feared Latifa was a victim of a kidnapping and that he had conducted 'a rescue mission'.

NSO denies the leaked list of numbers is that of 'Pegasus targets or potential targets' and says the numbers are not related to the company in any way. It said claiming that a name on the list is 'necessarily related to a Pegasus target or potential target is erroneous and false'.

Jauhiainen and Jaubert were released after a short period of detention, with the Finn relocating to London. Latifa was held under house arrest back home, and after a while managed to smuggle out fresh videos to Jauhiainen to tell more about her plight. 'I'm a hostage. I am not free. I'm enslaved in this jail,' she angrily said.

In the past three months there has been a notable change, involving two of the women Latifa tried to message from the boat. In May, Taylor posted a picture on Instagram of Latifa, sitting in a Dubai shopping mall, with her and Bouchiki, to show she was enjoying a degree of freedom at home.

Then, in June, a picture followed of Latifa inside Madrid's main airport, indicating she had been able to travel abroad. 'I hope now that I can live my life in peace without further media scrutiny,' the princess said in a statement released by her lawyers, suggesting after the years of conflict some sort of accommodation with her father had been reached.

With the passage of time, it may never be possible to establish definitively how Latifa was recaptured at gunpoint.

NSO said that the fact that a number appeared on the list was in no way indicative of whether that number was selected for surveillance using Pegasus. It also insists the database has 'no relevance' to the company, saying it may be part of a larger list of numbers that might have been used by NSO Group customers 'for other purposes'.

However, two people familiar with the operations of NSO who spoke individually to the *Guardian* and *Washington Post*, both on the condition of anonymity, said the company had terminated its contract with Dubai within the last year, and that the decision was at least in part the result of an investigation into claims that Dubai had used NSO technology to monitor members of Sheikh Mohammed's family.

As the latest revelations show, new information keeps emerging. A recent report from *USA Today* suggested that Dubai may have prevailed upon the FBI to demand that the US satellite provider KVH hand over location data on an emergency basis. Dubai and the FBI have declined to comment on that report, while KVH said it cooperated with law enforcement 'when compelled or permitted under existing laws'.

Jauhiainen and others who were campaigning for Latifa to be released have previously wondered whether the satellite uplink on the *Nostromo* was as secure as they thought – and it has already proved possible for the BBC to establish the course of the yacht from examining the headers of emails sent from the boat. But the disclosure that Latifa's friends and family are on the Pegasus project database could also prove significant in finding out how she was recaptured on the high seas.

24 July

'Be interested, be curious, hear what's not said': how I learned to really listen to people

ANNALISA BARBIERI

When I was a young girl, a fabulous woman called Pam who lived opposite us would come to do my mum's hair once a week. Pam was a retired hairdresser and beautician who had been taught partly by Vivien Leigh's mother.

I knew this because I listened as she and my mother talked. My mum would sit under the stand hairdryer with wads of cotton wool curling out from under her hairnet to protect her ears from the heat, and Pam would talk and talk: about Margaret Thatcher (my mum wasn't a fan); their early lives (Pam's in Yorkshire, my mum's in Naples); and about life up and down the London street where we all lived.

This arrangement started when I was about eight and continued until I left home aged 22. I would sit at the dining-room table reading the *Woman's Own* problem pages, stealing the biscuits my mum had put out for Pam, all the while observing how, so often, neither woman really listened to the other. My mother would wait for gaps in the conversation so she could say, 'Exactly', and then launch into her own, often unrelated, anecdote. I saw all the information missed like dropped balls: wasted opportunities for further exploration. My father was rarely present at these meets, but on the occasions he was there, he'd raise one eyebrow towards me in a knowing look.

Throughout my teens, I noticed how rarely people asked questions. Over many meals and catchups, I would watch as family members interrupted and road-blocked conversations, sending the chat on a detour that became all about them. We have one well-known culprit in the family: I can count on the fingers of a mitten how often, in the two decades we've known him, he asks anybody anything about themselves. As a child, I lacked the words to explain the way I felt, and was often shut down. Thus observing how not to do it, I resolved to be different.

It was only when I was appointed the *Guardian*'s agony aunt in 2008 that I realised I still had a lot to learn. As part of the process of replying to readers' letters, I would invite specialists (usually therapists) to work with me on compiling the answers. I was greedy for their insights into human behaviour, and soon learned that the basis of every problem I received was communication in some shape or form.

Listening, I discovered, wasn't just about waiting for the other person to stop talking, or asking good questions, or even not interrupting. It was about really hearing what the other person was saying, and *why* they were saying it. Being interested, but also curious. Sometimes that means looking for what's not said, what's left out, which words are used to mask emotions that are hard to acknowledge. Likewise, good listening is about approaching what has been said as if you've never heard it before. Put simply, it's about paying attention.

Listening is a skill that we could all do with sharpening. After all, for the past year, many of us have been conducting friendships and relationships entirely via social media or text message and email. It's not like real life. You don't have to concentrate as much; you can switch off and return to things when you want: it's an intermittent transmit and, you hope, receive. Real-time listening is different. For a new podcast series, I revisited trusted experts who have been part of my column for the last 13 years, asking them to distil their wisdom in a series of intimate conversations. At the core of all of them? The art of listening.

Becoming an advice columnist changed me within a few weeks. Just after starting the job, my eldest went to primary school, and life suddenly got more complicated. She was 'acting up', as the books would put it: being stroppy. I thought I was listening to her, but I was in a panic – I was tired, I was pregnant, and I thought the correct response was to descend into parent cliche mode, saying things such as, 'Don't you speak to me like that' and, 'Who do you think you're talking to?' These weren't phrases I normally used, but I've since learned that, when stressed, we often revert to what we've heard before; what we know. Then I remembered what I'd learned that week, talking to a child psychotherapist: listen to what you can't hear. What might her *actions* be telling me? When I zoned in on those, I realised that school hadn't turned her into a brat (my fear) but that she was worried and anxious.

So instead of berating her, I said: 'It sounds as if you've had a really hard day. Would you like a cuddle?' 'Yes, Mummy,' she said, suddenly soft and less furious as she burst into tears. If you don't listen to children, even when they are being 'difficult', the negative feelings they experience won't go away. They'll just stop bringing them to you.

Just a few weeks later, my daughter was telling me about a problem she had. I was five minutes into a prescriptive list of what she should and shouldn't do, embellished with my own stories to reinforce the points, when I caught her face. She was keen to listen, but I could tell I wasn't giving her what she needed. I remembered another child psychotherapist telling me that children wanted fewer solutions, and more empathy. Recognising and naming a child's feelings (in fact, anyone's) was crucial. 'That sounds like a really hard day,' I said, inwardly thinking how insubstantial it sounded, 'and I can see how sad it's made you.' 'It was!' she said, beaming. 'And I was.' And off she went. Could it really be that simple? Not always, but as a strategy it's more powerful than you think.

The psychotherapist I've spoken to most often for my columns is Chris Mills, a specialist in relationships. I've always been impressed with his ability to hear not simply what I'm saying, but what I can't hear myself (or, in the case of the column, what the reader is saying but hasn't acknowledged). He taught me that allowing a tiny silence after someone has spoken can enable them to say that bit more. Try it: resist saying something immediately after someone has stopped speaking and just do a gentle, mental, count to 10.

But listening is not about remaining resolutely silent. If it goes on too long, silence can make things awkward. The mistake a lot of people make (myself included) is filling the silence with their own anecdotes, offering platitudes or, worse, cliches

('Everything happens for a reason' should be struck from the annals of mankind. Ditto: 'What doesn't kill you makes you stronger'). Offering up the 'Oh, that happened to me/someone I know, too' stories seems empathic, and they do have their place if they're short, reinforcing the point your companion was making before you return to the original subject. But doing this without thought is called 'shifting', because you hijack the conversation and turn it on to you. The other person can feel shut down.

Instead, try supporting them, using responses such as 'That sounds tough', 'How did that make you feel?' or 'What a lot you have on'. I used to think these were lightweight, until once, after a high-stress day during which people tried to be sympathetic but actually offered me lists of what I should do, my Italian cousin simply responded to my text with one word: '*Capisco*' (I understand). I felt seen, heard, understood. Ever since, I've never forgotten the power of the short answer.

In well-worn conversations, often between couples, listening can falter, because you think you've heard it all before ('Oh, not this again'). Learning to listen as if the information is new is useful for hearing things differently and even, perhaps, making progress. Remember: a person saying the same thing over and over again is probably doing so because they don't feel heard.

The way information is delivered can also facilitate how well it's heard. Anger often overshadows detail so it's less about the message than the mode of delivery. If you make someone feel defensive they will rarely hear what you are saying, because little information is traded and certainly no progress is made when both parties are defending their positions. My very first (personal) therapist, the one I went to when I was barely out of my teens, was Gabrielle Rifkind. She's now a non-conflict resolution expert. She taught me how to look at things afresh: it is about letting someone see your vulnerable side, and being receptive enough to allow your conversation partner to do the same. Compassion, it seems, is an ideal listening companion.

Listening, as the psychoanalyst Avi Shmueli taught me, is also about looking beyond catch-all, overused masking words such as 'fine' and 'horrible'. We use these words a lot, but they don't actually describe feelings. Watch out for them in conversation and, if it's appropriate, dig a little deeper. What does your partner mean when they say they've had a horrible day? What are you not saying when you say, 'I'm fine'? What emotions could you replace those words with?

The child and adolescent psychotherapist Rachel Melville-Thomas taught me something else when we recorded a podcast episode called 'The Wonder of the Teenage Brain'. Teenagers interpret neutral faces as negative, she explained, no matter what's coming out of your mouth. With that age group, it's important not only to listen to them in all the ways described above, but to check on what *they've actually heard*. Teenagers also wait until you are busy doing something else to tell you important things – it's done on purpose, so it's not too intense. This is why big subjects can come out when you're not making eye contact – such as when you're driving, walking, or trying to cook dinner.

'This is all very well,' you may be thinking, 'but who is listening to *me*?' I understand this. Not being listened to is to not be seen; after a while you feel stymied, shrunken. Unfortunately, you can't make someone else listen to you. But I have learned that someone repeatedly not listening to you can be a form of control. As a child, I used to make adults look at me by physically moving their chins towards me. It's not socially acceptable to do that as an adult, and, anyway, it's no guarantee of being heard. If you do feel unheard, a good first step is to sit with the other person and say (always use 'I' statements): 'I feel we sometimes miss important details from each other. How do you feel about it?'

So has more than a decade of answering your questions and consulting the very best experts made me the mother of all listeners? Nope. But I do really try. Perhaps the most important thing I've learned is to listen to myself: that inner voice, my instinct, to listen to what I need and how someone makes me feel. I used to think that if I couldn't tell someone they weren't habitually listening to me, it was because I sensed a frailty in them. Mills taught me that, actually, it's about frailty in the relationship itself. That alone was worth hearing.

The good news is that listening is catching. If you feel listened to, it connects you to that other person, and those bonds grow. They, one hopes, will listen to you in turn. It was only after my dad died that I realised just how much he listened to me, and how valuable that was. He never paid me compliments, but he heard me, which is perhaps the greatest compliment of all.

29 JULY

The truth about fast fashion: can you tell how ethical your clothing is by its price?

HANNAH MARRIOTT

What is the true cost of a Zara hoodie? In April 2019, David Hachfeld of the Swiss NGO Public Eye, along with a team of researchers and the Clean Clothes Campaign, attempted to find out. They chose to analyse a black, oversized top from Zara's flagship Join Life sustainability line, which was printed with the Aretha Franklin lyrics 'R-E-S-P-E-C-T: find out what it means to me'. It was an apt choice, because the idea was to work out whether any respect had been paid to the workers involved in the garment's production, and how much of the hoodie's average retail price, €26.66 (£22.70), went into their pockets.

It took several people six months, involved badgering Zara's parent company, Inditex, over email, slowly getting limited information in return, and interviewing dozens of sources on the ground in Izmir, Turkey, where the garment was made. The researchers analysed financial results and trading data, and consulted with experts in pricing and production. It was, Hachfeld says on the phone, with dry understatement, 'quite a huge project'.

Their research suggested that the biggest chunk of the hoodie's retail price – an estimated €10.26 – went back into Zara, to cover retail space and staff wages. The next biggest slice, after VAT at €4.44, was profit for Inditex/Zara, at €4.20. Their research suggested that the textile factory in Izmir received just €1.53 for cutting the material, sewing, packing and attaching the labels, with €1.10 of that being paid to the garment workers for the 30-minute job of putting the hoodie together. The report concluded that workers could not have received anything like a living wage, which the Clean Clothes Campaign defined, at the time the report was released, as a gross hourly wage of €6.19.

When the research was covered by the media at the time, Zara said the report was 'based on erroneous premises and inaccurate reporting', that the €7.76 sourcing price was wrong and that the workers were 'paid more than the amounts mentioned in Public Eye's report'. But at the time and when I contacted Zara for this article, the company declined to set out in greater detail where the research was inaccurate.

It is clear that trying to find out the true production cost of a garment is a tortuous and potentially fruitless process – even when assessing a major high-street retailer's flagship 'sustainability' line.

Hachfeld points out that Zara is by no means uniquely opaque. It is doing more than many clothing brands and has long-term commitments in place to work towards living wages. 'They are launching initiatives and consultations with trade unions. But the question remains: when will they deliver on it?' he says. Vanishingly few retailers guarantee living wages across their vast, complex supply chains. According to the not-for-profit group Fashion Revolution, only two of the world's 250 largest fashion brands (OVS and Patagonia) disclose how many of their workers are paid a living wage – despite the kind of resources that make billionaires of founders. Forbes estimates that Zara's founder, Amancio Ortega, is worth $77 billion (£55 billion) and that H&M's founder, Stefan Persson, is worth $21.3 billion; the *Sunday Times* puts the wealth of Boohoo's co-founder, Mahmud Kamani, at £1.4 billion.

Throughout fashion, the numbers just don't add up. High-street clothing has been getting cheaper and cheaper for decades. A major reason why, according to Gordon Renouf, the CEO of the fashion ethics comparison app Good on You, is that so many western brands have 'moved from onshore production 40 years ago to larger offshore production'. Often, the countries they have chosen have 'much lower wage costs, weaker labour movements and laxer environmental regulations'. Of course, we know all this, but we have also become accustomed to reaping the benefits. Our perception of what clothing should cost – and how much of it we need – has shifted.

In 1970, for example, the average British household spent 7 per cent of its annual income on clothing. This had fallen to 5.9 per cent by 2020. Even though we are spending less proportionally, we tend to own more clothes. According to the UN, the average consumer buys 60 per cent more pieces of clothing – with half the lifespan – than they did 15 years ago. Meanwhile, fashion is getting cheaper: super-rapid brands such as Shein (which sells tie-dye crop tops for £1.49) and Alibaba (vest tops for $2.20) have boomed online, making high-street brands look slow-moving and expensive by comparison.

But the correlation between price and ethics is knotty, to say the least. The conversation about sustainable fashion tends to be dominated by expensive designer brands: at Stella McCartney, for example, a wool-cotton jumper costs £925; at Another Tomorrow, each $520 sustainable viscose carbon-offset scarf-neck blouse features a QR code in the label that outlines every stage of its 'provenance journey'.

On the high street, many who proudly opt out of shopping at Primark or Boohoo for ethical reasons may be unaware that most reassuringly mid-priced brands don't guarantee workers living wages or produce clothing without using environmentally harmful materials. A garment's price is often more about aspiration and customer expectation than the cost of production. Hachfeld points out that the Zara hoodie was priced higher in Switzerland (CHF 45.90; €39.57), where Zara is positioned as a mid-range brand, than in Spain (€25.95), where it is perceived as more mainstream and affordable.

Online, debates about the price of clothing can get heated. The sustainable-fashion writer Aja Barber, for example, uses the phrase 'exploitation prices' to refer to very cheap clothes, such as the 8p bikini offered by the Boohoo brand PrettyLittleThing last autumn. 'Either the company or the garment worker is taking the hit, and most likely it's not the company, because that wouldn't be a profitable business model,' she says.

Barber has a personal threshold in mind when she buys an item. 'Any time a dress is under £50, you really need to break down the labour on it,' she says. 'Think about what you get paid hourly – think, could a person make this dress in three hours?' She doesn't base this calculation on local wages in the global south, either, which are so much lower 'because of years of colonialism and oppression'. She buys new clothes infrequently and tries to avoid polyester, which is made with fossil fuels and generally used in garments to make them cheaper.

Barber gets annoyed by the accusations of snobbery that ripple through social media when anyone criticises super-cheap brands. Largely, she says, these comments come from middle-class people 'who want to participate in the system and not feel bad about it'. In her view, fast fashion is propped up not by those with very low disposable incomes, but by middle-class overconsumption.

The only way to tell if a garment has been ethically produced is by combing through the details on the manufacturer's website (although many give little or no information) and checking out its rating on Good on You, which compares fashion brands on the basis of their impact on the planet, people and animals. Even among brands that have launched with sustainability as their USP, greenwashing is rife. Renouf warns against those that talk vaguely about being 'natural' and 'fair', or bang on about recycled packaging, without giving details about, say, the materials they use or whether they engage with unions in their factories.

For the fashion retailer Sam Mabley, the idea that fashion can be ethical only if it is expensive is a myth. Mabley runs a sustainable fashion store in Bristol; he thought it was a shame that he was selling so many ethical T-shirts at around the £30 price point. Usually, he says, such T-shirts are created in small batches, by 'cool indie brands who do printed designs – a lot of the work is in the design'. He decided to invert that business model, ramping up the scale in order to get bigger discounts from suppliers and creating plain, organic cotton, ethically produced Ts in black and white for £7.99. With just a month of social media promotion, he secured 4,000 orders.

He believes it would be fairly easy for fast-fashion brands to use their buying power to 'drive change for millions of workers around the world' and guarantee their factories paid living wages, without drastically affecting their margins. He is not alone in this view: Jenny Hulme, the head of buying at the sustainable fashion mainstay People Tree, believes ethical production is necessary and possible in every part of the market. 'If you order in big volumes, it does reduce price – if a company really wants to improve, it can,' she says.

The reality of high-street clothes shopping is still very far from this ideal. Apart from a few 'sustainable' lines produced by the big fast-fashion brands – which I am loath to recommend, because of so many accusations of greenwashing – it is almost impossible to find new, ethical clothing at rock-bottom prices, because the business models that have enabled clothing to get this cheap rely on inexpensive, environmentally damaging fabrics and very low wages.

That may leave anyone wanting to dress ethically on a high-street purse feeling out of options. Buying fewer, but better-quality, items is the most consistent advice you will hear from fashion campaigners. 'Buy the best quality that you can afford, perhaps in end-of-season sales or by buying a thick jumper in the middle of summer to wear the next winter,' says Hulme.

Voting with your wallet will only go so far, however, and won't be possible for many people who are struggling, as the number of people in poverty in the UK soars to 15 million. Questioning the magical thinking of rock-bottom prices is not about blaming the consumer. Instead, you could write to MPs and CEOs and demand that they do something about living wages and the environmental cost of fashion. The responsibility lies with brands, and with the government, which should be held to account for a broken system.

5 AUGUST

Love, courage and solidarity: 20 essential lessons young athletes taught us this summer

SIRIN KALE

The Olympics are racing towards the finishing line, the Euros gave us euphoria and heartbreak and Wimbledon revealed that the true hero on Centre Court was not an Adonis in crisp tennis whites, but rather a middle-aged vaccine researcher. More than anything, though, this summer has thrown a spotlight on the inspiring and surprising strength and character of young people like never before.

We have watched elite athletes behave with the sort of dignity and respect that world leaders would do well to emulate. They have competed under intense global scrutiny at the highest levels and never lost sight of the fact that how you behave matters more than the goals you score or the aces you serve. Here are 20 things we learned about youth politics and culture from an astonishing summer of sport.

NAOMI OSAKA PUT MENTAL HEALTH BEFORE TROPHIES

When the 23-year-old pulled out of the French Open, then Wimbledon, to focus on her mental health, Osaka showed the world that elite athletes are people; that we cannot use them like arcade machines. In her Roland Garros withdrawal statement, she wrote that she experienced 'huge waves of anxiety' before interviews and had endured 'long bouts of depression'. Her bravery prompted a groundswell of support from tennis legends, including Martina Navratilova and Billie Jean King. Osaka destigmatised mental health concerns for a generation of athletes. For that, she should be commended.

THE ENGLAND TEAM ENDED THE CULTURE WARS (FOR A FEW WEEKS)

Once a fortnight, the UK collectively loses its mind over flags/ children's books/statues. It is an endless cycle of outrage in which the only winners are chattering pundits and merchants of hate.

When Gareth Southgate announced that England would take the knee before Euro 2020 games, bad-faith provocateurs accused the team of cultural Marxism – because multimillionaire footballers are always on the brink of trying to overthrow capitalism. Southgate, with characteristic decency, backed his players, explaining that they had 'a responsibility to the wider community' to use their voices on 'matters such as equality, inclusivity and racial injustice'.

With this, Southgate and his team helped to define a patriotism that is not boorish or rooted in rose-tinted nostalgia, but rather focused on trying your best for your country and giving back to your community.

This young, diverse team did not shy away from defending these principles. When Priti Patel condemned the racist abuse of Bukayo Saka, Marcus Rashford and Jadon Sancho after they missed penalties in the final, their teammate Tyrone Mings accused the home secretary of 'stoking the fire' by refusing to condemn those who had booed players taking the knee. His comments prompted much soulsearching among Conservative MPs, with Johnny Mercer and Steve Baker suggesting that the Tories needed to rethink their attitude to the gesture.

A squad of footballers – two of them teenagers – ended the culture wars (albeit temporarily). For that, we should be grateful.

THE DANES PROTECTED THE DIGNITY OF THEIR TEAMMATE

Christian Eriksen's cardiac arrest during Denmark's game against Finland was horrifying to witness: the hush descending as fans realised the gravity of the situation; the sight of his panicked partner. But the way Eriksen's teammates formed a human shield around their fallen friend, preserving his privacy while medics worked successfully to resuscitate him, was a spontaneous and heartfelt gesture of dignity – even as the cameras refused to cut away.

KYE WHYTE HAD BETHANY SHRIEVER'S BACK

With UK Sport no longer funding female BMXers, Bethany Shriever had to crowdfund even to qualify for Tokyo 2020. Nonetheless, she stormed her way to Team GB's first ever gold medal in BMX racing. Her friend and fellow Team GB BMXer Kye Whyte, who won the UK's first ever silver medal, was cheering her all the way. After Shriever crossed the finishing line, she collapsed with agonising leg cramps – so Whyte scooped her up and held her aloft, as triumphantly as she deserved. Did you have something in your eye? Me too.

MASON MOUNT MADE A LITTLE GIRL'S DREAM COME TRUE

A glow settled over England when Mason Mount spotted a young girl in the crowd after England's semi-final win over Denmark, climbed into the stands and handed her his shirt. She collapsed in ecstatic squeals while the spectators around her cheered. Properly heartwarming.

ENGLAND'S FOOTBALLERS REMINDED US THAT THE GAME IS FOR EVERYONE

From Harry Kane's rainbow armband – showing solidarity with LGBTQ+ people – to Jordan Henderson's tweet supporting a non-binary, queer fan who attended an England game in makeup, the conduct of the Three Lions this summer showed that football is for everyone – not just the beer-guzzlers and bum-flarers (look it up, if you must).

THE HIGH JUMPERS SHARED GOLD – AND HISTORY

The Olympics is not just about medals, but also, as the Games' charter puts it, 'friendship, solidarity and fair play'. Qatar's Mutaz Essa Barshim and Italy's Gianmarco Tamberi embodied this spirit after tying in an exhausting two-hour high jump final. They were offered the opportunity to have a jump-off. Instead, Barshim asked an official if they could have two golds. If you agree to share, came the response. 'History, my friend,' said Barshim, shaking Tamberi's hand. It was a joyous example of sportsmanship at its best.

KALVIN PHILLIPS RUSHED TO CONSOLE BUKAYO SAKA

Penalties are organised cruelty at the best of times, but during an international final they can feel positively medieval. After Saka missed the tournament-deciding penalty in the Euros final, the Italian team flooded past in glee. Saka was distraught, choking back tears. All alone, he looked like the teenager he was. Then Kalvin Phillips – a man who had just run for two hours straight – bolted towards his teammate and pulled him into a tight hug. In that embrace, Phillips reminded us that the best athletes have heart.

THE IRISH OLYMPIC TEAM SHOWED THEIR CLASS

The Irish consistently show up the British – in drinking ability, accents and devotion to the craic. At Tokyo 2020, they added manners, stopping to bow to their Japanese hosts as a token of respect during the opening ceremony. It was a gracious, Olympic-spirited move.

MARCUS RASHFORD WAS ... MARCUS RASHFORD

Marcus Rashford is not only a national hero but a national leader. At just 23, he has forced the government into two U-turns on free school meals, launched a nationwide reading initiative – and somehow found time to play for England and Manchester United.

What makes Rashford so remarkable is how he uses his experiences of growing up in a low-income household to destigmatise and advocate for such children today. He represents the very best of this new generation of principled athletes: never self-aggrandising, always quietly determined to use his platform for good.

TOM DALEY WEPT BEAUTIFUL TEARS OF JOY ...

Those two fat teardrops on Tom Daley's cheeks after he and Matty Lee took gold in the men's synchronised 10-metre platform dive represented the culmination of a lifetime's work. Hours training in the pool beside his beloved father. The bullying at school. The struggle of coming out. The heartbreak of his father's death before Daley won his first Olympic medal. His disappointing finish at the 2011 world championship. Crashing out of the 10-metre semi-finals in Rio in 2016. And then coming back from it all, to win the gold he had coveted his entire career. They spoke volumes.

... AND SHOWED US THE TRUE MEANING OF PRIDE ...

Daley has redefined what it means to be a man in sport, speaking about his sexuality with openness and sincerity. After taking gold, he spoke movingly about this. 'When I was younger, I always felt like the one who was alone and different and didn't fit ... I hope that any young LGBT person out there can see, no matter how alone you feel right now, you are not alone,' he said. 'You can achieve anything.' Thanks to trailblazers such as Daley, this has been a 'rainbow Olympics', with at least 172 LGBTQ+ athletes competing in Tokyo, more than three times as many as in Rio. Afterwards, he said he wanted to embrace his son and husband – and suddenly his tears were catching.

... AND BECAME A KNITTING ICON

Not content with being an LGBTQ+ Olympic champion with the torso of a mountain range, Daley also knits. At the women's springboard finals, he was serenely creating what looked like a purple scarf. At another event, it was a Team GB cardigan. On social media, Daley has shown off: a pouch for his gold medal, a cat couch, a doggie jumper and, best of all, a tiny Bernie Sanders. Daley's knitting reminds us why he is a hero of British sport – because he is utterly unafraid to be himself.

RUBY TUI ANNOUNCED HERSELF

The New Zealand rugby player is a charisma atom bomb. So under the radar that she doesn't have a Wikipedia page, Tui became a viral sensation after being pulled aside for a post-match interview after a stunning 36–0 defeat of Russia. After thanking her village, her family and God in Samoan, Tui grinned her way through the most charming, feel-great interview of the Games, congratulating her opponents on a well-fought fight, describing the Russians as 'really cool people, man', and revealing that her team had donated to the British team's fundraising efforts. Tui represents pure Olympic vibes: respecting your opponent, loving the sport and having a laugh.

Simone Biles showed that mental and physical health are the same thing ...

Simone Biles, widely acknowledged as the greatest female gymnast ever, arrived at Tokyo 2020 with the weight of the world on her shoulders. Commentators were predicting a clean sweep for the first woman to land a Yurchenko double pike.

But things began to go wrong in qualifying. They fell apart when she stepped out of bounds during her floor routine, then aborted her vault in mid-air during the women's team finals, narrowly avoiding serious injury and scoring one of the lowest marks of her career. Biles subsequently pulled out of the women's all-around and the women's team event, explaining that she had lost her air-awareness – a phenomenon known as the 'twisties' – and was struggling with her mental health.

She later said it 'sucked' not to be able to compete when she had spent the past half-decade preparing. But she explained that she had been inspired to talk about her mental health by watching Osaka and that she had quit to protect her 'mind and body'.

Some armchair experts would have preferred Biles to risk her neck for their viewing pleasure. But, overwhelmingly, the reaction was compassionate and supportive. Biles showed us that mental and physical health are connected – and that there is no shame in quitting to prioritise your wellbeing.

... and what it means to be resilient

Even as she struggled, Biles showed up to support her US gymnastics teammates, whooping and shouting from the sidelines. 'I'm proud of how the girls stepped up,' Biles told reporters. It was no less than we now expect from Biles, who has overcome incredible personal adversity (she was in foster care before being adopted by her grandparents) and trauma (she is a survivor of sexual abuse by the US team's former doctor Larry Nassar) to become one of the greatest athletes of her generation. After a week of nonstop speculation about whether she would pull out of the Games entirely, she took bronze on the balance beam. That single medal showed her deep resilience more than her embarrassment of golds.

NORWEGIAN WOMEN TAKE ZERO SEXIST NONSENSE

It is 2021, but still we expect female athletes to dress to titillate audiences. After campaigning to no avail for an astonishing 15 years to be allowed to wear shorts, the Norwegian women's beach handball team decided: enough. They went thigh-length, like their male peers, at the European championship in July to protest against the sexist dress code – and were fined €1,500 (£1,295). But the world – and the pop star Pink – was with them. She offered to pay their fine – and the officials of the sport's governing body looked like regressive dinosaurs.

ENGLAND'S FOOTBALLERS SHOWED WHAT IT MEANS TO BE ACCOUNTABLE

We live in the age of the political non-apology – which is why the astonishing statements put out by Saka, Sancho and Rashford after their missed penalties during the Euro 2020 final were stunning to behold. 'I would like to say sorry to all my teammates, coaching staff and most of all the fans who I let down,' Sancho wrote. Here were three young men apologising fully (even though they didn't need to), taking accountability and promising to work harder – all after coping with vile racist trolling online.

CHARLOTTE WORTHINGTON SHOWED US WHAT BRAVERY LOOKS LIKE

Charlotte Worthington had to work 40-hour weeks in a Mexican restaurant to support her biking career, competing during annual leave. Fast-forward to Tokyo 2020 and she tried a ground-breaking 360-degree backflip – but came off her bike. If she had completed it, she would have been the first woman to do it in an international competition. But Worthington took the risk, tried again – and nailed it. For these unbelievable levels of bravery and self-belief, she took gold.

Sky Brown became Britain's youngest Olympic medallist

A tiny, gravity-defiant, flying figure: at 13 years old, Britain's youngest-ever Olympian took bronze in the women's skateboarding. Tony Hawk has called her 'one of the best well-rounded skaters ever'. Sky Brown has the maturity of a competitor thrice her age – and the fearlessness of a babe of two. Refreshingly, there are no pushy parents or brutalising coaches in the background. Instead, Brown exemplifies the spirit of a new cohort of gen Z athletes: wildly talented and competing for the joy of the sport.

8 August

'If you talk, you live well': the remote Sardinian village with eight centenarians

ANGELA GIUFFRIDA

If there's one thing the remote mountain settlement of Perdasde-fogu ensures it always has a supply of, it's birthday candles. This year, 500 have been needed to decorate the birthday cakes of five residents who turned 100.

Each milestone usually means a celebration involving the entire town. The mayor, Mariano Carta, presents a medal to the centenarian. 'Whenever a citizen celebrates a 100th birthday, it feels as if I have a piece of history in front of me, a living monument,' he said. 'Here are people who tell small stories that are entwined with a bigger story. I feel very lucky.'

Some of that history is reflected in the 16 photos of centenarians that line the walls on either side of the town's main thoroughfare. There is Vittorio Palmas, who survived the Bergen-Belsen concentration camp during the second world war and died in 2019, aged 105.

There is also a mural dedicated to the town's longest-lived citizen to date – Consolata Melis, who died in 2015, aged 108.

Consolata was the eldest in a family of nine brothers and sisters who shot to fame in 2012 after entering the *Guinness World Records* as the oldest living siblings on the planet, with a combined age at the time of 818. Her sister, Claudina, died in 2016, aged 103, followed by Maria, who died at 100, and Antonio at 97. Another of the siblings, Concetta, turned 100 in February. A stone block at the entrance to Perdasdefogu, tucked high up in the rugged mountains of south-eastern Sardinia and accessible only by a narrow, winding road, celebrates the Melis siblings with the message: 'Perdasdefogu, world record for family longevity.'

The next of the siblings hoping to become a centenarian is 98-year-old Adolfo. The three youngest in the family – Vitalio, 90; Fida, 89, and Mafalda, who at 87 is called 'the baby' – live in the Sardinian capital of Cagliari. Their parents were Francesco Melis, who served during the first world war, and Eleonora Mameli, who was awarded a medal from Benito Mussolini's fascist government in 1939 for giving birth to so many children – 11 in total; two didn't make it to adulthood.

But the longevity streak is not limited to the Melis family. Perdasdefogu is currently home to eight centenarians – four men and four women – in a population of 1,740. Ten more citizens could turn 100 within the next couple of years. Across Italy, the number of people living to 100 or more is rising fast. As of 1 January 2021, there were 17,935 centenarians, up from 14,456 in 2019 and 11,000 in 2009, according to figures from Istat, the national statistics agency. Sardinia has been identified as one of five regions in the world with high concentrations of centenarians – it has 534, or 33.6 for every 100,000 inhabitants. The number of centenarians in Perdasdefogu is 13 times the national average for a town its size.

'There is of course the fresh air and the good food, but I believe one of the reasons for their longevity is their approach to stress,' said Luisa Salaris, a demographics professor at the University of Cagliari. 'They were born 100 years ago and certainly didn't have an easy life – there would have been hunger and war. But they are people who have managed to adapt – if there's a problem, they solve it quickly.'

Adolfo Melis, who worked on farms in his younger years, is convinced the main reason is diet. Food was scarce – a year before Consolata was born, there were protests against food shortages in Perdasdefogu – but their father was the first in the town to create a vegetable garden. 'Everything we ate came from the garden,' he said. 'What you put into your stomach is so important – if you abuse the stomach, it doesn't resist.' There is plenty of meat, as well as some fish (the sea is about an hour's drive away), but the trick was to 'eat little, but genuine food', he added.

At 102, Bonino Lai is still president of the town's football team. He lives with his wife, Elena, and one of his two daughters in a modest apartment. The ex-office worker said it is the simple activities that keep him going. 'Reading, walking, playing cards … the simple things are the best.'

Perdasdefogu is remote and most of the population elderly, but that doesn't mean the town is not lively. It hosts several cultural events, including a literary festival. Books are locally believed to be the key to longevity. Next to the photo of Palmas, holding a copy of Gabriel García Márquez's *One Hundred Years of Solitude*, is a sign that says: 'Reading keeps you alive.'

The literary festival is organised by Giacomo Mameli, a distant cousin of the Melis siblings. At the most recent event in July, Antonio Brundu, 103, was in the front row to listen to a discussion with Jonathan Hopkin, a politics professor at the London School of Economics. Other elderly people are equally active – Vittorio Lai, 99, still drives and hunts for wild boar.

'Our environmental conditions play a crucial role,' said Mameli. 'We live in a place where the air is clean. Our centenarians were in continuous movement in a healthy environment.

'Another important factor is that Perdasdefogu conserves the sense of community. The elderly still live at home and not in care homes. [It's] so important because if you have good social contacts, you remember, talk and evaluate ... you live well.'

9 AUGUST

IPCC report's verdict on climate crimes of humanity: guilty as hell

DAMIAN CARRINGTON

As a verdict on the climate crimes of humanity, the Intergovernmental Panel on Climate Change report could not be clearer: guilty as hell. The repeatedly ignored warnings of scientists over decades have now become reality. Humanity, through its actions, or lack of action, has unequivocally overheated the planet. Nowhere is escaping rising temperatures, worse floods, hotter wildfires or more searing droughts.

The future looks worse. 'If we do not halt our emissions soon, our future climate could well become some kind of hell on Earth,' says Prof Tim Palmer at the University of Oxford. This would be the sentence for these climate crimes, but it has yet to be passed down. The world can avoid the harshest punishment, but only just. Repentance is required in the form of immediate and deep emissions cuts.

The key aspect of the IPCC report is that the 42-page summary is agreed, line by line, by every government, with the scientists vetoing any politically convenient but unscientific proposal.

Governments that continue to fail to take action have nowhere left to hide. 'Too many "net zero" climate plans have been used to greenwash pollution and "business as usual",' says Teresa Anderson at ActionAid International.

The report exposes such plans with its stark statement that immediate action is the only way to avoid ever-worsening impacts. The action required is known and the IPCC report must be the spur for it to be taken, says António Guterres, the UN secretary general: 'This report must sound a death knell for coal and fossil fuels, before they destroy our planet. If we combine forces now, we can avert climate catastrophe. But, as the report makes clear, there is no time for delay and no room for excuses.'

Helen Clarkson, the CEO of the Climate Group, which represents 220 regional governments and 300 multinational businesses, covering 1.75 billion people and 50 per cent of the global economy, says: 'Every decision, every investment, every target, needs to have the climate at its core.'

The gravity of the situation laid out in the report blows away blustering over the supposed costs of climate action. 'It's suicidal and economically irrational to keep procrastinating,' says Prof Saleemul Huq, the director of the International Centre for Climate Change and Development.

For those governments and businesses that still chose inaction, the IPCC report may well end up being used as key evidence against them. 'We'll be taking this report with us to the courts,' says Kaisa Kosonen at Greenpeace. 'By strengthening the scientific evidence between human emissions and extreme weather the IPCC has provided new, powerful means to hold the fossil fuel industry and governments directly responsible for the climate emergency.'

Hope remains. Christiana Figueres, who was the UN climate chief when the Paris deal was sealed in 2015, says: 'Everything we need to avoid the exponential impacts of climate change is doable. But it depends on solutions moving exponentially faster than impacts.'

Political leaders are in the dock and the UN COP26 summit in Glasgow in November may be the last hearing at which they can avoid history's judgment.

10 AUGUST

The reform of prisons has been my life's work, but they are still utterly broken

FRANCES CROOK

Nobody really cares about prisons. They're so far removed from the experience of most people and are, apparently, full of horrid people. Occasionally the media will run stories about rat-infested cells or suicide rates, but because so few people have anything to do with prisons, the stories quickly fade and life for those on the outside continues as normal.

But prisons matter. It matters who goes into them. It matters what happens inside them. And it matters how much they cost. Although prisons too often function like black holes into which society banishes those it deems problematic, the state of our prisons tells a story about all of us. Prisons reflect society back to itself: they embody the ways we have failed, the people we have failed, and the policies that have failed, all at immense human – and economic – cost.

As chief executive of the prison reform charity the Howard League for the past 35 years, reforming prisons has become my life's mission. In October, I will leave my work with one sad but inescapable conclusion: prisons are the last unreformed public service, stuck in the same cycle of misery and futility as when I arrived.

If a time traveller from 100 years ago walked into a prison today – whether one of the inner-city Victorian prisons or a new-build – the similarities would trump the differences. They would recognise the smells and the sounds, the lack of activity and probably some of the staff. It is not only the buildings that have stayed the same, it is the whole ethos of the institution.

Prison is an unhealthy place. Most prisoners have come from poverty, addiction and social deprivation cemented by decades of failed social policy. Many arrive with long-term health problems, and in prison their health deteriorates further. While life expectancy and the quality of life for much of the country has advanced significantly in the past three decades, prisoners are considered 'old' at 50. In the 12 months to June 2021, 396 people died in prison custody – some from Covid, some from suicide, many from 'natural causes' that few of us on the outside would consider natural in middle age.

Even before prisons were locked down during the pandemic, it was normal for men – who make up 95 per cent of the prison population – to spend almost all day in their cells. Wing-cleaning or an education class might occupy a few hours on a weekday. A shower every few days might offer brief respite. Men spend the day, and sleep, in ill-fitting, saggy prison uniforms, unwashed for days on end, waiting to be released.

Mealtimes provide structure, but not sustenance. Breakfast is a pack of white bread, a small bag of cereal and a small carton of milk, provided the evening before. (Inevitably, it is consumed that night.) They wake hungry, and are without food until lunch at about 11am – usually a small, soggy baguette, a packet of crisps and an apple, if they're lucky. One hot meal comes with stodge and vegetables cooked beyond the point of identification at about 5pm.

The sheer monotony of life inside does nothing for the mental health challenges many prisoners face. Addictions worsen, with drugs readily available across the nation's prison estate. Lockdown may have ended what little human contact prisoners had with the outside world, but it did nothing to stem the flow of narcotics. On release, many face homelessness and joblessness. The people we step over in the street, for whom we sometimes buy a sandwich or a cup of coffee, are often people recently released from prison. It is hardly surprising that about half of those released are reconvicted of a further offence and end up back inside. It is a merry-go-round but without cheer.

Minister after minister has done nothing to address the central question haunting our prison system: what is it all for? Each new secretary of state arrives with a new idea – improving a handful of prisons, building a few new ones – and millions of pounds are duly splurged on the latest fad. But it does not face up to the problem that is the prison system as a whole.

At the heart of prisons is the fact that they are fundamentally unjust. They embed and compound social, economic and health inequalities. They disproportionately suck in men from poor, Black and minority ethnic backgrounds. We only have to look at the internal punishment system to see that unfairness is the name of the game, with Black people significantly more likely to be physically restrained and punished than their white counterparts.

The whole system needs radical overhaul, starting with a swingeing reduction in the number of people we imprison. Custody is the most drastic and severe response the state has at its disposal and should be used only in exceptional and rare instances – either for the most egregious crimes, or when someone poses a serious and continuing threat to public safety.

Abiding by that principle would virtually empty our prisons of women and children, and drastically reduce the number of men behind bars. Most women are either on remand or serving a short sentence. Many are survivors of domestic abuse. Vanishingly few have committed violent crimes that warrant incarceration; fewer still could be reasonably considered to pose an ongoing threat to society.

Along with the 500 children who are currently incarcerated, they should be managed in the community by specialist local authority-run services which provide the support, rehabilitation and education that will save them from further imprisonment. Thousands of men would benefit from similar support, whether that's community addiction services, decent housing or mental health facilities. The number of people in prison in England and Wales today sits at 78,600. That number should plummet – and swiftly. Margaret Thatcher, no softie on criminal justice, managed with less than half that number of prisoners.

A shrunken estate could be transformed so that prisons become places of purpose where people receive holistic support, quality care, meaningful skills and education, in an environment that is as similar as possible to the society that they will eventually re-enter.

Over the past 35 years, I hope that I have contributed to making things just a bit better. I am most proud of the work we have done with police forces to reduce the arrests of young people, saving hundreds of thousands of children from experiencing the trauma and lifelong damage of being arrested. But the state of our prison system – the leviathan that continues to devour lives and resources and contaminates political discourse – remains my most bitter regret. It does not have to be like this.

11 AUGUST

What has life taught me about exams? It's hard work, not grades, that really matter

ADRIAN CHILES

'I'll give you two separate marks for your work,' said many school-teachers to all of us at some stage. 'The first one will be for effort and the second will be for attainment. The one for how hard you work is more important than the one for how good the work is.' We would all think, 'Yeah, whatever,' or whichever phrase conveyed the requisite cynicism when we were at school. I was nearly 50 before it dawned on me what truth those teachers spoke.

The revelation came exactly five years ago, on the day my eldest daughter's GCSE results came out. On the way to get them I felt unusually relaxed. I wasn't sure why this was as I'm rarely relaxed about anything. If there's 1 per cent jeopardy in any given situation, I'll generally give it my fiercest focus. She had put a lot of work in and plainly cared about how well she had done, so why wasn't I on tenterhooks for her? It certainly wasn't because I thought great grades were in the bag, because I know life sometimes isn't fair.

Parked outside the school, I overheard a mother talking about her son's A-level results. 'He's a lucky bastard,' she said. 'He did no work, spent most of the time smoking dope and getting into trouble, and somehow he got four As.' While she couldn't completely disguise her pride, neither was she especially delighted. And quite right, too, because in my experience these are the types who can struggle in life. They're the kids who breeze through school, apparently without expending any significant time or effort on their studies, and yet always come through with flying colours. For added irritation they may well also be captains of sports teams, leads in school productions, prolific lovers and nailed-on choices for head boy or girl.

Without any great degree of schadenfreude (honestly!), I've noticed the problems that can ensue for them. I think it's because what they take from the effortless excellence they have enjoyed in their schooldays is an assumption that they can breeze through life just as easily. When this turns out not to be the case, it's a nasty surprise they're often not equipped to deal with. Winging it works for a while, but sooner or later they find themselves flying at lower and lower levels and perhaps even crashing completely.

Through work, I've been lucky enough to meet many people who are highly successful in all sorts of fields. Be it in sport, media, entertainment, business or politics, they have one thing in common: they all had to work incredibly hard for long periods of time. They got up early and went to bed late, often exhausted and not infrequently demoralised. They took orders from people they didn't rate or like but just had to nod and carry on. They ground it out. School can help teach you these skills, but not so much if you happen to be one of the gifted lucky ones who never had cause to work particularly hard. It's a hard habit to pick up – a new mindset entirely – if you've not had use for it in your formative years.

If I was in charge of hiring young people, I swear I would go for someone who worked their backsides off for three C grades over someone who never lifted a finger for their three A*s. Sadly, though, until someone decides to put grades for effort in brackets next to the actual results, it's going to be hard to find out who the grafters are.

So that, I realised, was why I wasn't as nervous for my daughter's GCSE results as I might have been: she had already demonstrated the key thing she would need to get on – a capacity for hard work. As it happened, she did really well. I suppose if she hadn't done well, then the challenge would have been to dissuade her from concluding that hard work doesn't pay after all. I may or may not have won that argument, but I would still have been pretty sure that she would do well in the end.

18 AUGUST

'We kept on hearing gunshots': my chaotic escape from Kabul's airport

RAMIN RAHMAN

The day the Taliban took over started with a call from my friend in Germany. He told me to get to the airport because there was potentially going to be a German embassy evacuation plane leaving that day. He had put my name on their evacuation list because I had worked for the German media, and I had been in the process of applying for a visa for the past year.

I didn't have time to think. It felt like a lifeline for me as a progressive, outspoken journalist with tattoos – basically the antithesis of what the Taliban stand for. I took my laptop and phone and nothing else. I felt scared the minute I left my home – I'd never felt so much pressure.

When I reached the airport, the initial checkpoint was eerie. The police had left, and the military was almost all gone. There was only private airport security checking bags. I didn't have a visa, so I was scared of being turned away – but I couldn't turn back.

When I reached the international terminal, I was shocked at what I saw, and I started to feel hopeless. There were thousands of people: women and men with their crying babies. They were fearful that the Taliban were coming. All these people, including foreigners, went to the airport not knowing what would happen.

The people all around me were panicking as they realised there might not be a plane for them. Even if they had tickets there was uncertainty around whether their flight would take off. They were frightened. So people started to damage the airport – windows and ticket booths. And from there the situation just continued to get worse.

I hid in a corner, even though I was also panicking. Looking out the window, I watched a whole scene unravel around an aircraft trying to leave for Turkey. People were streaming into the plane, and even hanging from the stairs. The aircraft was over capacity, and people were being pushed off the stairs so the plane could take off.

They were screaming so loud that we could hear them from inside the airport. 'We want to go, or we will die,' some shouted. I just watched in horror as I waited, pondering my fate. At around 8.30 or 9 in the evening someone shouted that the Taliban were inside the airport. People started screaming and running outside on to the tarmac. The airport was in utter chaos with nobody to control the situation. I heard firing outside the airport door. I kept thinking that the Taliban had arrived.

Everyone around me was scared and praying for the best. Nobody knew what to do. I called my friend in Germany again, and he said that the Germans would not start evacuations until the next day. This was terrible news, and I knew that I had to figure out what to do next.

I saw American troops leading a small group of people on to the military section of the tarmac. One of the soldiers told a group of foreigners: 'This is American soil and the Taliban will not come here.' I started to run after them with crowds of others. We kept on hearing gunshots, which felt so terrifyingly close.

In the next few moments, I felt like time had stopped. All I heard were the Americans saying: 'Let's go!'

I saw a stream of people getting on to a plane, and I followed. It was all I could do at the moment. I was rushed on to the plane, which had hundreds of people onboard. There was no room to sit – everyone was standing. People were clutching each other and their children. I couldn't breathe.

The American pilots were screaming that the plane could not go anywhere because there were too many people onboard. One of them shouted: 'Please get out, please get out!' Then soldiers came and started pulling people out from both the front and back doors. I was in the middle.

It was chaotic, uncomfortable and stressful. People were pushing and there was no air. The entire scene was so hopeless, sad and scary. I looked at the mothers with newborns around me, and I felt so guilty. I decided to get off so the plane could take off.

But as I made my way towards the door to get off, I saw American troops circling the plane in Humvees. One of the soldiers told me to stay put because there were perceived threats. Another 20 minutes passed. Then suddenly, the Americans told those of us standing around the door to get in the plane. This was the only chance. We rushed into the plane, and they closed the doors.

I couldn't see out because there were no windows, but in my head, they had started fighting outside. The plane remained on standby for an hour. All these different thoughts went through my head of what could happen next.

And then, without warning, the plane started moving. It started flying. We took off.

It was one of the happiest moments. Everyone was clapping and cheering. There was a feeling of appreciation for the American pilot who took off. There was a general sentiment in the air that we probably would have died if that plane had not come. But the flight was challenging. There were many babies onboard, and parents were holding them above their heads to ensure they would not be stepped on. There was no food, water or breathing room for hours.

We landed in Qatar at the US air base, and we have been transferred to a military base. When we arrived, I felt several emotions – happiness, sadness, confusion, exhaustion and frustration. I have tried to help people who could not speak English to explain their situations and get medicine.

I took a chance to change my life from what could be a very terrible situation. I am just looking forward to the next steps and what will come. I'm sad that I left everything. I'm sad for Afghanistan. But I'm so happy that I'm alive.

Ramin Rahman was interviewed by Robyn Huang.

3 SEPTEMBER

'Everything has vanished': For Afghan women, bad days are back

EMMA GRAHAM-HARRISON AND AKHTAR MOHAMMAD MAKOII

When Taliban fighters moved into Herat city in western Afghanistan last month, one thing mattered more to some of them than the battle itself. As gunmen faced off around the governor's office, militants came to Shogofa's workplace and ordered all the women home. 'They hadn't even taken all the city, but they came to our headquarters. The manager called an emergency meeting and they told the women to leave,' she said.

As the main breadwinner for her widowed mother and disabled brother, losing her job means destitution. So on Thursday she decided to publicly challenge Afghanistan's new rulers. With 40 or 50 other women, she walked to the seat of city government chanting 'no fear, we are united'.

'We hoped we could tell the governor how we are struggling, but they let us stand there for some time then removed us. We couldn't even meet him,' she said.

Since seizing Afghanistan, Taliban spokesmen and officials have promised to respect women's rights to work and education, albeit in an Islamic framework they refuse to define. These pledges have led to a discussion about how much the Taliban have changed since they ruled with an extreme misogyny in the 1990s, barring women from almost all work and education.

There have been calls from abroad to give the group time to form a government and lay out its policy before pressing too hard. But there is increasing evidence from on the ground across Afghanistan that the biggest changes may be in messaging, rather than ideology.

Women protesting in Herat had been stripped of their jobs two weeks ago; reports from elsewhere include gunmen ordering bank tellers out of their jobs in Kandahar.

The Taliban have asked most women to stay home, claiming it is a temporary measure for 'security reasons', but that explanation has an ominous ring to Afghan women whose memories stretch back to the last time the group held power.

'We heard some of these explanations in 1996 to 2001, when the Taliban said the reason girls couldn't study and women couldn't work was because the security situation wasn't good, and once the security situation was better they could go back. Of course that moment never arrived,' said Heather Barr, associate director of the women's rights division at Human Rights Watch. 'This indicates that even in the 1990s the Taliban felt the need to disguise some of their misogyny.'

Other rules from that time that have resurfaced unofficially, according to accounts from Afghan women, include a requirement for a male guardian, or *mahram*, to accompany them in public spaces.

Bano, another protester in Herat, works in healthcare, one sector where the Taliban have called on women to come back to their jobs, but says she was ordered home for commuting alone. Her husband, a soldier, has been missing in action for three years and with no adult sons or brothers nearby, she has no one to fill this role. She has been sole breadwinner for three children since her husband disappeared and she is getting desperate. 'I am borrowing money from my friends and relatives in the city. We cannot go on like this.'

In education too there are clear signs that women will face extensive and damaging exclusion, even if restrictions do not go as far as the total ban of the 1990s.

The new higher education minister says women and men must be separated at universities, and the historical consequences of such services within a discriminatory system strongly suggest women will be pushed out or get a lower quality education.

A labyrinthine new decree to private universities, seen by the *Guardian*, lays out a long list of rules to prevent male and female students even glimpsing each other's faces. Women must be transported in buses with covered windows and a curtain separating them from the driver. They must stay in 'waiting rooms' before and between classes, and female students and teachers must dress in black. All new classes must be segregated, and in current classes with fewer than 15 women, a 'sharia partition' must be erected to keep men and women apart. Ideally, teachers too will be separated by gender, the rules say.

Some women have already given up on their education. 'I'm scared of their rules and I'm concerned to lose my life for no reason under their control,' said one student, who lived in a hostel while studying in Kabul. 'I had a plan to accelerate my studies and take more classes. I went to the gym after university. I had a plan to launch a small business for myself in Kabul but everything vanished in a matter of hours. Words cannot describe my current depression.'

All names have been changed.

13 SEPTEMBER

The rise of Raducanu: What next for tennis's new star?

SEAN INGLE

Most fledging British stars spend years trying to crack America. Emma Raducanu did it in three giddy weeks. And such was the skill and scale of her first grand slam victory – which ended with her blitzing an ace before collapsing and rubbing her eyes, as if to make sure she was not in some impossible dream – it felt natural to immediately speculate where it ranked in the pantheon of the nation's great sporting triumphs.

High, for sure. Perhaps even highest of all. Certainly for an individual. After all, never in tennis history has anyone fought through three qualifying rounds of a grand slam before winning the tournament. Let alone an 18-year-old rated as a 400-1 outsider. And she did it at the US Open without dropping a set. If a young writer dared pitch such a script to Hollywood, it would have been fastballed into the nearest bin.

Yet it was all true. The $2.5 million (£1.8 million) prize. The praise from legends such as Martina Navratilova. The peak TV audience of 9.2 million Britons willing her on to her 6–4 6–3 victory over the Canadian Leylah Fernandez. Even a message from the Queen, one ER congratulating another. 'I don't feel any pressure,' Raducanu said afterwards, with a conviction that was as startling as her stunning tennis. 'I'm still only 18 years old. I'm just having a free swing at anything that comes my way.'

Later, with a natural ease, she joked that her first goal at the US Open had been to earn enough money to replace her lost Airpods. Now, though, her sights are being recalibrated. The PR guru Mark Borkowski, who has worked with Michael Jackson and Led Zeppelin, reckons Raducanu has the talent and charisma to be Britain's first billion-dollar sports star.

'This is the start of something epic,' he said. 'She is a billion-dollar girl, no doubt about it. She is the real deal. It's not just that she plays extraordinary tennis, it's also her background, her ethnicity, her freedom of spirit. People also love the fact that she is vulnerable, but laughs the pressures away.'

Forbes noted that another tennis player, Naomi Osaka, the world's highest paid female athlete, made $60 million in 2020 – $55 million of which came from corporate sponsors. Raducanu has Max Eisenbud, who guided Maria Sharapova, in her corner. And the fact that Raducanu, who was born in Canada to parents from Romania and China, can speak Mandarin will not hurt. After her win she used her second language when speaking to the US Open official Weibo site to thank the Chinese public for their support.

Remarkably it is only three months since she made her WTA Tour debut at the Nottingham Open in June, losing in the first round. It is barely two months since she retired during a fourth-round match at Wimbledon with breathing difficulties. Afterwards a succession of middle-aged men, including the TV presenter Piers Morgan, suggested she couldn't cut it. But she could. And how.

'Nobody does it this fast, this well,' said Navratilova. 'Her rise has been beyond meteoric. I have never seen it before, that is the truth.' And while it has been a stunning year for British sport, thanks to the Olympics and Euro 2020, nothing compares to Raducanu. No wonder she is the overwhelming favourite to be the BBC's Sports Personality of the Year. She would have to shoot Bambi to not win.

Her emergence also comes at the perfect time. With Roger Federer and Serena Williams turning 40 and Rafael Nadal and Novak Djokovic in their mid 30s, tennis needs fresh heroes. And in Raducanu, bright enough to gain an A in A-level maths and an A* in economics, but normal enough to appeal to almost everyone, it has the perfect candidate. Unsurprisingly the Lawn Tennis Association is already noticing anecdotal signs of the 'Raducanu effect', with more girls asking for tennis lessons.

Matt James, an LTA coach assigned to her full time from 15 to 17, said: 'She will inspire a lot of people, and especially young girls. She has such a great attitude. She's going out and saying "I'm just going to enjoy the experience". But at the same time she is a fierce competitor who can be composed under enormous pressure.'

In another measure of her popularity she doubled her Instagram followers to 1.4 million in less than 48 hours. Charlie Beall of the digital consultants Seven League noticed something else too. 'In the last week she has had an Instagram interaction rate of 38 per cent, which is extraordinary,' he said. To put it into context, most brands would be delighted with 1 per cent.'

Such engagement, Beall believes, is not only down to Raducanu's success on the court. 'Young people are interested in people like them,' he said. 'She's 18 years old and she's digitally native; it feels intuitive to her.'

And this is just the start. As Tim Henman, predicted: 'She is going to win more of these. This is not some flash-in-the-pan fairy tale... It is going to be one hell of a ride.' Time to buckle up.

Index